John Widdicombe

Fourteen Years in Basutoland

A Sketch of African Mission Life

John Widdicombe

Fourteen Years in Basutoland
A Sketch of African Mission Life

ISBN/EAN: 9783337121013

Printed in Europe, USA, Canada, Australia, Japan

Cover: Foto ©ninafisch / pixelio.de

More available books at **www.hansebooks.com**

IN

BASUTOLAND

A SKETCH OF

African Mission Life

BY

JOHN WIDDICOMBE,

Rector of S. Saviour's, Thlotse Heights, and Canon of Bloemfontein.

WITH FOUR PORTRAITS AND AN ILLUSTRATION.

LONDON:
THE CHURCH PRINTING COMPANY
11, BURLEIGH STREET, STRAND, W.C.

PREFACE.

South Africa is so much in the minds of Englishmen at the present time, and claims and occupies so large a share of their attention, that little or no apology is needed for the appearance of the present volume.

Nevertheless, I should not have ventured to write it had I not been urged to do so by several whose opinion on such a point I felt bound to respect, and whose reiterated wishes had for me almost the force of a command. They thought that the story of the Thlotse Mission ought to be known, and it is in deference to their judgment that these pages see the light.

Yet it seemed to savour somewhat of egotism to write so much about a work which, in the Providence of God, has become so largely identified with my own life and labours, and I may be pardoned if I shrank from the task. But other and better men have had to perform a like duty, and have succeeded in doing it; and I hoped that the interest evoked by the story I had to tell might perhaps pardon the apparent egotism involved in the narration of it.

The greater part of my life has been spent in South Africa. I have lived in various parts of it for thirty years, and in Basutoland for the last fourteen. So long an experience of South African life in its varied phases—more especially of life in a large and not unimportant native territory—ought to bring with it a knowledge, large or small, of the habits and customs of tribes and peoples, and of the history of at least our own times, if not of preceding ones. Whether I can with any show of reason claim to possess such knowledge, in a greater or less degree, it is for this book to testify.

When I sat down to write it I did so with the intention of avoiding politics as far as possible, if not altogether. I found this to be almost impossible as the narrative proceeded, but trust nevertheless that I have not obtruded my own political views and feelings, if I have any, upon the reader; nor dealt unfairly with the opinions and aims of those statesmen to whose fostering care the government of Basutoland has at various times been committed. The old motto "Ne sutor ultra crepidam" is, I venture to think, an excellent one for the missionary.

I should indeed be sorry if anything in these pages could be construed into a reflection, much less a slur, upon the ability or the integrity of a man so eminent and so justly respected as Sir Bartle Frere. Few, I should think, would deny that that great man had the interests of South Africa at heart, and that, could his policy of confederation have been carried out, not by the arbitration of the sword, but peacefully and naturally, it would have resulted in permanent good to the whole country.

That he was throughout his life an earnest supporter of Christian missions, and a devoted admirer of missionary effort, no one will venture to dispute.

Mission work, in each and all of its phases, ought to be dear to every Christian heart; and if my readers do not feel called to venture out themselves into the "great deep" abroad, or even into the "highways and hedges" at home, they can at least pray for the extension of the Kingdom of God. Most, if not all of them, can do more: they can aid with their alms the "Forlorn

Hope" who have gone out in their Master's Name, and at His command, to storm and destroy the many strongholds still, alas, existing of the empire of Satan.

Great opportunities are ours. We live in a day when " the fields are white unto the harvest." Basutoland is one of such fields. There, as in so many other places, " the harvest truly is plenteous, but the labourers are few." " Pray ye the Lord of the harvest that He would send forth labourers into His harvest."

London,

Easter, 1891.

CONTENTS.

CHAPTER I.
	PAGE
INTRODUCTORY	1

CHAPTER II.
THE BASUTOS	13

CHAPTER III.
SOCIAL LIFE OF THE BASUTOS	41

CHAPTER IV.
RELIGION	59

CHAPTER V.
S. SAVIOUR'S, THLOTSE HEIGHTS	72

CHAPTER VI.
LENGTHENING THE CORDS	97

CHAPTER VII.
LOSS AND GAIN	108

CHAPTER VIII.
VIA CRUCIS	114

CHAPTER IX.
NEW WORKERS	125

CHAPTER X.
THE REBELLION	133

CHAPTER XI.
Dreary Days 172

CHAPTER XII.
Patching up a Peace 189

CHAPTER XIII.
Reorganization 198

CHAPTER XIV.
Inter-tribal Warfare 214

CHAPTER XV.
Gleams of Hope 240

CHAPTER XVI.
Quiet Progress 253

CHAPTER XVII.
Sunshine and Shadow 267

CHAPTER XVIII.
Tribulation and Joy 286

Fourteen Years in Basutoland.

CHAPTER I.

INTRODUCTORY.

The Switzerland of South Africa—Physical Characteristics of the Country—Climate—Fauna—Flora—Mineral Wealth—Natural Mountain Fortresses—Inhabitants.

IF we look carefully at the map of South Africa we shall observe a little lozenge-shaped purple patch, about an inch in length, not far from the south-eastern corner of it.

This purple patch represents Basutoland—the Switzerland of Southern Africa. It is a country elevated some 6,000 feet above the level of the sea, and full of lofty mountains, which are tossed about all over it in endless and picturesque confusion. It is watered with countless rivulets, brooks, springs, and fountains, and possesses a soil second to none in richness and fertility. Lying to the west of Natal, and separated from that colony by the lofty range of the Drakensbergen, whose peaks range from 8,000 to 10,000 feet in height, it slopes gradually down to the great western table-land, which now forms the Southern Boer Republic—the Orange Free State. From the latter country it is easily accessible; but the Drakensbergen effectually shut it out from Natal, forming to the east an almost impassable barrier between the two countries. Physically regarded, Basutoland stretches from the Drakensbergen westwards to beyond Thaba 'Nchu, in the Orange Free State; and in the palmy days of Moshesh's rule that powerful chieftain claimed, and often exercised, dominion over the whole of this large tract of country. But time has brought with it great changes in Southern Africa; and at the present day what is known as Basutoland is, roughly speaking, the comparatively small territory lying between the river Caledon on the west—which separates it from the Orange Free State—and the Maluti mountains. These Malutis, or double mountains, as they are sometimes called, are the inner and most westerly peaks of the Drakensbergen. The country is thus much longer from north to south than from east to west. Its extreme length is a little less than 300 miles, and its breadth varies from fifty to nearly 120.

If South Africa is a land of extremes, Basutoland is emphatically so. Its climate is probably the roughest, the severest, and the most bracing to be found anywhere throughout the whole vast continent of Africa. The atmosphere in this elevated mountain region is highly rarified, and marvellously clear and pure. For the greater part of the year it is dry and exhilarating, and pulmonary complaints are unknown. The thermometer ranges from 105 degrees in the shade in the height of summer to fifteen degrees in the depth of winter. But in summer the extreme heat does not, as a rule, last for more than a very few weeks, and it is frequently tempered by cooling thunder showers during the months of November, December, and January. Towards the autumn, especially in February and March, copious rains fall for weeks together, rendering travelling well-nigh impossible. The spruits and mountain torrents roar, the brooks babble, the rivers are full to overflowing. Innumerable rills and fountains spring up all over the country. The rainy season has set in in its strength: the great heat has passed away, to be succeeded by a short, bright, calm, mellow autumn, very similar to the Indian summer of North America.

The winter is the dry season. The days then are usually warm and bright, the nights piercingly cold. Now and then, when the wind sets in strongly from the South Pole, something approaching to a blizzard is experienced, and not unfrequently, snow falls. Indeed a snowstorm is usually looked for towards the end of June, and perhaps once in six or seven years the snow falls fast and thick for a distance of 150 or 200 miles. On most mornings in the winter large masses of ice may be seen floating in the rivulets and spruits, but they quickly melt away under the heat of the sun. Before noon all traces of the night's frost have disappeared: the sky is cloudless, the sun warm and genial; and the natives of the country—true lovers of sunshine —creep out of their huts to squat on the sunny side of their "Khothlas," and drink in at every pore the delightful warmth of the luminary of day.

Fifty years ago Basutoland was full of wild animals. The lion roamed over the plains, retreating to the mountains when pursued. Old Basuto hunters love to sit at night around the winter watch-fire and recount the stirring scenes and adventures of bygone days, before fire-arms had found their way into the country, when twenty or thirty of the young braves of the tribe, led on by their elders, would with the assagai attack the monarch in his lair and despatch him; but only after a furious contest, in which some of their number would fare by no means well. Troops of quaggas galloped over hill and dale; elands, springboks, blesboks, reeboks, rietboks, and other antelopes were to be seen on almost every hill side; and gnus, hyænas, panthers, ounces, jackals, wolves, baboons, and wild dogs abounded. Almost all these are now gone. The eland and one or two smaller antelopes are still to be found, but only far away in the mountain fastnesses of the Malutis. The rest have retreated northwards or north-west, where they may still be met with on the plains of Bechuanaland, or in the solitudes of the Kalahari desert. The white man and the black have both combined to exterminate them; indeed, of the two, the black man is their most deadly foe. The South African native leaves very little alive except his flocks and herds, and of course his dog—ever the friend of man—wherever his foot holds sway. Birds, beasts, and reptiles, all go down before him. His hand wages perpetual war against them, and destroys them all. In Basutoland you may search the rivers now in vain for a crocodile, or a hippopotamus, and serpents and other reptiles are diminishing in numbers day by day. Happily for the human race, in a few years these last will have perished altogether. The conies in their " stony rocks," and the suricates (*miercats*) of the open country are almost the only wild animals now left to greet the eye of the traveller. The former are scarce and shy; the latter, engaging and timid little creatures, may be seen in the summer everywhere, peeping cautiously out of their holes in the veldt, or standing erect on their hind legs sunning themselves at noonday.

Most of the birds too have disappeared, but birds of prey, such as vultures, carrion crows, and hawks are still plentiful. Pigeons also are numerous. Partridges, wild duck, and quail are scarcer; while the kingfisher, the scarlet chaffinch, and others of the feathered race, so numerous in former years, are now but rarely seen. The sparrow, of course, is everywhere wherever man fixes his habitation, and, together with other competitors, makes serious depredations in the corn fields and orchards. The plovers in their wheeling flight, a few cranes, a little company of locust birds, a solitary secretary bird, with now and then a ring dove cooing to its mate, still claim the attention of the wayfarer, and remind him of the splendour of glories long since departed.

To the native his cattle is the most valuable of his possessions. He loves his flocks and herds above all things, sometimes even above his wives and children. The horse, the ox, and the goat now fill the vacant places of the lion, the panther, and the antelope. As a rule the native takes diligent care of his cattle. The small boys of each village soon learn to become patient and careful neatherds, and the cattle learn to know their guardians.

One of the prettiest sights in the Lesuto (to give Basutoland its native name) is the return home of the cattle each afternoon a little before sunset. Strings of cows and oxen, with here and there a grave-looking bull marching by their side, and a troop of calves frisking in their rear, may be seen coming home from their mountain pastures ; each string *following* its herd-boy as in the East ; while the boys chant their pastoral songs, or display the dawn of musical genius upon the lesiba. Now and then some of the lads, by way of variation, will mount the calves, and then ensues a mad frolic—an amusing merry-go-round—which usually terminates in the riders being pitched ignominiously into the veldt amid the laughter and banter of their companions. It is altogether a happy, healthful, peaceful scene, and one that helps us to realise and appreciate the pastoral life and occupations of the Basutos.

Not much more than a generation ago each river and almost every rivulet (so the old men tell us) was fringed with indigenous willows. These were alive with chaffinches and ringdoves; while the air around resounded with the cries of wild duck and teal. A few charred or waterworn stumps are all that now remain of these noble trees, for noble they must have been judging from the girth of these stumps at their base. In the extreme south east, the Quiting district, there is a good deal of bush and scrub still remaining, and the spruits and watercourses are still clothed with the wild willow on either side ; but elsewhere, except in remote mountain gorges, there is no large timber left, and hardly any bush or scrub except the olive, which remains in abundance in the more secluded and hilly districts.

But though the indigenous woods of the country have nearly all perished, a great many new trees have been introduced, especially since Basutoland has become a British possession. Many of the native Christians and some of the chiefs have endeavoured to make amends for the wanton destruction of former days by planting the eucalyptus (blue gum), the Cape poplar, and the willow, round their huts and villages; while the mission stations and the magistracies may be detected at once by the leafy screen which surrounds them. The officials of the British Government have done a good work by distributing from time to time the seeds of various kinds of trees, especially the eucalyptus, which grows readily almost everywhere.

Owing doubtless to the barbarous custom of grass burning which takes place annually at the end of winter, there are but few wild flowers to be seen in the country. But in the nooks and crannies which escape the flames and remain unravaged one finds quantities of gladiolas, daffodils, geraniums, lobelias, and daisies. Ferns are abundant in these hidden glades and recesses, and some of the loveliest specimens of the graceful maidenhair may be easily gathered in the clefts of the great rocks which lie along the precipitous sides of the mountain gorges. The ever-welcome clover and the homely buttercup are found in profusion in the meadows. Mingled with evergreen scrub, and gracefully covering the boulders on the hill sides, the clematis may sometimes be found, its charming white flowers filling the air around with their delicious perfume.

In August the whole country presents a gruesome and ghastly spectacle. Veldt there is little or none, the ground is charred and black for miles upon miles as far as the eye can reach, while dense volumes of smoke ascend in every direction. The old grass is being burnt off to force on the development of the new. Should rain fall during the process, as is often the case, the young grass will rapidly appear, and will be available for pasturage some six weeks or even two months before its ordinary time. But unfortunately veldt burning is by no means an unmixed good. While it ensures an early pasturage it tends to keep the grass rank and sour, and therefore unfit for sheep. Hence the grass of Basutoland is almost all "sour feldt," and but few sheep are seen in the country. But cattle thrive and multiply exceedingly, and throughout the greater part of the year look fat, sleek, and vigorous.

Of indigenous fruits there are none except the blackberry (monōkōmetsi), and the wild raspberry (monōkōtsuai); but both of these are inferior in size and insipid in flavour. European fruits have been largely introduced into the country, chiefly by the missionaries, and flourish abundantly. Of these the peach, the nectarine, the apricot, the plum, the apple, the pear, the cherry, and the strawberry are the most successful and the most prolific. The peach is found at almost every village, and when the trees are in full blossom at the beginning of September a peach orchard is a lovely sight. The peach, nectarine, and apricot are not wall fruits as in England, but are planted in rows in orchards like the plum or the apple. Oranges require great care and nursing owing to the severe frosts, and the fruit is inferior to that of the Cape Colony or the Transvaal. Figs do fairly well, but do not attain the size or the luscious flavour of those of the western province of the Cape. Grapes are grown with success on walls with a sunny northern aspect, but do not answer in vineyards; while guavas, pineapples, bananas, loquats, and other fruits which do so well along the hot coast districts of Natal and the eastern province of the Cape Colony are here unknown.

Vegetables of all kinds are plentiful and good. Not only the ordinary kinds of English vegetables may be grown most successfully, but the more tender varieties, such as cucumbers, tomatoes, asparagus, vegetable marrows, pumpkins, and indeed the whole gourd and melon tribe flourish vigorously in the open air, and are of excellent flavour.

Nearly all English flowers thrive in Basutoland, and some, especially roses, when once they have had a good start, will grow everywhere almost as rapidly as weeds.

The chief cereals are millet (mabèle) and maize. The former is indigenous to Africa, and is found throughout the entire continent; the latter was probably introduced by the white settlers of the Cape as they gradually pushed their way northwards and eastwards among the various native tribes. Wheat is beginning to be largely grown in the central districts, and the cultivation of oat-hay is extending. Besides these cereals the Basutos raise large quantities of pumpkins, beans, and water-melons; and most of them contrive to find room also for a small patch of *infe*—a sweet cane—which matures at the end of summer, and the juice of which is wholesome and nourishing.

The harvest, both of millet and maize, is in midwinter; the grain being allowed to stand for three or four weeks after it has ripened. When fully ripe the frost is said to benefit both millet and maize (or *mealies*, as the latter is called everywhere in South Africa); but should an early frost set in before they are thoroughly matured both crops may be frost-bitten and ruined in a night. It is but seldom that such a dire calamity takes place, though almost every year partial frosts will destroy patches of grain, especially in low-lying fields and gardens.

Basutoland is, as has been said, a well watered country, though its rivers, like the others of South Africa, are none of them navigable. They are mountain streams or torrents, at times, especially in the winter, almost dry, but during the rainy season full, deep, and swiftly flowing. Sometimes in the spring a single thunder shower will suffice to fill them, though perhaps only for a few hours, so rapid is their course. Some of the largest rivers of South Africa take their rise in Basutoland, in the very heart of the Malutis, at the foot of the Mont aux Sources, a dome-shaped mountain over 10,000 feet in height. Among these are the Orange, the Caledon, and the Tugela; while of the lesser streams the most important are the Kornet Spruit, the Putiatsana, the Thlotse, and the Hololo. In addition to these, and helping to feed them, innumerable streamlets flow forth from the Malutis, and render the country one of the most fertile in the world. It is by far the best watered portion of South Africa, and though now almost destitute of trees its pasturage is everywhere good, and its valleys, especially those drained by the tributaries of the Caledon, contain a rich and fertile soil admirably adapted for agriculture.

Of its mineral wealth little is at present known. Coal has been found in many places, and one seam has been recently opened up and worked by the Government with the concurrence of the Paramount Chief. Iron abounds in several districts; while old Australian diggers and other mining experts assert that rich gold reefs are to be found in many parts, especially along the spurs of the Malutis. Some maintain that diamond deposits exist, and others profess to have discovered quicksilver. The streams of water wash down annually great quantities of quartz, crystals, agates, cornelians, and other stones. For obvious reasons it has hitherto been the policy of the British Government to forbid all prospecting for minerals, and this rule has been rigidly enforced, the country being held in trust by the Queen of England for the Basuto people.

But above all, Basutoland is emphatically a land of mountains. As the reader already knows it lies along the inner slope of the Drakensbergen, whose western peaks, running parallel with the eastern or Drakensbergen proper, form the magnificent range of the Malutis. But detached from this latter range and from its spurs, often at a considerable distance, solitary mountains rise, flat-topped, like huge fortifications, to the height of from 800 to 2,000 feet. These isolated mountains are frequently from ten to twenty, or even thirty miles in circumference, and are usually of an oblong shape. They are in fact table-lands, the plains at their summits being crested with a crown of grey sandstone rock which hardens by exposure to the atmosphere. The horizontal strata of this sandstone often lie one above the other with striking and beautiful regularity. These natural mountain fortresses are almost impregnable. Their sides of bare, naked rock are wellnigh perpendicular, and their summits are inaccessible, except at perhaps two or three points where a narrow pathway may be found between huge overhanging cliffs. In wartime a dozen bold and determined men on these heights have been known to keep a whole army below at bay, and to hold their mountain fort against all assailants. The tops of these mountains are quite flat, and form table-lands several miles in extent. They are often well watered with springs and natural fountains, and afford such excellent pasturage that they are constantly covered with herds of cattle, especially during the summer season. In times of invasion or war these solitary mountains are the refuge of defeated chieftains and their followers, and may be held for months and even years, as was the case at Thaba Bosigo during the Basuto-Dutch war, and later on in the Quiteng during the Morosi campaign. The base of these mountains is generally surrounded by huge blocks of sandstone, which were formerly covered with the wild vine, the clematis, convolvulus, and other creeping plants; but these have for the most part been destroyed by veldt fires, or ruthlessly plucked up for fuel by the natives. Besides these large detached mountains, isolated " koppies " are frequently to be met with, and enormous rocks, often of the most fantastic shapes, abound on all sides. Huge crags with a perfectly round cap—like mammoth mushrooms wrought in stone; grotesquely shaped blocks perched aloft upon colossal bases, like so many griffins or quaint caricatures of man; great splinters of rock resembling in shape tables, vases, or broken obelisks—all these and more meet the eye of the traveller, and form constantly recurring objects of astonishment and delight. These flat-topped mountains are indeed one of the most striking features of the country. Usually they are, as I have said, detached, but sometimes they are united together for long distances, and form sub-ranges of their own, which stretch away for miles and miles from the foot of the Malutis westwards until they are lost in the great plateau of the Orange Free State. Some of these sub-ranges, like the Platbergen, are so extensive, and their summits so well watered and so thickly covered with soil and clothed with grass, that large farms are to be found upon their tops. These farms often possess many acres of rich arable land, and their owners are, as may be supposed, a hardy, sturdy race, living as they do in exposed, breezy homesteads built at an elevation of 6,000 or 6,500 feet above the level of the sea.

Speculation has been rife as to the origin of these flat-topped hills. If I might venture to put forth an opinion upon such a subject, I should say that, after a long residence in the country and much thought and careful observation, the conclusion which most commends itself to my mind is that the flat tops of these mountains—stretching away as they do westwards—were centuries ago *the ordinary level of the country.* The present level must therefore be some 800 feet or more below the original one, and this I believe to be the fact. The mighty rush of water from the Malutis, often continuous for months together during the rainy season, must have eaten out deep channels during its vehement onward flow, and as time went on these channels gradually became wider where the ground was softest. More and more of the soil was perpetually carried downwards towards the great table-lands of the west, thus causing the sloping and undulating belt of country lying between these table-lands and the mountainous region to the east of them. But the solid rock—often, as we have seen, for miles in extent —remained disintegrated, resisting the force and solvent power of the rushing waters, and in the end forming this remarkable series of detached and elevated plateau or solitary flat-topped mountains. It must, of course, have taken ages to effect such a result, but anyone who has lived long in the Lesuto can easily imagine the process—nay, can even now see it going on, and continued still further. Year by year new shoots, ravines, and fissures are being formed by the downward rush of the waters along the hillsides in the rainy season, and the old ones are becoming wider and wider. Some of them, indeed, have already become so broad that the rich, loamy soil on their sloping sides is utilised for cultivation, and long, irregular patches of the finest maize may often be seen far under the ordinary level of the land. Old Basutos, after a long absence from their birthplace, will often exclaim on revisiting it: " *Hele!* where has this *lengope* (sloot, watercourse) come from ? It was not here when I was a boy. The ground was flat and level, where now I see a deep and yawning chasm. *Hele!* God is great, and His works are wonderful."

No wonder the Mosuto loves his country. It is, indeed, a fascinating land—a land of lofty mountains and smiling plains, where the grass is often as green as in England or Ireland ; a land of rushing rivers, babbling brooks, and flowing fountains ; of beetling crags and bewitching waterfalls—one of these latter (the Malutsuanyane) being nearly 700 feet in height. It is the natural home and abiding-place of countless flocks and herds, signs to the native of peace and plenty ; where often and often when the rest of South Africa is parched and dried with drought, there is "a sound as of an abundance of rain," when the great thunder clouds floating over the Drakensbergen from the Indian Ocean, big and black with pent-up moisture, burst, and shower their welcome freight upon the waiting, grateful earth.

The climate, too, though, as I have said, rough and extreme for Africa, is nevertheless magnificent. To the Englishman it is especially so : cold, dry, bright and bracing in winter ; hot, but seldom unendurably so, in summer. And if, in springtime, boisterous winds and drifting storms sometimes combine to make one feel that nothing perfect is to be looked for on earth, the passing unpleasantness is more than compensated for by the gentle, balmy days of cloudless sunshine that follow, and the moderate, genial warmth of the calm and restful autumn.

But who are the inhabitants of Basutoland? Whence did they come, and what manner of people are they?

These questions are important enough to demand a separate chapter for their answer.

CHAPTER II.

THE BASUTOS.

The Bushmen—The Bantoo Races—Their Origin—The Basuto Branch—Sebetoane—The Bamonageng—The Basutos of to-day—Moshesh—His Career and Conquests—Moselikatse and Thaba Bosigo—The Korannas—Basutoland a British Protectorate—Wars with Boer Settlers—With the Barolong—With the English—Berea—Sikonyela—The Basuto-Dutch War—Intervention of England—Settlement by Sir Philip Wodehouse—the Sons of Moshesh—Letsie—Masupha—Molapo.

THE first inhabitants of Basutoland were Bushmen. Where they came from, and how long they occupied the country, are questions which probably can never be answered. It is enough to say that when the Basutos first made this mountain land their home they found the bushmen already there. They conquered them, or rather, little by little exterminated them. Bushmen drawings and paintings, flint and iron arrow heads, and the names of many of the mountains and hills, bear witness to the fact that the Lesuto was once the abode of these "human scorpions," as the Basutos term them. Their paintings abound in the many caves and grottoes of the country, and under the gigantic overhanging rocks of the mountains. These drawings are usually sketches of animals, the ox and the antelope being the most frequent, and are often neatly, nay cleverly, done in coloured ochres and clays, the dark reddish brown of the oxen being the most conspicuous.

The Bushmen were apparently, for the most part, a race of cave dwellers—veritable troglodytes. Perhaps they fled to these strongholds and took refuge in them through fear of the darker and more powerful northern tribes which, as time went on, began to bear down upon them, and threatened gradually to exterminate them. Perhaps they made these caves and dens of the earth their homes and dwelling places from idleness, or from want of skill in building : for we know that nowhere did the Bushman construct any habitation other or better than a rude and temporary shelter—it could hardly be called a hut—made of twigs and bushes ; a human nest indeed, but neither so softly lined nor so deftly woven together as that of a bird.

Like the untamed creatures, the lion and the panther, which he hunted and laid low with his poisoned arrow, the untamed and untameable Bushman has disappeared from his former home. When I first went to reside in Basutoland, a few of these outcast Ishmaels of the human race were still to be found, dragging out a precarious existence in the innermost fastnesses of the Malutis ; and from time to time, when their depredations became too audacious, and the choicest cattle had been carried off by them, the Basuto chiefs would organise a commando and literally track them to their dens, and hunt them down there. One chief, the renowned Morosi, a vassal of Moshesh, and the head of the Baphuti, living in the mountains in the south, used to shoot down the men, but spare the women and children. The young girls and women were carried off to his harem, or divided among his warriors. The children grew up side by side with those of their conquerors, and learnt their language, habits, and customs ; but rarely did any of them remain for more than a few years. On the first favourable opportunity they would escape to their old haunts, and wage war against every man, until they in turn perished by the bullet or the assagai.

The great majority of the present inhabitants of Basutoland are Basutos, the remainder being Zulus, Fingoes, and people of mixed blood from among the Kafir races.

The Basutos are one of the main branches of the great Bantu

family. Bantu is simply the Kaffir word for *people*, and it is the name now usually given by European writers to the section of the human race inhabiting South-Eastern Africa. "In the division of mankind thus named are included,"* says Mr. Theal, "all those Africans who use a language which is inflected principally by means of prefixes, and which, in the construction of sentences, follows certain rules depending upon harmony in sound. The Bantu family is divided into numerous tribes politically independent of each other. Each tribe is composed of a number of clans, which generally have traditions of a common origin at no very remote date; in some instances, however, the tribes consist of clans pressed together by accident or war, and whose relationship is too remote to be traced by themselves."

That these tribes came originally from the north, travelling southwards, probably by successive migrations, from the coast districts of the continent, there can, I think, be little doubt. They vary in colour from light brown to the deepest black. Not only among the same tribes, but even in the same families, these differences of hue present themselves; some individuals being of the lightest brown, indeed almost tawny, while others are as black as the purest negro. And this difference as to degree of colour manifests itself strikingly in their physique. Some of the Bantu—notably those of lighter hue—are almost Arab in their appearance; tall, beautifully built, with aquiline noses, upright foreheads, and lips almost as thin as those of Europeans. Indeed, but for the colour of their skin, and the texture of their hair, which is always woolly, they might be taken as fine examples of the Caucasian type of man. Others have the thick lips, flat noses, and low receding foreheads of the negro. The Bantu can hardly be said to be purely African. They are probably a mixed race, sprung from the intercourse of Asiatics— Arabs or Persians, or both—many centuries ago with the

---

* Theal, Hist. of the Boers, Cap. I., p. 1.

Africans of the eastern coast lands, and having both Asiatic and negro blood flowing in their veins. " Ordinarily they present the appearance of a peaceable, good-natured, indolent people; but they are subject to outbursts of great excitement, when the most savage passions have free play. The man who spends the greater part of his time in gossiping in idleness, preferring a condition of semi-starvation to toiling for bread, is hardly recognisable when, plumed and adorned with military trappings, he has worked himself into frenzy with the war-dance. The period of excitement is, however, short. In the same way their outbursts of grief are very violent, but are soon succeeded by cheerfulness." *

When these tribes migrated from the north and began to occupy the lands in which they now dwell it is impossible to say, but there are reasons for supposing that it was at no very remote period. But in their progress as they pushed their way southwards, they came upon the great range of mountains which separates Central South Africa from the low-lying lands of the South-Eastern coast. Here they would seem to have divided; one section of them going to the left, and occupying the warm fertile region between the mountains and the Indian Ocean; the other keeping to the right, and still advancing southwards on the western side of the mountains, seems after a time to have become separated into two large parties. The first of these kept close to the Drakensbergen and the Malutis, taking possession of their slopes, and of the undulating country between these ranges and the plains of the central plateau; the other spread out in a south-westerly direction, and eventually occupied the elevated table-lands which extend for hundreds of miles between the undulating country on the east, and the Kalahari desert on the west.

We thus get three great branches or divisions of the Bantu race: The Coast Tribes, the Mountain Tribes, and the Western Tribes.†

---

* Theal. Ibid., p. 2.   † Cf. Theal. Hist.

The first of these comprises all those tribes known to Europeans as *Kafirs*—viz., the Amakosa, the Pondos, the Tembus, the Pondomisi, the Xesibes, the Bacas, and others of less importance, together with the Fingoes, and the more northerly tribes of Zulus, Matebele, and Swazies.

The group of Mountain Tribes consisted of the Bamonageng, the Batlokoa, the Baphuti, the Makhoakhoa, the Baramokhele, and perhaps some others; and the descendants and representatives of these, welded together as a nation by Moshesh, are named Basutos.

The Western Tribes, inhabiting the great central plains, comprised the Baharutsi, the Bangoaketsi, the Bakuena, the Barolong, the Batlaping, and others. But the Batlaping, the most southerly and the most degraded of these tribes, can now hardly be called pure Bantu, intermarrying as they have done with Korannas and other races of Hottentot extraction. These Western Tribes are known as the Bechuanas.

These two last great divisions of the Bantu family—the Basutos and the Bechuanas—though they differ from each other in many important respects, have much more in common than either of them has with their brethren of the coast lands. The great mountain range which separates these latter from the western clans must have often formed a serious barrier to intercourse between the two sections. Such intercourse as did exist was confined for the most part to the coast tribes and the Basutos; and hence these latter came to occupy an intermediate position, not only geographically, but also as regards language and customs, between the two extreme sections of the Bantu race. The three divisions now speak three languages, or more strictly, three dialects of a common language. But between Sesuto and Sechuana, the languages of the Basutos and the Bechuanas, there is much less difference than between Sesuto and Setebele—the language of the Coast Tribes. A Mosuto and a Mochuana will understand one another without much difficulty, but a Masuto and a Zulu find it very hard, in fact almost impossible, to converse together, so greatly have the two dialects diverged as time has gone on. Of the three languages Setebele or Zulu is generally considered the grandest and most sonorous, Sesuto the softest, and Sechuana the least euphonious. The leading vowel of the first named is u (oo), of the second e (a), and of the third o; the chief consonants of each being respectively v, ng, and z; l and t; and k and a hard guttural g. "Zulu is the language of bold men and warriors; Sesuto of polite men and diplomatists; Sechuana of hunters and peasants." This is, of course, a Basuto estimate of the three, and must be taken accordingly.

The Basutos and Bechuanas are, as a rule, inferior to the Kafirs in physical strength and beauty of form. Being less warlike and caring less for violent exercises, they lead a more pastoral and sedentary life, and perhaps their physique has suffered in consequence. But they often make up for this physical inferiority by superior mental power, more refined social habits, and a greater aptitude and desire for civilised employment.

The Mountain Tribes, that is to say the Basuto clans in their entirety, may be traced to-day from Kaffraria in the south, northwards through Basutoland and the Transvaal to the banks of the Zambesi. Nay, they are even found beyond that river, for the Makololo, mentioned so often by Livingstone and other African travellers, are a section of the Mautati, one of the leading clans of the Basutos, who migrated northwards from the borders of Basutoland under the leadership of the celebrated chief Sebetoane in 1824, and who have contrived to hold their own up to this present day against the savage hosts of the Matebele.

Before going further it may perhaps be well to explain the meaning of the more important prefixes of some of the native names which have already been used, and which will of necessity recur from time to time in this narrative. The following explanation will help to make these names and terms clear to the reader :—

Mo is the *singular* prefix to Personal Substantives.

Ba the *plural* to the same. But some words take *Le* and *Ma* instead.

Se refers to the language or customs of a people.

Le to the country belonging to a tribe.

A few examples will make these rules quite clear.

Mosuto. A single individual of the Basuto tribe. This word is spelt in Sesuto *Mosutho*, and pronounced Mo-soo-to, with the addition of *an aspirate* thrown in *between the t and the o*, there being no sound in the language equivalent to the English *th*. The accent is on the *penultimate*, and each syllable ends in a vowel; and this is the case with nearly all words in the language.

Basuto (Basutho). Two or more members of the tribe.

Morolong. A single individual of the Barolong people.

Barolong. Two or more of the Barolong people*.

Letebele. A single individual of the Kafir or Zulu tribes.

Matebele. Two or more individuals of these tribes.

Lekhoakhoa. A single individual of the Makhoakhoa tribe.

Makhoakhoa. Two or more of that tribe.

Mochuana. A single individual of the Bechuana tribes.

Bachuana, or more often *Bechuana*. Two or more of the above.

Sesuto (Sesutho). The language, laws, or customs of the Basutos.

Setebele. The language, &c., of the Kafirs or Zulus.

Sechuana (or Secoana). The language, &c., of the Bechuanas.

Lesuto (Lesutho). The country of the Basutos, *i.e.*, Basutoland. The names of foreign nations and their languages follow the same rules. Examples :

Lekhooa. A white man.

---

* These two words are exceptions to the general rule just given as to accent and vowel ending. The accent here is on the *ultimate*.

Makhooa. White men.

Moroa. A Bushman or Hottentot.

Baroa. The plural of the above.

Seroa. The language, &c., of Bushmen or Hottentots.

Sekhooa. The language, &c., of white men.

In the same way the Basuto Christians are called derisively by the heathen *Mayakane, the people who have changed their chief.* But among themselves they are known as Bakreste (plural of Mokreste), *those of the Christ*; or Badumedi (plural of Modumedi) the *Believers,* or *the Faithful.* The Basuto Christians in communion with the English Church are called *Machurche*; those of the French Protestant Mission, *Mafora*; and those of the Roman Catholic Mission *Baroma.*

In the latter half of the last century the Paramount Chief of the Basuto people, which then consisted of five principal clans, was Motlomi. He was held in great veneration by the whole tribe, and exercised paramount power over it until his death, which took place in or about the year 1814. These five clans were the Bamonageng, the Batlokoana, the Baramokhele, the Makhoakhoa, and the Mayiane, and they occupied what is now known as Basutoland, together with the eastern and north eastern parts of the present Orange Free State. After the decease of Motlomi, there seems to have been no one with sufficient ability or force of character to take his place, and accordingly some of the nearest Coast Tribes, chiefly the Amahlubi and the Amangoane, after fighting with one another, suddenly fell upon the Mountain Tribes, who, from want of a leader and head, had to meet this sudden onslaught and invasion as best they could, each clan for itself, without any common plan of action. But a young and somewhat obscure chief was rising, and even then coming into prominence, who, against desperate odds and many reverses, was destined to weld together the whole of the mountain clans and form them into what has since become known everywhere as the Basuto nation. The name of this young chief was Moshesh.

Moshesh was born about the year 1786* at Dinchuaneng, on the River Thlotse (Tlotsi), not far from my own mission station of St. Saviour's. Born at a time of dissension and disturbance, he was called at first *Lepoko*, "Dispute." At his circumcision, when attaining to manhood, he took the name of *Tlaputle*, "The Energetic," because of his activity and prominence in public affairs, youthful as he was. He was rapidly coming to the front; and when, some years afterwards, he had established for himself a name and reputation as a leader of men, he received from the tribe the name of Moshesh (Moshueshue), "The Shaver"—a fitting appellation, and the name by which he was ever afterwards known.

By birth he was not of the highest, or even of a very high rank; his family being of so little repute that it is now difficult to trace his lineage very far back with anything approaching to certainty. He was the son of Mokhachane, the younger son of Pete, who about the year 1823 was eaten by cannibals. Pete was the son of a widow of the chief Sekake, and accordingly took legal rank as that chief's son, though his actual father was, it is believed, a native of one of the Coast Tribes, to whom his mother had been given in marriage after Sekake's death.

I have often conversed with relatives, counsellors, and companions of Moshesh, and the mention of his name never fails to evoke the greatest enthusiasm for his memory. One of his most trusted and favourite nephews, Nathanaele Makotoko, the son of his brother Makhabane, has been for the last ten years residing at Thlotse Heights, the headquarters of my own mission station, and I am proud to reckon him among my closest friends. Nathanaele is not only an able chief and a man

---

* Theal makes the date "about 1793," but I am inclined to place it earlier. As far as I can ascertain the young chief was circumcised in 1803, and he must then have been about seventeen years of age.

of wise and ripe counsel in all the affairs of the nation; he is also the "hero of a hundred fights." Best of all, he is a good and sincere Christian. He was converted to Christianity more than twenty years ago through the influence of one of the French Protestant missionaries, and has proved himself worthy of the name he bears. He is, too, emphatically a "nature's gentleman," as all who know him can testify. He is an old man now of over seventy years, but his intellect is unclouded, and his memory as clear and retentive as ever. Many a pleasant evening have we spent together in my study or under the verandah of the mission house, chatting over old times and scenes in which the old man bore a prominent part. It is from him more than from any other source that the leading details of Moshesh's life and career which I here desire to place before the reader are derived. The career of the great Mosuto is well known to thousands, and has been described by several writers; but it may not, perhaps, be amiss to record it once more as briefly and succinctly as possible, from testimony thus received at first hand from one on the spot so eminent in character and abilities as the son of Makhabane.

Moshesh, according to the testimony of all who knew him, both European and native, was a man of commanding and dignified presence, with pleasant, attractive features, and a well-formed person. In his youth he was, like most other young chiefs, addicted to the chase, brave and fearless, and especially fond of hunting the elands and other large animals which were then found in the mountain gorges near his own birthplace. These hunting excursions must have done much to exercise and develop his activity and strength, and doubtless contributed to make him wary as well as bold in the almost incessant warfare in which the earlier years of his manhood were to be spent. He was by birth but a petty chief of little rank or standing in the tribe, though distantly related to the royal house of Monageng; but unaided and by his own abilities he saved the Basuto clans from destruction, and raised himself to be their leader and king. Take him all in all he was probably the greatest native that South Africa has produced. An intrepid warrior, cautious as well as bold on the battlefield, an astute, far-seeing statesman, a strong and sagacious ruler, a consummate diplomatist—unscrupulous and crafty where his interests or those of his people were concerned—he was nevertheless a firm and faithful friend to all who sought his protection or espoused his cause. He was not a Christian, and must not be judged by a Christian standard. The first half of his life was spent in the dreary darkness of African heathenism. Before a single ray of the Gospel of Jesus Christ had shone upon his path his career had been half run, and had already marked him out as a born leader of men. No doubt he could be untruthful and unscrupulous in his dealings with others when it served his purpose. A heathen African chief, born and brought up as he was, would naturally act upon the maxim that "language was given to man to enable him to disguise his thoughts" as occasion might serve. He was a savage, ruling over savages more barbarous than himself, some of whom, indeed, were even cannibals. Judged by the standard of his own time and circumstances, it must be allowed by all that he was a remarkable man—a man towering head and shoulders above his fellows.

Moshesh's first military attempts were not altogether successful. Upon the invasion of his country by a section of the warlike tribes of the coast he took up a strong position at Buta-Bute, a mountain to the north of his birthplace, and at no great distance from it, and endeavoured, by the aid of a few chosen warriors, chiefly companions in the chase, to make a stand there. He must then have been in the full vigour of his manhood. He appears to have held his own against the invaders, who were Fingoes under Pakalita, and Zulus under Mateoane. These latter were fugitives from their own land, who had long groaned under the iron yoke of Chaka. But the Batlokoa, a mountain tribe on the Caledon, under Ma-Ntatisi, were at feud with the house of Monageng, and being much more powerful than such a petty chief as Moshesh, they succeeded, after several hand-to-hand encounters, in driving them from his advanced position at Buta-Bute. This was probably in the winter of 1824. He and his people, indeed the Bamonageng generally, seem at this time to have been reduced to great destitution. The inroads of the two Matebele tribes under Mateoane and Pakalita, and the havoc committed by the Batlokoa, had reduced the land to desolation and anarchy. The result of this incessant strife was that the fields and gardens were uncultivated, no corn could be grown, food became scarcer, and the horrors of famine were added to those of war. Some sections of the tribe were altogether ruined, and brought to abject want. "Hunger is a sharp thorn," and, as old Moroka, the chief of the Barolong at Thaba 'Nchu, once expressed it, " a hungry man does not know what he might do. He might eat his own grandfather." Some of the Basutos did this. There had been cannibals in the land before the war, and now their numbers began rapidly to increase. In their utter extremity many of the people gave themselves up to murder and rapine. The ties of kindred and friendship were forgotten. Bands of famished wretches roamed about pillaging and destroying, and then feasting upon the victims laid low by the tomahawk and the spear. Those who did so, having once tasted human flesh, began, horrible as it may seem, to conceive a liking for it, and ended by forming themselves into separate parties, whose one object was to wage an inhuman war upon their fellow creatures. They laid snares and ambushes for the wayfarer, and spared neither high nor low. Their lurking-places were usually the caverns of the mountains. One of these "cannibal caves" is only a short day's ride from my own mission station. Its ground is still thickly covered with half-roasted skulls and broken bones; while large red blotches are clearly perceptible upon its walls, against which the bleeding corpses of the hapless victims had been piled up. In some places the blood has stained the rock so deeply that it will perhaps take centuries to efface the traces of it. Cannibalism ceased in Basutoland nearly half a century ago, but here and there some old and degraded-looking creatures may now and then still be met with who are known to have been man-eaters. One is told so, at any rate. " You see the old man sitting up against the wall yonder, Monere? Well, he was in his youth a *ledimo*—cannibal. There are not many of them left now. Moshesh put them down, and we thank God that such a dreadful custom has come to an end." You ride on with a sigh, the words of the Christian poet coming unbidden to the mind :—

"Where every prospect pleases,
And only man is vile."

Upon his retreat from Buta-Bute Moshesh took up a strong position upon Thaba Bosigo (" The Mountain of Night "), a mountain fortress some two days' distance to the south-west. This mountain fortress, though often attacked, has never been taken, and is regarded by the Basutos as impregnable. On its summit Moshesh set up his Khothla, and from hence he bore sway over many a tribe and people as the great " Chief of the Mountain," and here, too, he died. Here also the most celebrated members of his family are buried, for Thaba Bosigo has ever since been the last resting place of the royal house. When Moshesh first established himself upon the mountain there was a Baphuti village at its foot, inhabited by None and his people, but he and they were promptly " eaten up " by Mankoniane, Moshesh's chief captain, and driven away southwards.

Moshesh now endeavoured with all his might to strengthen and consolidate his position. He was surrounded by enemies. His own subjects were nothing better than a horde of plundered and starving fugitives, with cannibals among them literally " biting and devouring one another." The Matebele and the Fingoes were a standing menace in the north; the Baphuti, by no means peaceably inclined—and no wonder—in the south while the Batlokoa, his most deadly enemies, were ever on the alert close to his very birthplace. In addition to these, Griqua and Koranna, marauders from the plains of the west, mounted on horses and armed with guns (animals and weapons as yet unpossessed by Moshesh or his people) were constantly roaming along the banks of the Orange and the Caledon, and swooping down upon the Lesuto when least expected. But in the end he subdued them all.

His first stand against the Matebele and the Fingoes had been so successful that, notwithstanding his retirement from Buta-Bute, numbers of his countrymen began to flock to his Khothla, recognising in him the leader so much needed at the present crisis. The hour had produced the man. His fame was quickly spread abroad among the Basutos, and Thaba Bosigo became the rallying-point of the shattered fragments of the tribe. These now speedily united together, and acquired fresh confidence and strength under their new leader and head.

Moshesh always knew when to wait. Wary and sagacious, when war was not advisable diplomacy was employed, and often with the best results. Nay, he was even ready to humble himself before a too-powerful enemy in order to gain time. Thus, before his position was firmly established, he paid homage to the chief of the Amangoane, acknowledged himself as his vassal, and rendered him a regular tribute from the spoil taken in his numerous and varied expeditions. Fortunately for him and his people some of his most inveterate and most formidable enemies began after the lapse of a few years to quarrel amongst themselves. Two of them, Pakalita and Mateoane, fought not far from the banks of the Caledon at a spot close to the present village of Ladybrand, with the result that the Amahlubi were routed, and their chief, Pakalita, followed up and slain. But the victorious Mateoane and his warriors soon afterwards themselves sustained a severe defeat from another and more powerful foe. They fell into the hands of an army sent against them by Chaka, the Zulu King, and were compelled to retire altogether from this part of South Africa. Thus the Amahlubi and the Amangoane troubled Basutoland no more.

Moshesh now turned his attention to the Batlokoa. The chief of this tribe was Sikonyela, the son of Ma Ntatisi. He had only lately succeeded to the chieftainship, and was a man not wanting in ability. But, according to Basuto testimony, he was as ferocious as he was faithless and crafty. He was defeated by his rival in two well-organised and ably-conducted expeditions, and soon afterwards the two chiefs made terms of peace together. The Batlokoa were at that time the most powerful of all the mountain tribes, and were destined to be a thorn in the side of Moshesh for years to come.

But the Basuto chief had foes in his own household. His most formidable domestic enemies were the cannibals, and he resolved to put them down if need were with a strong hand. He exerted all his energy and all his influence to abolish the cannibalism which prevailed so largely amongst a section of the people. But he was loth to shed the blood of his own subjects, and trusted more to moral suasion than to the force of arms. Seeing that this inhuman practice had crept into the tribe in the first instance through want, and knowing that it was foreign to national customs and traditions, he relied upon the growing prosperity of his people more than upon anything else for its extinction. And the event proved that he was right. With increasing prosperity and assured peace and safety the horrible custom gradually died out. Yet there were not wanting among his advisers many who urged him to exterminate the men-eaters at once and at all risks. He saw, however, that this would in all probability lead to a civil war, and help to depopulate still more a land already half denuded of its inhabitants, and he had no wish to light up by his own direct action the flames of domestic discord. On the contrary, feeling that unity is strength, his chief aim was to cultivate peace and harmony at home, that thus he might be able, by a united front, to defend his subjects from the invasions of the many enemies by whom they were so constantly menaced.

In connection with this subject there is a well-known story told of him which illustrates at once his adroitness and sense of humour. On one occasion, when his counsellors urged him to deal summarily with a party of cannibals who had only lately way-laid, killed and eaten an inoffensive traveller, the chief manifested, for reasons best known to himself, a clear disinclination to follow their advice. Chagrined at his apparent callousness, they went on to remind him that it was to such wretches that his own grandfather owed his death. "You are doubly bound," they said, "to exterminate these men-eaters. Not only the safety of your people, but also the honour due to your ancestor requires that you should act promptly and at once. Instead of which you treat these human tigers with such consideration that, did we not know you, we should be almost tempted to say that they were your special friends and protégés." "Well," said the chief, with that grave and effective irony, for which in after days he was so celebrated, "I have always been told that *a man ought to venerate the tombs of his ancestors.*"

In 1825 the Baphuti were conquered and reduced to submission, their chiefs from henceforth acknowledging the headship of Moshesh. A few years afterwards the great chief himself, finding that the Zulu King was becoming jealous of his increasing power and meditating an expedition against him, humbled himself to Chaka, and appeased his wrath by sending him as a vassal the usual subsidies of karosses and ostrich feathers. Indeed the old men tell me that the Basutos have always owned the Zulu monarch as, in some sense, their suzerain, and sent him annually their tribute of homage either in the shape of cattle or of plumes and furs.

Almost every Englishman at all acquainted with the history

of South Africa has heard of the terrible Moselekatse, but few, I think, know that the only check his forces ever received at the hand of a native potentate was given to them by Moshesh. It was in 1831 that these redoubtable warriors were sent by their master against the Basutos. The ferocious Matebele chief, a runaway, rebellious captain of Chaka's, had already devastated the greater part of the vast territory between the Limpopo and the Orange ; eating up the unhappy Bechuana tribes in the same way and on the same scale that the Tartars of the Middle Ages invaded and laid waste the cities and towns of Russia. Moselekatse and his invincible hordes were the scourge of all the tribes north of the Orange until they received their final check and were driven to the north of the Limpopo by the Boers in revenge for several atrocious massacres which the latter had suffered at their hands. Moselekatse was not himself at the head of the expedition against the Basutos, or perhaps events might have turned out differently. The Matebele, having plundered and laid bare the country along their line of march, at length halted under the willow trees which lined the banks of the Putiatsana, a pretty little stream not far from the foot of Thaba Bosigo. There they sat down and rested after the fatigue of their long three hundred mile journey ; bathing themselves daily in the cool, limpid water, sharpening their assagais, arranging their head-plumes, and dancing their war dance preparatory to investing the stronghold of the man they were sent to conquer. The Basutos watched it all from the heights above, and did all that lay in their power to prepare for the onslaught of their dreaded foe. They barricaded the few entries to their stronghold with huge boulders, and carefully repaired and strengthened the breast-works at the top of the mountain, erecting strong and substantial *schansen* at any point where an ascent seemed possible.

On the morning of the attack the Zulu—or rather Matebele—host divided itself into two columns, which delivered the assault simultaneously from two opposite points. The rush was terrific, and seemed irresistible. Regarding themselves as invincible Moselekatse's warriors, pressed forward with the utmost confidence up the precipitous sides of the mountain, heedless of the rocks and stones hurled upon them from above. But the mountain was so steep, the paths so thoroughly blocked with boulders, and the *schansen* so well guarded, that, in spite of every effort, they were unable to reach the summit. Then there ensued a general crash. Avalanches of stones and showers of well-directed javelins—the short, light assagai of the Basutos—forced back the assailants, and compelled them to retreat in haste and disorder. Their leader and his lieutenants, mad with rage and fury, rallied the fugitives, trampling their plumes and war trappings under their feet. Once more they led them to the assault, this time delivered with even greater force and fury than before. But it was all in vain. The besieged rained torrents of rocks, stones, boulders, and spears down upon them, and the hitherto " ever victorious army " was compelled to retire. The victory was a decisive one for the Basutos, for next morning the Matebele retreated homewards.

Then Moshesh did a noteworthy deed which the Basutos to this day never fail to relate with pardonable pride and pleasure. Seeing the dreaded hosts of his adversary thus turning their backs upon him crestfallen and in sullen despair, partly no doubt from motives of policy, but also—we can hardly doubt it—with that fine sense of humour which so distinguished him, *he sent their commander a handsome present of the finest and fattest oxen,* with the following message:—" Moshesh salutes you. Supposing that hunger has brought you into his country, and feeling sure that you must be exhausted after your prodigious and fruitless efforts, *he sends you these cattle as a reward of your bravery, that you may have food for yourselves on your way home.* He desires to live in peace with you and with all men."

They accepted the gift, and went away singing the praises of so great and magnanimous a chief; vowing at the same time that they would never more molest him. And they kept their word. Whether from fear or from admiration of a character so unique, I cannot say; but they never again appeared in Basutoland, though its inhabitants were for years to come in constant dread of them.

But no sooner was one enemy got rid of than another appeared. Bands of marauding Korannas and Griquas swooped down upon the flocks and herds of the Basutos, carrying off the choicest cattle. For years did these ravages continue; but at length these ferocious robbers were chastised and subdued, nay, almost exterminated. Fragments only of them remained. The remnant of the Griquas was dispersed among the tribes to the westward, and the Korannas retreated to distant hills, where they learnt to respect their neighbours and live with them in peace.

In 1833, at the desire of the Wesleyan missionaries, Moshesh ceded the western portion of his territory (the country round Thaba 'Nchu) to the Barolong, a fugitive Bechuana tribe which had fled southwards to escape annihilation at the hands of the hordes of Moselekatse. These Barolong, under their chief Moroka, were thus saved from destruction, and continued to possess the Thaba 'Nchu territory until the troubles of 1884 ended their national existence.

With the expulsion of Moselekatse by the Boers and the dispersion of the few remaining Griqua and Koranna marauders an era of comparative peace set in, and the "Chief of the Mountain," as Moshesh was now called, was not slow to take advantage of it. The Basutos became prosperous, and their chief turned his attention more than ever to domestic matters—to questions connected with the social well-being, as he understood it, of the people. If we are to believe the testimony of the old men—his contemporaries and counsellors—law and order were enforced throughout the Lesuto as they had never been before, and as they have not often been since. Men lived and moved freely and in safety; life and property were respected and protected; cannibalism became extinct.

But this was not all. A new sphere of labour and influence was opening out to the quenchless energy of the chief; a sphere which, while it satisfied his ambition, was fraught with splendid possibilities for the future of the nation which he had built up at the cost of so much toil, and in the teeth of so many hindrances and reverses. Henceforth he became the astute diplomatist, as well as the successful warrior. Seeing the advancing power of the English all over the southern portion of Africa he desired to enter into a treaty relationship with them, perceiving, doubtless, that in this lay one of the greatest safeguards of his people for the future that might await them. He was far-seeing, and his judgment in this not misplaced. His wish was made known to the Secretary of State for the Colonies by the Governor of the Cape, Sir George Napier, in 1842, and from that time forward the Basutos were regarded as under the "protection" of the British Government. As time went on treaties were entered into between the Chief and the Governor purporting to regulate the relationship between the former and the emigrant Boers, who were day by day taking possession of the unoccupied tracts of land north of the Orange, and were thus becoming his neighbours on the west and south-west. Delimitations were also made and altered from time to time of the territory claimed by his old rival and enemy Sikonyela on the north-eastern banks of the Caledon.

I have neither time nor space to follow in detail the career of this remarkable man, and indeed to do so would be foreign to the main purpose of this book. It will suffice to say that with increasing prosperity as time went on many of the Basutos, forgetting the bitter experiences of early days, themselves became marauders and "cattle lifters." If adversity tries a man, prosperity does so still more. And as with the individual man, so it is with the nation. "Jeshurun waxed fat and kicked." *

---

* Deuteronomy xxxii. 15.

The Basutos, swollen with pride and fulness of bread, became involved in acts of aggression upon their weaker neighbours, especially upon the emigrant Boers (then few in number), the Barolong, and the Batlokoa. But this state of things could not go on indefinitely, and so in the course of time they came into collision, not only with these, but also with the British officials who ruled, or professed to rule—for they usually had no force wherewith to ensure obedience to their proclamations—the territory north of the Orange, then known by the name of the Orange River Sovereignty. Alas, that it should be said, Moshesh began to get a bad name. He was regarded as treacherous and untruthful, and Major Donovan was sent to punish him and bring him to book. The British Commander's force was made up of Boers, English settlers, Fingoes, Barolongs, Griquas, Koraunas, and Half-castes, and this motley body was hopelessly defeated and scattered by Moshesh at Mount Viervoet in June, 1851. The victorious chief then proceeded to ravage the Barolong country (the territory which, it will be remembered, he had made over to that tribe nearly twenty years before), carrying off many thousand head of cattle, and driving Moroka and his people far away across the Modder river. Moreover, by his diplomatic skill, as the Basutos love to put it, or his astute unscrupulousness, according to the version of his enemies, he succeeded in outwitting the Special Commissioners, Major Hogge and Mr. Owen, and frustrating all their efforts to effect a permanent settlement of affairs or a lasting peace. Matters had evidently come to a crisis, and as the British Government seemed bent upon holding the Trans-Orange Territory at all risks, the Governor of the Cape, Sir George Cathcart, himself proceeded next year to chastise the refractory chief.

The British Resident of the Sovereignty and the Special Commissioners appointed to report upon the raids of the Basutos estimated the losses sustained by the Europeans, the Barolongs, and others at £25,000, and recommended that a fine of 10,000 head of full-grown cattle, and 1,500 horses should be imposed upon Moshesh as compensation for these losses; and also that he should be required to surrender 500 stand of arms (for by this time fire-arms had found their way into the country), in token of his submission and his desire for peace. The boundary line laid down before by Major Warden, the former British Resident, was also to be preserved intact.

The force with which the Governor advanced against Moshesh was the finest that had ever been seen north of the Orange. It was also admirably equipped, and consisted of about 2,000 infantry and 500 cavalry, with two field guns. No doubt the Governor hoped that the mere presence of such a body of troops would be sufficient to overawe the chief, and compel his submission without recourse to hostilities. But in this he was mistaken. His Excellency sent an ultimatum to Moshesh, of which the following were the main provisions:—

"10,000 head of cattle and 1,000 horses to be delivered within three days.

The restoration to Sikonyela of the cattle taken from him.

The restoration of Platberg to the Half-castes.

The cessation of cattle raids, and the observance of peace for the future with all the neighbouring tribes and peoples."

After some fruitless negotiations an extension of time of one day for the collection of the cattle was granted. There is no doubt that Moshesh dreaded above all things a war with the English. He saw that such a war would almost certainly result in the ruin of himself and of his people as an independent tribe. But he was overruled by his sons and the younger men generally. They had put to flight the commando of Major Donovan at Viervoet: why should they fear the red-coats of Sir George Cathcart?

Moshesh did what he could to meet the Governor's demands, feeling, no doubt, that they were just. But he warned His Excellency that "a dog, when beaten, will show his teeth," and then proceeded to collect together what cattle he could. These he sent to the Governor, and they were delivered to the British on December 18, 1852, at their camp on the western bank of the Caledon. These cattle were distributed to the Barolongs and other claimants, and driven off at once to Bloemfontein, the headquarters of the British Resident. No more cattle having come in, the English General crossed the Caledon on the Monday following, and, forming his forces into three divisions, proceeded to sweep off the vast herds of cattle which were known to be grazing on the heights between Berea and Thaba Bosigo. Though the action which followed was claimed by the English commander as a victory, it was regarded as a defeat both by his own soldiers and by the Basutos.* The casualties on the English side were two officers and thirty-five men killed, and fifteen wounded; while it was subsequently ascertained that the Basuto loss amounted to no more than twenty killed, and about the same number wounded. During the fight part of a troop of the 12th Lancers, who were collecting cattle on the heights, suffered severely. They were surrounded by Molapo's horsemen and their retreat cut off, and the "Lancers' Gap" at Berea, down which they threw themselves, only, in many cases, poor fellows, to meet with certain death, is still pointed out with pride by old Basuto warriors. It is not necessary to go further into the details of this unfortunate engagement, or to do more than glance at its results. It will be enough to observe generally that the worst of all possible policies towards the black man is to promise without performing, or to threaten punishment without inflicting it. Sir George Cathcart, no doubt with the best intentions, was led to do both these things. He had promised the Barolongs and others compensation for their losses, and had entered the Lesuto at the head of a splendidly equipped body of troops to enforce payment of it. He had sent an ultimatum to the Basuto chief, threatening him with condign punishment if

---

* Theal, *vide supra*.

its provisions were not at once complied with; and now, having failed to enforce at the point of the sword the payment of the fine he had inflicted—10,000 head of cattle and 1,000 horses—he seized the first opportunity of withdrawing from the position he had taken up. That opportunity was not long in presenting itself. Though the British forces had been vastly outnumbered in the engagement the Basuto horsemen had noted with awe, as well as admiration, the splendid discipline of the small body of infantry which advanced against them, and the obstinate stubbornness with which it held its own against such desperate odds. This made a deep impression upon Moshesh, and there was one marked trait in his character which availed him greatly at the present juncture, if indeed it did not save him and his people from national extinction. It was said of him that " he always knew when to humble himself"; and accordingly, seeing the peril of his position, and the certainty that the English would attack him with redoubled force and determination on the morrow, he sent to the Governor the following characteristic epistle* :—

"Thaba Bosigo, Midnight, December 20, 1852.

"Your Excellency,—This day you have fought against my people and taken much cattle. As the object for which you have come is to have a compensation for Boers, I beg you will be satisfied with what you have taken. I entreat peace from you—you have shown your power—you have chastised—let it be enough, I pray you; and let me be no longer considered an enemy to the Queen. I will try all I can to keep my people in order for the future.

"Your humble servant,

"MOSHESH."

---

* This letter was, I think, first made public and given to the world by Mr. Theal in his "History of the Boers of South Africa," p. 324. He makes the date the 29th, but this is probably a misprint for the 20th, the latter being the correct date. I would here take the opportunity of acknowledging my obligations to this able and attractive writer. And I may, perhaps, be permitted to add that it has been a great satisfaction to me to find that my own researches, made independently, and for the most part several years before the publication of his volume, have been fully borne out by a writer of such undoubted authority.

This letter had the desired effect. The Governor, though he had been practically worsted by the chief, and had failed to take more than a small portion of the 6,000 head of cattle still due to him in accordance with his demand, began to realise the fact that he was face to face with an enemy of no ordinary native type, to subdue whom would involve, in all probability, a protracted and costly war. He was unwilling, for many reasons, to enter upon such a contest. He thought that Moshesh had already felt the power of English arms; and when the chief thus humbled himself before him and besought his clemency he at once resolved to accord it, and to retire with the best grace he could and with the spoils he had gotten from his unenviable position. He therefore accepted the chief's submission, and after exhorting him to good behaviour for the future, withdrew his forces and returned to the Cape. It is not for me to blame him. Sir George Cathcart was a brave soldier, and he met, we know, not long afterwards a soldier's death in the battlefields of the Crimea. But undoubtedly his action in retiring from the Lesuto so hastily with his mission only half accomplished, after the threats he had held out, was fraught with evil results to the settlers of the Sovereignty and to their native allies, as the event testified. In the eyes of every native Moshesh was regarded with more pride and veneration than ever. Had he not succeeded in defeating and driving away the armies of England, with no less a personage than the great Governor himself at their head? The Barolongs and other fragments of tribes friendly to the white man had been but barely half compensated for their losses; the Europeans looked upon the Governor's proceedings with ill-concealed indignation and disgust; and these feelings were intensified when it was known soon afterwards that the British Government were preparing to abandon altogether the whole of their territories north of the Orange. This determination was carried out early in 1854 by the British Special Commissioner, Sir George Russel

Clark, notwithstanding the indignant protest of the great majority of the settlers, and from henceforth the Orange River Sovereignty was known as the Orange River Free State.

While Sir George Clark was making arrangements for the abandonment of the Sovereignty, and doing his best to induce its inhabitants to form an independent Republic of their own, Moshesh, seeing his opportunity, and with all his recent laurels fresh upon him, suddenly fell upon his old and troublesome enemy Sikonyela, and completely routed him, taking not only his stronghold, but all his cattle, waggons, and everything else of value. Sikonyela and his people, together with his allies the Koraunas, were completely eaten up. Vast numbers of the Batlokoa perished on the battlefield, Makitikiti, Sikonyela's eldest son, being among the number. The whole tribe was, in fact, wiped out. The fragments that were left were most of them incorporated among the Basutos, intermarried with them, and are to-day scarcely distinguishable from them. Only a tiny remnant, Ledinyane's people in the northern corner of the Leribe district, still retains some of its own tribal customs. Sikonyela himself escaped with a handful of his followers, taking refuge first in the Sovereignty, and afterwards at Herschel in the Cape Colony, where he died in 1856.

Moshesh was now completely master of the situation, and it redounds to his honour that for some years he lived for the most part in peace and amity with the Barolong and also with the Boers of the new Republic. But after 1860, when he had become an old man, the scene again changes. He was more and more swayed by his sons and nephews, who in their turn were influenced by the warlike speeches and the braggadocio of the young braves who were continually thirsting to "wet their spears." Marauding exploits once more became frequent. The homesteads of the white settlers in the south-eastern districts of the Free State were attacked and pillaged, and the choicest cattle carried off. Lesooana, or as he was more commonly called Ramanella, a nephew of Moshesh, was one of the most prominent leaders in these scenes of outrage and robbery, and the chief did little or nothing to restrain him. Whether in the pride of power he believed himself invincible and secure on his mountain throne, or whether old age had weakened his energies, I cannot say. It is enough that this rapine and violence remained unchecked by him. And doubtless there were faults on the side of the white settlers too. But these strained relations could not long continue; war was the inevitable result. From 1863 to 1868 war raged everywhere between the Basutos and the Boers. At first the former were the victors, ravaging nearly every farm along the border, and for many miles to the west; but at length the tide began to turn, and the Boer commandos entered Basutoland and made themselves masters of the whole country, with the exception of Thaba Bosigo. The Basutos were now at their last extremity. The Free State forces had made two ineffectual attempts to take the mountain fortress and were meditating a third when, at the prayer of Moshesh, Sir Philip Wodehouse, the Governor of the Cape Colony, intervened, and in the Queen's name proclaimed the Lesuto British territory, requesting the President of the Orange Free State to disband his commandos, and at once leave the country. Thus, by the intervention of the British, the Lesuto, or at any rate the greater portion of it, was spared to the Basutos, and the tribe once more secured a new lease of national existence.

The Governor himself arrived soon afterwards at Thaba Bosigo, and was received by the whole nation with demonstrations of unfeigned gratitude and joy. Moshesh in an earnest exhortation entreated his people, in the symbolic language so well understood by natives, to take shelter in the "cave" which their "mother," the Queen of England, had so graciously provided for them, and never on any account to leave it. Should they ever dream of doing so, he warned them that their destruction was certain.

After gaining back the greater part of their country for them, and laying down, in conjunction with Mr. Brand, the President of the Orange Free State, a new boundary line between the two territories, Sir Philip Wodehouse made what arrangements he thought wisest for the government of Basutoland, and appointed Mr. Griffith as his representative in the country.

The "Chief of the Mountain" did not long survive the transfer of his power and authority to the Queen of England. He died on March 12, 1870, leaving his eldest son, Letsie, to succeed him as Paramount Chief, and his sons Masupha and Molapo as chiefs of the districts of Thaba Bosigo and Leribe.

It is doubtful how far Moshesh embraced the Christian faith. He was never baptised, and would never consent to make any public confession of the faith of Christ, though often exhorted to do so by the Christian missionaries then in the country. He kept close to most of the old ideas and customs of his tribe, but he invited missionaries to enter the Lesuto, and steadfastly protected and defended them. He respected the sanctity of the Lord's Day, and through his influence Sunday was known far and wide as the day on which no unnecessary or servile work ought to be done. He was the one strikingly great man the tribe has produced. His sons were in every way greatly his inferiors, and the only one of his house who at all resembles him in capacity and force of character is his grandson, Jonathan Molapo, the present chief of the Leribe district.

After Moshesh's death the Basutos continued in peace and prosperity under British rule until the revolt of Morosi in 1879, and the outbreak of the rebellion of the following year.

During the last ten years thousands of natives of various tribes, chiefly Kafirs from the Transkeian territories, and Barolongs from Thaba 'Nchu, have emigrated into Basutoland with the consent of Letsie and the other chiefs, and now even the remote valleys of the Malutis are rapidly becoming populated. A census was taken in 1875, but it was a first attempt, and necessarily imperfect and incomplete. It gave the number of inhabitants as 127,000, and there has been no census since. It is thought that the present population cannot be far, if anything, short of a quarter of a million. The European population of the country is a little over 800.

CHAPTER III.

SOCIAL LIFE OF THE BASUTOS.

Government—Land Tenure—Common Law—Occupations—Circumcision Rites — Marriage — Polygamy — Habitations — Food — Clothing—Amusements.

THE reader is now in possession of the leading facts connected with the career of the great Chief of the Basutos; but before going further it may, perhaps, be well to say a few words concerning the social life of this mountain tribe—their manners and customs, usages and laws.

And first, a word as to their system of government. The details of this have naturally been somewhat modified since 1868, when the Basutos were first taken under direct British protection, but its essential characteristics remain the same.

The chief is regarded as the source and fountain of all authority, the father and ruler of his people; but he is by no means in all respects an absolute monarch. He may not infringe the social usages or common laws of the nation, or introduce new laws or customs, or make war without the consent of at least a majority of his councillors. If he does so, as will sometimes happen when he is a man of more than ordinary force of character, he must take the consequences. At the present time, now that the country is under British jurisdiction, the Paramount Chief (Letsie), is guided, and to some extent controlled, in the administration of affairs by a Resident Commissioner, appointed by the Governor of the Cape Colony in his capacity of High Commissioner of the native territories of South Africa. Or the Commissioner may be sent out direct from Downing-street; and in any case the Imperial Secretary of State for the Colonies has a veto upon the appointment, and is responsible for it.

The Resident Commissioner alone has power to inflict capital punishment, and that only in accordance with the sentence of the Combined Court of Assistant Commissioners; the chiefs having no longer the power of life and death in their hands. These latter deal with all petty cases in their own Khothla, and with graver ones also if requested to do so by the Commissioner or his local representatives; and all measures affecting the social welfare, or the usages and customs of the tribe, are usually submitted to the Paramount Chief for his approval before being promulged by the Government. New laws or regulations are not as a rule adopted before being considered and approved by the great Pitso, or National Assembly of the people. This Pitso is convened by the Resident Commissioner, and is held annually at Maseru, the Government capital, or in the neighbourhood. All the great chiefs are cited to it, and every Mosuto can attend it if he pleases. Anyone may speak, but the common people rarely do so, leaving the oratory to their superiors. As a rule, they content themselves with endorsing or dissenting from the remarks made by the chiefs or their counsellors.

This dual system of government, which may be characterised as Home Rule in its broadest form, rests mainly, under the present circumstances of the country, upon the personal character and ability of the Resident Commissioner, Sir Marshall Clarke, K.C.M.G., and his subordinate officials. These gentlemen have been called upon to undertake the task of keeping in order, through their own native chiefs and headmen, nearly a quarter of a million of savages, or, at any rate, people just emerging from barbarism; and they have to do this without any force at their back, or authority at their disposal, beyond that which is conveyed by the mere name of the Queen of England. They have to rule, as far as they can be said to rule at all, by moral force alone. That they have to some extent succeeded in this difficult and delicate task is a sure evidence of their integrity as well as their ability, since the native is quick enough to notice the least indication of anything crooked in policy or conduct, and appreciates above all things moral rectitude on the part of his European rulers. "Is he a straight man?" is the question asked at once by the native on hearing of the appointment of some new official.

The revenue is derived from hut tax (ten shillings per annum for each hut), traders' licenses, and a Colonial subsidy not exceeding £20,000 per annum. The expenditure—always within the income—is devoted to the payment of the officials and those of the chiefs who act as magistrates, the native mounted police (150 in number), the making and repair of roads, and grants in aid of education.

The system of land tenure is what may be broadly termed socialistic. The land belongs to the tribe as such, and individual ownership is not permitted. This principle is respected by the British Government, which holds the territory in trust for the people. Wardmasters appointed by the chiefs allot, from time to time, to each family patches of arable land sufficient for its support. This is usually done in the spring, before digging or ploughing has commenced; and ordinarily a family retains its right to the same fields for many years in succession. Uncultivated land is public property, and is used for grazing purposes by the people generally. Lines of demarcation and delimitation are laid down between the districts of the greater chiefs, and these are subdivided into wards over which minor chiefs and headmen are appointed with certain rights of their own, but in strict subordination to the chief of the whole district. The fields are unenclosed, hedges or fences between the gardens and corn lands of the different families being unknown. That the rights of each family are rigidly respected goes without saying. Infractions of these rights are of very rare occurrence, but when they do take place they are punished promptly and severely. No title deeds to any land whatever are granted either by the Government or the chiefs. Even the mission property at the various mission stations, as well as the Government offices and buildings, and the shops and houses of traders, are erected on land to which no legal claim of ownership can be made. The land is simply "assigned" to certain individuals *for specific uses* by the authorities. A missionary, a trader, or any other European permitted to settle in the country is regarded as the absolute owner of any buildings erected by him; he may sell them or remove them, but he possesses no legal right to the ground on which they are built. The very ground on which the mission churches are erected cannot be alienated from the tribe, though it is understood that, being devoted to the service of God, it will never be disturbed, or reclaimed for secular purposes. In the absence of legal title deeds to the land, the churches cannot of course be consecrated, and they are therefore simply dedicated to Divine worship by an appropriate service authorised by the Bishop of the diocese, and usually performed by him.

Certain portions of the pasture lands, especially of those in the valleys of the Malutis, are marked out by the chiefs as winter pastures, and are preserved accordingly. Footpaths are, of course, free everywhere to all. The chiefs derive no revenue from the land, but their fields are larger than those of the common people. Their cattle, in which their wealth mainly consists, are distributed among various families, especially those of headmen, who herd them, and are responsible for them, taking the milk as a reward for their care and labour.

It is obvious that such a system of land tenure is only fitted to a nation in its infancy, or to a pastoral and agricultural community in a thinly-populated country. Even in Basutoland there is scarcely room under this system for the increasing numbers of the people, and land and grazing disputes are very common. In olden days, before the tribe came under British jurisdiction, such disputes would be settled by the assagai, and the increase of population kept in this way within certain limits; but this cannot, of course, be the case now. While this primitive and simple system of land tenure is hardly compatible either with the perfect fulfilment of the Divine command to "replenish the earth and subdue it," * or with the natural and unchecked increase of the population; it nevertheless prevents pauperism on the one hand, or the acquisition by any one individual of thousands of broad acres on the other. There are many poor men amongst the Basutos, for "ye have the poor with you always, and whensoever ye will ye may do them good." † But there are no paupers; and the extremes of wealth and poverty which mark, more than ever in our own day, highly advanced and civilised communities do not exist in Basutoland.

The common law of the Basutos, as of all the Bantu tribes, has come down to them from a remote period of antiquity. Its details, as well as its leading principles, have been carefully preserved from generation to generation. All trials are held in public in the open Khothla, to which every full grown man has access, and hence the methods of procedure become known to all. Every man is a born orator, and pleads his own cause. Cases are always, if possible, decided according to precedent, and this again would help to stamp the traditions and usages of the tribe upon each member of it. Like the system of land tenure, the leading principles of their common law are adapted only to a people in its infancy. They are largely identical with those of the patriarchal dispensation of the Old Testament. The modern

---

* Genesis i. 28.   † St. Mark xiv. 7.

Englishman sees every day in the Lesuto Old Testament scenes and customs enacted before his eyes, and lives, so to speak, in the atmosphere of the patriarchs of old. He finds that here the law holds the head of the family responsible for the conduct of its members, the village for that of its households, and the clan for the behaviour of each of its village communes. Individual rights, such as we have come to possess under the influence of matured Christian teaching, and as the result of it, are unknown to the Basutos.

The occupations of the people are, in the present day, almost entirely agricultural or pastoral. There is now very little to be done in the way of hunting, nearly all the game having been killed out. The chiefs usually make up annual hunting parties in the Malutis, chiefly with the object of securing the eland; but as year by year goes by the hunters have to go further and further into the innermost recesses of the mountains in order to find any sport worthy of the name.

From time to time numbers of the younger men leave their homes and go away to the Diamond Fields, or the Gold Fields, to work in the mines for periods of six months or a year, hoping to save sufficient money out of their earnings wherewith to procure the much coveted rifle, or the still more coveted wife. It is to be feared that these poor fellows learn more of the vices of civilization than its virtues. They return to their homes with their wits sharpened, and their cunning developed, but also, in most instances, with constitutions enfeebled, and habits more depraved than ever. Those who go out thus to work are, for the most part, "raw" heathens, but with them there will often be a sprinkling of Christian natives—usually those under Church censure, in fact, the off-scourings of the mission stations. These, on the principle of *corruptio optimi pessimi*, will generally prove themselves to be leaders in all kinds of evil courses, becoming in time adepts in rascality and wickedness. Boasting of their Christianity, but carefully concealing the fact that they are out of communion, and under censure at the mission stations to which they belong, they bring discredit on the Christian name, and cause the finger of scorn to be pointed at the "School Kafir," as native Christians are usually called by the more irreligious among the colonists.

Vast tracts of land are cultivated in the Lesuto. As a rule every valley is full of corn fields, mealies and Kafir-corn being much more largely grown than wheat. The two former, especially the second, form the principal food of the people. As has been already observed the soil is very prolific, manure being never used; yet in good years it will literally produce "some thirty, some sixty, some an hundred" fold.* In most years large quantities of grain are sold to the traders in the country and sent by them to Kimberley, Johannesburg, Bloemfontein, and the other principal towns of Griqualand West, the Transvaal, and the Free State. The field work was formerly almost entirely performed by the women, but since the introduction of Christianity into the country the men have gradually learnt to take their share in it; and at the present time both men and women work hard in the fields during the ploughing and harvest seasons. The plough is largely superseding the native pick or mattock; indeed, the young girls are already beginning to stipulate that the man who asks them in marriage—that is to say, who asks their father for them—should both possess a plough and know how to use it. They say that "a man who has not got a plough has no business to have a wife."

The ploughing is always done with oxen, four being usually inspanned for the purpose. The fields of each chief are ploughed, sowed, and weeded by his men, who render this service very willingly as an act of homage to their lord. He orders a "letsema"—a "garden party," in the Sesuto and literal meaning of the term—and every able-bodied man responds cheerfully and at once to his summons. The next morning's dawn sees

---

* St. Mark iv. 8.

them all hurrying to the scene of action. It is a pretty sight at such times to watch, in the case of the greater and more influential chiefs, hundreds of ploughs going at once over the extensive unenclosed fields. The furrows, it is true, would hardly pass muster in England, but the work is done effectually and with a will. The first *letsema* of the season usually takes place in September, and in November or December a second is held, which is even a more interesting sight than the first. You may then see a thousand or fifteen hundred men all hoeing the lands together. They are divided into companies of a hundred and fifty or two hundred, and all of them keep perfect time with their hoes as they chant the quaint and expressive songs and calls to labour appropriate to the occasion, which have come down to them from generation to generation.

The harvesting is a slower business, and is still done almost entirely by the women. The fields are not reaped as with us, the stalks of maize and millet not being cut, and no sickle being needed. The rich, full ears, or rather bunches, of millet are broken off with the hand, and the cobs of maize are detached from the parent stalk in the same manner. All are taken home, and the grain is carefully rubbed out of its sheath, the smallest children even assisting in the work. The reader must remember that the millet and maize harvest takes place, as I have already said, at midwinter, the wheat harvest being at midsummer, that is to say as early as possible in January.

During the two months of the mid-winter harvest the women work very hard. A woman will leave her home a few minutes after dawn, carrying her infant on her back, and a large *Seruto*— a basin-shaped basket—on her head. She will trudge along bravely and patiently until she reaches her corn patch, at perhaps four or five or even seven or eight miles distance. In that corn patch she will work with scarcely any interval of rest until the long slanting rays of the declining sun warn her to return home. Then she piles her basket to the brim with maize cobs or bunches of millet, and with her little one still at her back cooing out in the prettiest and most engaging way its baby accents, she will plod diligently homeward. Arrived at her cabin she will at once, without a moment's intermission, commence the preparation of the family meal, having herself partaken of nothing but a cup of *leting* before starting for the harvest field, and a mouthful or two of bogobe during the whole of the day.

The wheat is threshed out and winnowed on the threshing floor so familiar to every reader of the Old Testament, the grain being trodden out by horses or bullocks. The wheat almost always finds its way to the trader, being in fact grown with that intention; the Basutos not having yet learnt the art of making bread after the European fashion. The mabele required for the year's supply of the family is carefully stored away in huge, globular, almost air-tight grass baskets made for the purpose, the small mouths of which are covered with a flat stone carefully plastered round with clay. The grain intended for sale is usually conveyed to the trading station in enormous bullock skin bags dangling at the sides of some stout fat pack ox, which the owner never fails to ride on his return journey.

The pastoral life of the Basutos is a very pleasant one. The herding of both cattle and horses falls, as we know, to the lot of the young men and boys. As to the men, they are "veritable lords of creation," having for the greater part of the year little to do and plenty of time to do it in. Most of the older men spend their time mainly in the Khothla, listening to the cases before the court, gossiping, or simply squatting on the ground doing nothing. In the ploughing and sowing seasons all are busy. The time that used formerly to be spent in hunting or war is now devoted to the more prosaic and peaceful pursuits of improving their dwellings and planting fruit trees. Every man is in his way a tanner and a tailor, and here and there one may find a smith. But the handsome karosses so common in days

E

gone by are now only rarely seen. There is very little left to dress besides bullock skins and goat skins. The neatest of European furriers could barely hold their own against the Basutos and Bechuanas in the dressing of the skins of wild animals, and the preparation of those robes of fur so justly and universally admired by all who have seen them. These lovely and graceful furs are beautifully stitched together with sinews simply by the aid of a small awl. The men are still very fond of this sort of work. The dressing is performed by a number of them working together in groups, all of them chattering away like so many parrots until the skin becomes in their hands as supple as a glove.

Many of the women, when not engaged in their domestic duties or in their fields and gardens, occupy their time in making pottery. They mould drinking and other vessels of clay with the hand, and then bake them on a slow fire of *disu*, the ordinary fuel of the country. Some of these vessels are of really graceful shape and design, and are much sought after by the Europeans in the country.

At the age of seventeen or eighteen the youths undergo the rite of circumcision. This ceremony is regarded by them as the entrance into the rights and privileges of manhood. Among the Kafir tribes of the coast there is little or nothing that is secret about the rite, nor does it seem in any way to be very objectionable. The Zulus abolished it among themselves during the reign of Chaka, and at his command. The Basutos cling to it still with great tenacity. "The youths," says Mr. Theal,* "are formed into guilds or lodges with passwords. The members of these lodges are bound never to give evidence against one another. The rites of initiation are kept profoundly secret, but certain horrible customs performed on some of these occasions have become known. One of these customs is that of infusing

---

* Hist. Boers. p. 17.

courage, intelligence, and other qualities. Whenever an enemy who has acted bravely is killed, his liver, which is considered the seat of valour, his ears, which are considered the seat of intelligence, the skin of his forehead, which is considered the seat of perseverance, and other members, each of which is supposed to be the seat of some desirable quality, are cut from his body and baked to cinders. The ashes are carefully preserved in the horn of a bull, and during the circumcision ceremonies are mixed with other ingredients into a kind of paste and administered by the tribal priest to the youths, the idea being that the virtues which they represent are communicated to those who swallow them. This practice, together with that of using other parts of the remains of their enemies for bewitching purposes, accounts for the mutilation of the bodies of those who fall into their hands in war, a practice which has more then once infuriated white men whose friends have been thus treated, and caused them to commit deeds from which they would otherwise have shrunk." "The corresponding ceremony through which young females pass," says the same writer, "as practised by the coast tribes, might be deemed the most degrading rite that human beings have ever been subject to, if it were not known that among the mountain tribes it is even more vile. All that the most depraved imagination can devise to rouse the lowest passions of the young females is here practised. A description is impossible."

These are very sweeping assertions, and it is possible that they may be too highly coloured. I sincerely trust that this may be the case, though from my own experience of the country I fear that they are, in the main at least, only too true. The recipients of these rites generally remain in the lodges for about three months, during which time the discipline which the young men undergo is so severe that they sometimes die under it. Anyone who has heard their howlings at night in the awful solitudes of the Malutis, echoing and reverberating from glen to glen and crag to crag, like the wailings of lost souls, will hardly ever think of them without a shudder. The girls, during the time of their sojourn in the lodge, are daubed from head to foot with white clay as a sign of their uncleanness, and wear a curious veil of reeds over their eyes. They may be encountered from time to time in small bands, marching along in solemn procession near the roadsides, uttering as they go a series of doleful sounds in a minor key. Being almost naked, the sight of these poor creatures thus daubed and plastered is a ghastly and repulsive one. They look like so many moving spectres, calculated to frighten an Englishwoman out of her wits. This circumcision ceremony may be characterised as *the initiatory rite or Sacrament of heathenism*, and Christian youths and maidens are forbidden to take part in it.

Marriage among the Basutos is usually a mere affair of convenience. The parents or guardians of the young people arrange it with little or no regard to the feelings of the young people themselves. There is a wedding feast, but no religious ceremony —indeed no ceremony at all worthy of the name. The binding force of the marital contract, as far as it may be said to be a marital contract and to possess any force at all, depends upon the transfer, or more plainly, payment of a stipulated number of cattle to the father or guardian of the bride. This secures to the girl the rights and privileges, such as they are, of a wife. The wife is the mere serf of her husband, but he cannot sell her, nor has he a right to maim or maltreat her. The payment of the cattle is regarded as a guarantee against ill-treatment; for should the husband ill-use her she may return to her father or guardian, and her husband would lose both his wife and his cattle. The chief objection to this system of marriage is that it permits a man to give his daughter in marriage to the highest bidder for her, without any necessary reference to her inclinations. Human nature being what it is, the result is, of course, in most cases lamentable; the marital tie is often utterly disregarded, and the purity of domestic life sapped to its foundations.

But the crowning social evil of the Basutos is polygamy, the chiefs being the greatest transgressors in this respect because of their superior wealth. No one who has lived for any length of time in Basutoland can be insensible to the gigantic evils which polygamy entails. It is the parent of jealousies, heart-burnings, dissensions, murders, and wars. The half brothers of a family are taught by their mothers to hate each other from their very infancy; and should they be the sons of a chief there is nearly always a war of succession upon the death of the father. War thins out the male population, thus causing the female to preponderate more than ever, and this disproportion leads again inevitably to further polygamy. And so the ball keeps rolling on. In fact, among the many devices of Satan for the degradation of the human race, I know of none more seductive, and in the end more potent, than the evil of which we are speaking. The possession of many wives brings to the possessor of them great wealth and influence. Each wife or concubine has her own hut, works in the fields allotted to her, and supports her own establishment, the husband reaping as he chooses the fruits of her labours. When a chief has many wives and concubines he sometimes bestows some of them either permanently or for a time upon a needy friend, or upon the hangers on and parasites of the Khothla, who are too idle or too poor to procure a wife for themselves. Divorces are of frequent occurrence, especially among the ruling caste. In fact the whole subject—like the two preceding ones—is so unsavoury that we will dwell no longer upon it.

The houses of the Basutos are built of sods, well cemented together with clay; the walls being about five feet high, and the roof of poles thatched with reeds and grass. Most of these huts are round in shape, but oblong structures are beginning, on account of their greater convenience, to make their appearance everywhere, especially among the Christian converts. They are entered by one small aperture, sometimes not more than two feet in height, through which one has to wriggle one's way like a snake in order to get inside. Chimney there is none, the cooking being done outside in the open air. These huts are used only for sleeping purposes or in times of sickness or in bad weather, open air life being the one most natural to the native. Surrounding the hut and protecting it from the wind, there is usually a high screen of reeds, substantial, and in its way even handsome; and within the courtyard of this screen the cooking is done. Here also in the hot afternoons of summer men, women, children and dogs all lie huddled together in sleep. The doorways of the huts almost always face east or north-east, so as to catch the first rays of the rising sun. The poorer families have only one hut, the more well to do two, or perhaps even a third, which latter is usually reserved for visitors.

The villages of the people—some large, some small—are spread all over the country; and one may constantly find good-sized villages perched up on the ledges running out from the spurs of the Malutis, or even built along the mountain slopes. There are barely half-a-dozen villages in the whole country which contain a settled and resident population of over a thousand souls; and in the absence of anything whatever in the way of sanitary arrangements, this dispersion of the people all over the land in small clusters of huts is a great blessing, contributing as it does to keep the whole population healthy.

I have said that the native prizes his cattle above all things. And, indeed, it is no wonder, for they not only work for him, but provide him with food and clothing. Animal food he rarely eats, but milk enters largely into his daily diet. It is, however, seldom used when fresh; but sour, and especially when fermented in the form of curds, it is in universal request, and certainly there are very few things more delicious than a dish of *mafi*. Delicately white in colour and sub-acid in taste, it is most grateful to the palate as well as nutritious to the system on a hot summer day.

The women are everywhere the cooks; the men are mere clumsy, unclean bunglers in the preparation of food. The Basutos, however, do not excel in the culinary art. Their dishes are few and simple, the pot being in universal recognition to the exclusion of the gridiron or the frying-pan. They boil nearly everything, and a London or Parisian epicure would fare badly at their hands. Porridge, made either of mabèle or mealies, and thickened and flavoured with sour milk, mafi, or herbs, constitutes the usual daily food of the people. They make a peculiar kind of bread (bogobe), a pasty, insipid, unappetising mess, resembling a cannon ball in size and form. Europeans rarely, if ever, take to it kindly. Of fermented drinks there are two kinds—one, a light, refreshing beverage of a sub-acid flavour called *leting*; the other a much stronger and highly intoxicating liquor—*joala*, or native " beer," as the whites term it, which, when newly made and very pungent, is almost maddening in its effects. Both these are prepared from fermented mabèle. During the summer and autumn, vegetables, especially gourds and pumpkins, enter largely into the daily diet; while the young green maize, boiled and served with melted butter, is esteemed for its delicacy not only by natives, but by everyone. Africanders regard " green mealies " as a dish fit to put before a king; and certainly it is a delicious food, and as nourishing and wholesome as it is delicious.

In the matter of clothing the coloured blanket or rug is becoming universal throughout the country. It has taken the place of the kaross, now so seldom obtainable. Dressed bullock skins are worn sometimes for the sake of warmth in the depth of winter, especially by the men. When prepared, shaped and finished, and worn according to native fashion, they are by no means so ungraceful in appearance as one would imagine. Indeed, I remember only last winter one of our Christian converts—old Simeone Dichakana—coming into church one Sunday morning clad in a deep chocolate-coloured bullock skin cloak, which looked exactly like *a cope*, clasp, and all complete! The old man might have passed for an Abyssinian ecclesiastic of high rank, so venerable and dignified did he look. Sheep skins are constantly worn by the herd boys as cloaks, and in winter the lads make themselves shoes of the same material, the wool being inside for the sake of warmth. The women and girls use beads very largely as ornaments. They make them into necklaces and armlets with charming taste, the bead-work of the Zulu girls being [in its way really beautiful. Bangles of fine copper or brass wire, deftly interwoven, are largely affected both by men and women. A desire for finery of European make and pattern is greatly on the increase, the shops of the traders being now full of "costumes" of the most gaudy and extravagant types direct from London; and these are eagerly bought up by the wives and daughters of the more well-to-do members of the community. In vain does the missionary set his face against, and oppose this extravagance and love of display. The tide of fashion is too strong for him, and he has to content himself with the reflection that, objectionable as this finery is, it is at any rate not worse than the tattooing and the daubing with red clay and pig fat which are still universally in use among all but a fraction of the people.

All natives are fond of dancing, most of them passionately so, and the Basutos are not behind in this matter. Almost any pretext will suffice for a "mokete"—a feast—which, of course, usually ends with a dance. Sometimes, when there is a great "beer-drinking" going on at a heathen village, the dance which accompanies it terminates in an orgie. The dancers of both sexes become thoroughly intoxicated, and then ensues a scene of bestial revelry, such as can hardly be imagined, much less described. Yet, intoxicated as they are, many of the dancers will dance on until they drop from sheer exhaustion. Now and then some of them have been known literally to drop down dead. But, happily, all the dances are not of this description, though it is doubtful whether the best of them are such as a modest Christian youth or maiden ought to take part in. The Zulus dance in their way exquisitely, with much more perfect time and grace than the Basutos; but the postures and gestures employed are, it is to be feared, equally licentious in both cases.

The national war dances are remarkable spectacles, producing nothing less than a thrilling effect upon the spectator, whether he be black or white. Some two thousand warriors or more, plumed, and in their war trappings, and armed to the teeth with the weapons of their tribe, form themselves into a circle, and commence a weird, unearthly chant in a minor key. This is rendered with perfect rhythm and intense feeling. Then follows a recitative, when suddenly some well-known brave will spring with what seems to be a single bound into the centre of the circle, stab the earth with his assagai, leap frantically into the air, then stab the earth again, uttering as he does so a loud *hiss*, which is taken up by the thousand throats as one overwhelming, blood-curdling *shzz* again and again repeated. This is supposed to represent the annihilation of all enemies of the tribe by the repeated stabs of the assagai, and is accompanied by the stamping of each naked, horny foot upon the ground by a simultaneous movement which seems to make the very earth around tremble. Then ensues a deafening babel of sounds and clattering of tongues, such as no words can describe, each and every man in the vast circle yelling the direst threats, anathemas, and imprecations against the enemy; and then again the warrior in the centre brings his foot to the ground, stabbing the earth and breathing out, as only a native can, his deep-chested resonant *hiss*, which is again immediately taken up by the multitude as before. The number of stabs he inflicts upon the earth shows the number of enemies he has killed; and when he has ended the recital of his heroic deeds, the refrain in the minor key is taken up and repeated again by the whole circle with the most perfect solemnity, and continued until a second warrior leaps into the midst of the throng, and recounts his heroic deeds on the battlefield with the same gestures as the first. A third succeeds, then a fourth, and so on, until, on great occasions, the whole regiment or regiments will be so wrought upon by the intensity of their feelings that they will continue the dance for hours and hours together; the lugubrious, doleful refrain of their song, and the thud of their stamping feet being heard to a great distance. These war dances are held before going to battle, and with still greater enthusiasm and intensity of feeling after a victory.

The Basutos have three musical instruments, the drum, the *lesiba*, and the *tomo*. The first of these, which produces a hideous and deafening noise, is made by simply stretching a piece of dried sheep skin to its utmost tension over an earthenware or wooden pot. It is often accompanied by the second, the *lesiba*, a curious little instrument made by stretching a string like that of a violin along a short piece of slightly curved bamboo. At one end of the string a quill is placed, slit in two lengthwise, and considerably flattened. The instrument is usually played by a boy, who draws with his lips a series of sharp, shrill, nasal sounds from the vibrating string and quill, which would be nothing less than an utter terror to anyone possessed of "nerves." Sometimes the women and girls will dance to these instruments, keeping time by singing and clapping their hands. On such occasions one of the females, generally a wizened old hag with a stick in her hand, acts as conductress and mistress of the ceremonies; and the women with their contortions, their horrible grimaces, their hand clappings, their shrill piercing voices, and the flapping to and fro of their short stiff leather petticoats look like so many witches—an African rendering of the well-known scene in "Macbeth."

The *tomo* (thomo) is something like the lesiba, but larger

and more curved. It has no quill, but the string is fastened upon a bamboo attached to a calabash with a hole in it. The performer holds it by one end in his left hand, leaving his thumb and fore-finger free to touch the string. In his right hand he holds a thin stick, with which he strikes the string from time to time. The sound, swelling as it passes through the calabash, can be varied and raised higher or lower by touching or striking the string at different heights. The tomo is thus a primitive guitar; and as human nature is essentially the same everywhere, this instrument is a favourite one with the young men. They will spend hours at a time over it, and grow to be intensely fond of it. When they have mastered it, they are never weary of playing it. Above all they will, we may be sure, seek opportunities to "make it sing" to some gentle though dusky damsel the same song of love, ever old yet ever new, which is not unknown, though rendered it may be with sweeter strains, and a more polished diction, to their more favoured relatives in distant Europe.

CHAPTER IV.

Religion.

Religious and Moral Ideas of the Basutos—Superstitions—Witchcraft—Diviners and Rain Doctors—Siboko—Moshesh and the French Protestant Missionaries—Results of their Mission—The Roman Catholic Mission—Room for more Christian Workers—Moshesh and Bishop Gray—Basutoland attached to the Diocese of Bloemfontein—Tentative Efforts—Resolution of Bishop Webb to carry out Moshesh's Wish.

The Bantu races have no buildings dedicated to religious worship, and no public rites or ceremonies. The traveller may pass through all the various territories inhabited by them without seeing the slightest indication of any religious belief or worship.

The natives of Central Africa have at least a fetish; these have none. No doubt it was this singular spectacle of a people without any apparent religious belief and any object of supreme worship which made the Arabs give them centuries ago, in their dealings with the Coast Tribes, the name of *Kafirs* or Infidels—a name which has clung to them ever since. Yet the Bantu peoples are not destitute of religious or moral ideas; and though it is true that they have no temples or structures of any kind dedicated to religious uses, they have, nevertheless, objects of reverence and supreme worship. They worship the spirits of their ancestors. They have "exchanged the truth of God for a lie, and worshipped and served the creature rather than the Creator." *

The Basutos, in common with the other Bantu tribes, believe that the spirits of their ancestors interfere in their daily affairs, and influence their destiny. Accordingly they endeavour to worship and propitiate them with prayers, incantations, and sacrifices. Such worship as they render to these departed spirits is based upon fear; love does not enter into it. Some of them may perhaps have a dim idea of the existence of a supreme, all-powerful Being; but if so, He is for practical purposes an abstraction to them. They do not regard Him as interesting Himself in their affairs, nor do they imagine that they stand in any direct personal relationship to Him. What religious instincts they possess have become so perverted that it is doubtful whether it can be said with truth that they are "a power which makes for righteousness."

But this is a large subject as well as a deeply interesting one, about which a whole volume might be written. We can but barely glance at it here.

M. Arbousset, one of the first French Protestant missionaries to the Basutos, has recorded in graphic language a touching

---

* Romans i. 25. Rev. Version.

conversation which he had with a Mosuto shortly after his arrival in the country.* Sekesa, the Mosuto in question, said to him one day :—

"Your tidings are what I want; what I was seeking before I knew you, as you shall hear and judge for yourselves. Twelve years ago I went to feed my flocks. The weather was hazy. I sat down upon a rock and asked myself sorrowful questions; yes, sorrowful, because I was unable to answer them.

"Who has touched the stars with his hands? On what pillars do they rest? I asked myself.

"The waters are never weary: they know no other law than to flow, without ceasing, from morning till night, and from night till morning; but where do they stop? and who makes them flow thus?

"The clouds also come and go, and burst in water over the earth. Whence come they? Who sends them? The diviners certainly do not give us rain, for how could they do it? and why do I not see them with my own eyes, when they go up to heaven to fetch it?

"I cannot see the wind, but what is it? Who brings it, makes it blow, and roar, and terrify us?

"Do I know how the corn sprouts? Yesterday there was not a blade in my field; to-day I returned to the field and found some. Who can have given to the earth the wisdom and the power to produce it?"

"Then I buried my face in both my hands."

Doubtless there have been at all times many such seekers after truth among these people, and I suppose that every missionary must have met with cases similar to the one just recorded. Let us thank God that their yearnings have been answered, and that the true light of the Gospel of Christ now

---

* Quoted in Casalis, The Basutos, p. 239. An interesting volume, but one dealing with a state of things that has largely passed away.

shines upon these souls who have so long dwelt "in darkness and the shadow of death." Not of course that no one glimmer of light had ever before reached them. Sitting there in that *shadow* of death, Conscience was nevertheless present within them. Go to the most ignorant and debased heathen man in the deepest recesses of the Drakensbergen, and ask him: "Is it right to steal, to murder, or to lie?" and he will at once answer you "No"; though perhaps he might not be able to tell you why.

The superstitions of the Basutos are almost innumerable, and they are firm believers in the efficacy of charms, spells, and amulets. They will fasten about their persons the most repulsive, ridiculous, and filthy objects, in order to escape from some danger, real or imaginary, or be cured of some ailment, or obtain some "stroke of good luck." In fact, they seem to have a remedy for every imaginable evil. But these superstitions are of little moment compared with the far more serious one of witchcraft.

"The belief in witchcraft is to this day the cause of a terrible amount of suffering among the tribes that are independent. All events that cannot be readily comprehended—sickness in man, murrain in cattle, blight in crops, even casual accidents—are by them attributed to the agency of wizards and witches, and not the slightest compassion is felt for any unfortunate wretch whom the recognised witch-finder of the community points out as guilty. Confiscation of property, torture, death, are the penalties of being charged with this ideal offence. It is believed that one man can bewitch another by means of any such thing as a few hairs from his head, a clipping of a finger-nail, a piece of clothing, or, indeed, anything whatever that belongs to him, or can be brought into contact with him, or can be concealed in or about his hut. Occasional cases of real poisoning undoubtedly occur, and each such case is additional proof to them that their belief is correct." *

---

* Theal, Hist. Boers, p. 9.

RELIGION.

It is pleasant to be able to say that these words do not apply, without at least some qualification, to the Lesuto of the present day, now that it has become in some sense a portion of the British Empire. But even now cases of "smelling out" do at times occur at the dictation of the chiefs—or at any rate with their connivance—though such doings are for obvious reasons kept as quiet as possible. Still there is reason to hope that the power of the diviners and witch doctors is, slowly it may be, but surely on the decline, though I regret to say that the rain-makers still flourish, and that, too, under the patronage of the chiefs. A well established and highly reputed rain maker in good practice will often receive during droughty seasons five, six, or even ten fat bullocks at a time for his incantations. These are generally muttered over a venerable and greasy pot, containing a decoction of herbs and a mixture of filthy and disgusting substances all boiled up together—a number of charms being cast in during the process. Even intelligent chiefs like Jonathan Molapo will sometimes patronise and pay these impostors, so great is the force of habit and superstition combined.

One superstition, harmless compared with others, is the veneration in which the Basutos hold the crocodile. Each of the Bantu tribes has its own *Siboko*, or object of reverence, which in former days it was said to *dance to*, though not actually worship. The Siboko, or, as we should say, the crest of the Basutos, and of some other tribes also, is the *kuena*, or crocodile, formerly found in great numbers in the rivers of Basutoland, but now almost, if not entirely, extinct there. The Basutos called themselves the *Bakuena*, or people of the crocodile, and they are still proud of the title. It is still the custom to address them by this name at public meetings, or when greeting a number of them together at their villages or in the fields. Other branches of the Bantu took the lion (tau) for their Siboko, like the Bataung; some are Baphuti, those of the blue antelope; some

Batlaping, those of the fish; or Bathlou, those of the elephant. They venerated these creatures, and endeavoured to preserve them from harm. To the present generation of Basutos the crocodile is little more than a name. Occasionally a skin of this reptile finds its way into the country and is eagerly bought up by the "medicine men," cut into fragments, and used as a charm against accident or disease.

In common with the Bechuanas, the Basutos have a curious superstition about thunder and lightning. They believe that both the thunder and the lightning are caused by a bird! A colossal bird with plumage as of shining silver comes out of the unknown, and poises itself above the dense, dark, lowering clouds. It flaps its wings and commands the clouds to burst. The sheen of its silver plumage lights up the sky in dazzling streams of light. It sweeps onward, and the motion of its pinions produces the thunder which man hears reverberating through the mountains or pealing over the plains. Then, in a moment, the clouds are rent asunder, and pour the fulness of their treasures upon the earth.

The year 1833 was a bright one for Basutoland, for it was in that year that Christian missionaries first found their way into the country. Moshesh had long known of the existence of white men, and had even made the acquaintance of a small party of them—Boers from the Cape Colony on a hunting expedition—some fourteen or fifteen years before. As time went on he heard more of them, and was naturally impressed with their superior knowledge and resources. One day a visitor—a half-caste Hottentot from the West—who had often been brought into contact with Christian missionaries, told the chief that some of these teachers had lately arrived north of the Orange river. They were, he said, white wizards who were wonderfully wise and knew the secrets of the universe; and he advised the chief to invite them into his country. Moshesh caught eagerly at the idea. He was anxious above all things to consolidate his newly-acquired power, and no doubt thought that these white teachers would be of use to him in carrying out his darling scheme of welding together the fragments of the mountain tribes into one strong, united people. He accordingly sent to Phillippolis, a station of the London Missionary Society far to the west among the Griquas, to invite these new teachers into his country. Two missionaries, M. Casalis and M. Arbousset, together with an artisan, M. Gosselin, attached to the mission, at once responded to the summons. All three were Frenchmen, members of the French Protestant Church, and had been sent to South Africa by the Paris Evangelical Mission with the object of evangelising the heathen tribes north of the Orange. All three were men of ability, as well as earnestness and piety, and they left an abiding mark for good in the district in which they settled. They were soon joined by other like-minded men, who established mission stations, with the consent of the chief, in several parts of the country, especially in the centre and the south. Their efforts have been largely blessed, and at the present time this French Protestant Mission has some twelve or thirteen stations with a number of out stations attached to them. At Morija, their principal centre of work, several admirably conducted educational institutions have been established, chiefly through the zeal and ability of M. Mabille, the missionary of the station; and there is in addition a printing establishment, which has been a powerful auxiliary to the work of the mission. Moshesh throughout his long career was faithful to his word: he promised to protect the missionaries, and he consistently fulfilled his promise. He gave them lands on which to settle, and insisted upon their being treated with respect by the people; and this friendship and protection he accorded not only to the French Protestants but to all Christian missionaries with whom he was brought into contact. It was, I suppose, inevitable, though the fact is to be regretted, that

F

these first missionaries, good and devoted men as they were, should become involved in the politics of the country in which they settled. That they acted for the best no one can doubt, but as time went on they became more and more identified in the eyes of the surrounding peoples, both black and white, with the schemes and plans of Moshesh, until, rightly or wrongly, they came to be regarded by the growing European population of the Orange Free State as the political agents of the chief. During the Basuto-Boer war they were expelled from the country on that ground by the victorious Free State forces, who, strong Protestants as they were, and Presbyterian in creed like the missionaries, nevertheless did not molest the Roman Catholic Mission, no charge of political partisanship or interference having been brought against it.

The Roman Catholic missionaries settled in the Lesuto in or about the year 1862, with the approbation of Moshesh. These were also Frenchmen, and members of a religious order. They came with a Bishop, Mgr. Allard, at their head, and accompanied by a strong contingent of nuns. The clergy and lay brothers of this mission are all "Oblates of Mary Immaculate," the sisters being nuns of the order of the "Visitation of the Blessed Virgin." They settled in a lovely spot—a "hoek," or recess in the hills—not far from Thaba Bosigo, which has become their headquarters. They likewise have large institutions, educational and industrial, which are not less admirably conducted than those of their Protestant brethren. The station is now known to Europeans by the name of Roma, though the Roman Catholic converts call it the "Motse oa Ma-Jesu"—the town of the mother of Jesus. Other stations have since been founded elsewhere in the country, and at the present time the Roman Catholic missionaries are making further efforts to extend their sphere of labour. They have made many converts, and have considerable influence in the neighbourhood of Roma; but, considering the staff of workers, both male and female, they have had and still have at their disposal, their success has not been, as far as man can judge, as great as that of the other Christian bodies in the country.

In the presence of such an overwhelming mass of debasing heathenism as exists in the Lesuto, any Christian agency is welcome. Better, a thousand times better, that the Basutos should be brought to the knowledge of the Redeemer in any way—whether by the agency of the most ultramontane Romanism, or by the efforts of the most extreme partisans of Calvinism—than that they should be suffered to remain a prey to the snares and delusions of wizards and rain doctors, without Christ, and without the knowledge of God.

But, though the Roman and the Presbyterian missionaries have done much, there is yet more, far more, to be done. Basutoland is still emphatically a heathen country, as the subsequent pages of this narrative will help to show. Not a single chief of the front rank is a Christian. All the great chiefs are either heathen or French Protestant converts, who, after a short profession of Christianity, have relapsed into their old habits and superstitions. Of chiefs of the second rank I know of only one in the whole country who is a Christian. This is Nathanaele Makotoko, with whom the reader is already acquainted; and he, amid evil report and good report, and the severest trials and temptations, has continued steadfast and faithful to his Lord and Saviour.

Two things more than any others have contributed to keep the chiefs heathen, or to tempt them back into heathenism. These are the "lust of the flesh," and the "pride of life." The first of these, in the shape of unlimited polygamy, has been, and is still, a most potent influence for evil; the second, the fear of loss of chieftainship or power, has been hardly less baleful in its effects. But few of the chiefs have at any time embraced the teaching of Jesus Christ, and most of these few have lacked force of character. In the hour of trial they have been carried away by the stream of passion, or have yielded to the fears inspired by the warnings and threats of their heathen counsellors. A young chief is told that he must choose between Christ and his chieftainship. The old men declare plainly that if he follows this new teaching he is lost. His people will regard him as a traitor, or at least as a coward dominated by the fear of the white man's God. The spirits of his ancestors, of whose brave deeds he has so often heard, but of whom he has proved himself unworthy, will wreak their vengeance upon him, and his people will desert him. He is told to make his choice, and he makes it. Alas! he does not choose Christ and His Cross. He cannot bring himself to " suffer," if need be, " affliction with the people of God," rather than to " enjoy the pleasures of sin for a season."* On the contrary, he yields to the same alluring voice that said of old: " All this will I give thee if thou wilt fall down and worship me." †

Assuredly there is room, ample room, in Basutoland for all the Christian energy and influence that can be brought to bear upon it; whether Catholic or Protestant, Anglican, Roman, or Presbyterian.

But what has the English Church done for the evangelisation of the Basutos? Has it done anything? Let us see.

It was in the year 1850 that Moshesh first heard of the English Church. In that year the Bishop of Capetown, Dr. Gray, the lion-hearted founder of the Church in South Africa, made his first great visitation journey through the Cape Colony, the Orange River Sovereignty, Natal, and Kaffraria. Three years before he had been consecrated to the see of Capetown, his vast diocese embracing all the territories I have named. While in the Sovereignty he received an invitation from the Chief of the Mountain to visit him at his stronghold at Thaba Bosigo, but was unable, from want of time, to accede to the Chief's wish. Moshesh had heard that the Bishop was a man of exalted position among the " Baruti " ‡—that he was, in fact, the head

---

* Hebrews xi. 25. † S. Matthews iv. 9.
‡ Teachers: the name usually given by the Basutos to Christian missionaries.

of them; and had been sent to South Africa, not only by the chief Baruti of England, but also by Queen Victoria, to teach her subjects in the countries subject to her sway. He was then, with his people, under the protectorate of the Queen; and when he heard that a chief minister of " the Queen's Church " was actually near his borders, his curiosity was awakened, and he desired to see the " Bishopo " for himself. Failing to do this, he sent messages to the Bishop inviting, nay urging, him to send Christian teachers of " the Church of the Queen of England " to his people. He spoke gratefully of the French Protestant missionaries, the only ones then in the country, and of their efforts on behalf of his subjects; but they could only reach a few of the people, and he was anxious to have in addition English teachers, especially as he regarded himself as the child of the Queen. He offered to give the clergy sent by the Bishop a warm welcome, protection, and land on which to settle. Moreover, the Episcopal constitution of the Church commended itself to his mind. He now, for the first time, became aware of the existence of a Church with " chiefs " among the *Baruti;* all being under the Supreme Chief and King of all, Jesus Christ our Lord. The Bishop was unable to respond to his wishes. Basutoland was too remote, and the wants of the Cape Colony and Natal were too pressing to allow a mission to the Basutos to be even thought of. But he did what he could. He told the chief that he would bear his application in mind, and that some time in the future—he hoped in the near future—he might be able to send some of his missionary clergy into the country. He could not do so now, but he would endeavour to do so as soon as he had men to spare for the purpose. The promise was fulfilled long afterwards, but Moshesh did not live to see it. Meanwhile, the Chief sent two of his sons down to Capetown to be educated at the Church's native training institution, recently established at Zonnebloem by the efforts of the Bishop, seconded by those of Sir George Grey, the Governor of the Cape Colony. One of these young men made great progress at the school, and became a convert to the faith of Christ. After his baptism he desired to become a missionary to his own people, and was accordingly sent to England to be prepared for the sacred ministry at S. Augustine's College, Canterbury. But his wish was not to be fulfilled. After a short residence in England he died at S. Augustine's, and thus the hope of evangelising the Basutos through his efforts was lost.

But the Bishop kept his promise in mind, and upon the foundation of the see of Bloemfontein in 1863 (then called the Missionary Bishopric of the Orange Free State), Basutoland was included in that diocese; and the first incumbent of the see was urged by the Bishop (now become the Metropolitan of South Africa), to establish a mission in the country at the earliest opportunity. His lordship was anxious to accede to the Metropolitan's request, and paid a visit to the Chief of the Mountain at Thaba Bosigo soon after his arrival in his diocese. Moshesh received him with the utmost cordiality, asked him to send him "teachers," and offered to give them land in any part of his territory in which they might wish to work. "Here is my country," he said; "it lies before you: choose out your own ground, and I will give it you, and gladly welcome the teachers you may be able to send."

But the Bishop had neither men nor means at his disposal for the task. The few clergy he had brought with him were imperatively needed for the scattered European members of the Church in the Orange Free State. Moreover, war had just been declared between the Free State Government and the Basutos, and a mission to the latter under such circumstances, having its "chief" and its "headquarters" at Bloemfontein, the capital of the Free State, would be almost, if not quite, an impossibility. Still the Bishop bore this great need in mind, and a few years afterwards, as soon as peace was restored, he established a "missionary brotherhood" under the Rev. Canon

Beckett, at Modder Poort, a farm in the " conquered territory," near the borders of Basutoland. It was hoped that this society might grow in numbers, and be able ere long to redeem the promises made to Moshesh. But the community did not increase, and the few members or associates of it had more than enough to do to minister to the Europeans in the villages of the eastern part of the diocese, and to evangelise the heathen who came to work on the brotherhood farms. Canon Beckett paid an annual visit to the magistracies established in Basutoland after the cession of the country to England in 1868, and through his efforts services were held from time to time at Maseru, the official capital of the country, for the men of the Frontier Armed and Mounted Police stationed there. In 1875 an itinerating chaplain to the Europeans was appointed, but nothing had been as yet done by the Church for the evangelization of the Basutos, and the promises to Moshesh remained unfulfilled.

Meanwhile a new Bishop, Dr. A. B. Webb, had succeeded to the see of Bloemfontein, and the Metropolitan had not forgotten to urge the claims of Basutoland upon his consideration. Bishop Webb, however, could do nothing for some years from lack both of means and men. At length, in 1876, a way seemed to be opening out for the establishment of a mission in the country. It ought certainly to have been done at least twenty years before, and we may believe that it would have been done had the Church possessed the power to do it. But, as we have seen, she had not. Vast territories had to be covered, and arrears of work to be made up before she could attempt the evangelization of a distant tribe like the Basutos. But now, at last, the way seemed to be opening out. As has been so often the case under like circumstances, it was the Society for the Propagation of the Gospel in Foreign Parts that came to the rescue; and without its efforts the English Church would, as far as I can see, have been unable even to the present moment to bear any part or lot in the evangelization of these multitudes of heathen. But in 1875 the Society, at the Bishop's request, very generously voted an annual grant-in-aid, for the support of direct mission work to the heathen in the Lesuto, and two priests of the diocese offered to go into the country in response to an appeal from their Bishop. These two clergy were the Rev. E. W. Stenson, who had been residing for a year at Maseru as chaplain to the Europeans, and myself. The Bishop desired Mr. Stenson to commence a mission at Mohale's Hoek, in the southern part of the country, where there were already two or three families of native Christians in communion with the Church; and he directed me to proceed northwards to the district of Leribe.

CHAPTER V.

S. Saviour's, Thlotse Heights.

Leribe—Leaving Thaba 'Nchu—Modder Poort—Prospecting—Molapo—Settlement at Thlotse Heights—Hut Building—Chapel and School—Services—Heathen State of the Country—Ntoana—Dedication of the Chapel.

The district of Leribe thus assigned to me as my future sphere of labour was by far the most heathen in the whole of Basutoland. There was but one mission station in it, that of the French Protestants at Manamasoane. This station had been in existence about twenty years, and had been founded and superintended by M. Coillard, an earnest and devoted man who has since gone to the north of the Zambesi to proclaim the Gospel of Christ to the Banyai and other tribes in those regions. M. Coillard's labours had not been without fruit, though almost ninety-nine per cent. of the population still remained in their heathenism. Moreover, the chief of the north, Molapo, the third son of Moshesh, whose name has been already mentioned, had, after a few years' profession of Christianity relapsed, and was now living a life of heathenism in every way more degraded than that of his father or his brothers.

The responsibility thus laid upon me by my Bishop was indeed a great one. I was commissioned to be, in however poor and lame a way, a "pioneer and founder" of the mission work of the Church among these multitudes of heathen; a task honourable indeed, but yet one from which I naturally shrank, knowing not only my own weakness, but keenly realising the fact that I had little or no experience of Basutoland, or of the Basutos, to guide me. Then, too, I hardly knew six words of Sesuto, and I felt that anything like a serious mistake at the inception of the work might be fraught with disaster to it, and possibly even wreck it altogether. Still the command had come to me from the chief pastor of the diocese to "go forth in the Name of the Lord," and I felt that it was my duty to "gird myself" and obey, "nothing doubting." I had been sixteen years in South Africa, and had taken part in various kinds of Church work, but pioneering was new to me. Still, though I was going out into heathenesse among a strange people speaking a strange language, I felt that it would be cowardly and wanting in faith to shrink from the responsibility. I had spent the previous year—a very happy one—at our mission station at Thaba 'Nchu, working side by side with "brethren beloved in the Lord" among the Barolongs of Moroka; and I had visited the central districts of Basutoland from time to time during the preceding five years, but the northern districts were unknown to me. My year's experience at Thaba 'Nchu stood me in good stead, having given me an insight into the ideas and habits of a kindred tribe to the Basutos. Thaba 'Nchu also gave me a fellow-worker in the person of a young layman, William Lacy, who had been in the diocese for some years, and was now looking forward to ordination. He was an earnest and devout young man; a good singer, a patient, painstaking schoolmaster, and possessed a remarkable aptitude for acquiring the native languages. He spoke Serolong with an unusually pure accent, and would no doubt rapidly acquire a knowledge of Sesuto, so that when he volunteered to go with me into the Lesuto I accepted his offer gladly and at once.

Mr. Lacy and I made our "good byes" and left Thaba 'Nchu at the end of June, 1876. One of our last visits was paid to the family of a small trader who had formerly lived in Basutoland; and his wife, a kind-hearted soul in her way, wished, I suppose, to say something cheering to us by way of a final farewell. "You needn't be afeard of going, Sir," said she, "I once lived among the Basutos myself, and got quite to like them. You needn't be afeard, Sir, they don't often eat one another now, *and they always spares the missionaries.*" Well, at any rate it was comforting to know that there was such method in their madness! Of course I could only smile in reply, and assure my good old lady friend that cannibalism had been extinct in Basutoland for the last thirty or forty years—a fact of which she appeared to be ignorant, though residing in a territory which had once belonged to Moshesh himself.

Our plan was to go first to the Brotherhood farm at Modder Poort. We hoped to be able to pick up some information there as to the northern districts of the country for which we were bound, and we proposed to spend the remaining month of winter in learning what Sesuto we could, and in making copies of such translations as Canon Beckett possessed of the Baptismal and other offices of the Church.

We started on a bitterly cold morning in an open transport waggon, the only vehicle at hand. In the afternoon a biting wind set in from the south pole, and we were glad enough when night came to outspan, and roll ourselves up in our blankets on the veldt under the waggon. We slept soundly, notwithstanding the frost and cold, and arrived the next evening at Modder Poort. The wind was now piercing in its coldness, and in the night snow began to fall. It continued snowing as steadily as in England for six or seven hours, by which time the whole country from the Drakensbergen to the confines of the Kalahari desert was one scene of Arctic whiteness, the snow lying in some places three feet deep. It was a beautiful sight—to an Englishman at least—and one that is not often seen in South Africa, even in the neighbourhood of the Drakensbergen.

Canon Beckett received us with his wonted kindness, taking the keenest interest in the proposed mission, and giving us valuable information as to the condition of the Leribe district, the European residents of which he regularly visited every year.

While at Modder Poort I pondered much over the various conversations I had had with the Bishop before leaving Thaba 'Nchu, and embodied them in the following rules for our guidance in the future. I give these as showing the spirit in which, I trust, the new mission was to be undertaken :—

1. To keep aloof from politics, and not to take part in the *pitsos* or public political meetings of the tribe.
2. Not to write letters of a public or political import for any of the chiefs.
3. Not to identify the mission in any way with the government officials, lest the natives should think it to be a department of the civil service, and the missionaries paid or subsidised by the Queen; the Church of England being in their eyes "the Church of the Queen of the English."
4. To respect the labours of those missionaries already in the country, who, in the present divided state of Christendom, are, unhappily, not in communion with our own branch of the Church Catholic.
5. To abstain entirely from controversy unless attacked; and to endeavour then to speak the truth in love, and in the spirit of meekness.

6. Not to receive into the communion of the Church, should they desire to enter it, Christians of other religious bodies under censure for evil conduct, or any whose motives for wishing to unite with us were not, as far as could be judged, pure, and above reproach.

I venture to think that these resolutions were wise and salutary; at any rate, I am sure that they have been uniformly acted upon, and with good results, by all the workers in the mission.

At the end of July Mr. Lacy and I started on a fortnight's prospecting tour through the Leribe district. How we fared, the following notes of our journey, made at the time, will show.

Monday, July 31, 1876.—Started after breakfast from S. Augustine's, Modder Poort, with Mr. Lacy, the catechist of the mission, in an open bullock cart—a small, rough, strong, springless vehicle, the only one that could be obtained. It was drawn by two oxen, kindly supplied to us from the Brotherhood team. We took with us a trusty Christian Mosuto, named Willem, as driver, and a heathen boy as leader of the oxen. Willem was also to act as our guide, though I fear he was not strong in that capacity. He had been born and bred on the borders of Basutoland, but nevertheless knew little or nothing of the northern districts: very much like those Cockneys of Whitechapel who have never seen Westminster Abbey, and have only a vague idea where it is. Our blankets, food, pots and pans were all packed into the cart, together with a good-sized tarpaulin, or "sail," which could be unfolded and let down by the side of the vehicle at night as a screen from the wind. The nights were still frosty, and would probably remain so during our journey, and as we had usually to sleep in the veldt, the sail proved to be a great boon. We trudged along by the side of the cart in high spirits, the "yek" of Willem to his diminutive team sounding pleasantly in our ears. About an hour after sunset we reached the Caledon, and outspanned above the heights of Omega. A fire was soon kindled, the coffee kettle steamed and hummed, and we were soon regaling ourselves with a substantial meal of bread, meat, and coffee—the latter without milk, which was not to be had, but with plenty of sugar to make up for the absence of it. It being still winter, we feared that we should find the bare veldt a not very attractive couch. Fortunately, a brother of Willem's, who lived under a neighbouring hill, very kindly allowed us to put our bullocks into his kraal for the night; and this enabled us to spread our blankets under the cart, where we could sleep securely and soundly without being exposed to the frost, which proved to be still severe.

Tuesday, August 1.—A bright beautiful morning. After an early breakfast we in-spanned and crossed the Caledon safely, the water being low, and the drift in fairly good order. We were now in Basutoland, and our hearts rejoiced in the thought of having crossed the Rubicon, and being actually in the country in which we were to become witnesses for Christ, and which was to be our future home. We passed many kraals or villages, all of them heathen, and were constantly mistaken for "smouses," or itinerating traders; the people noticing our coloured rugs and blankets, and thinking they were for sale. At mid-day we outspanned near a village not many miles from Advance Post, the police station between Maseru and Leribe. A number of children came out to us, and when they found that we were *Baruti* they gathered us quite a large quantity of fuel, wherewith we kindled a fire and prepared our noonday meal.

Wednesday, August 2.—It is marvellous with what security one travels in a country like this. Highway robbery and violence are here unknown, and one lies down to rest in the veldt at night with a stone for one's pillow, like Jacob of old, far away from any earthly habitation. The Southern Cross keeps its silent watch over one's head, and one is penetrated with the thought that though man is absent, God is near. With that thought one feels as secure, and as much at ease, as if one were dwelling in some great city at home, even in London itself.

Thus the week passed on. We told the people everywhere that we were not *smouses*, but teachers, and were paying a visit to Molapo, their chief, with the object of settling in the country to teach them about God and the Saviour of mankind. We found them quite civil, and many of them asked us why we would not stay at their villages and teach them; to which we replied that we could settle nowhere without the permission of the chief, and that we wished to see him, and hear from his lips in what part of the country he would like us to establish our mission. "Ka sebele," said they assentingly, leaving us to proceed on our way with many expressions of friendship. We had been provided by Canon Beckett with a letter of introduction to Major Bell, the British Resident of the district, whose headquarters were near a small village not far from Leribe itself—the town of Molapo, which gives its name to the whole northern division.

After a five days' *trek* we arrived at a trading station, close to the "great place" of the chief, and Saturday morning found us at the door of the Residency. Major Bell received us with the greatest courtesy and kindness, inviting us to stay with him until the *locale* of the new mission should be decided upon. Glad indeed were we to accept his kind hospitality, and to find ourselves once more between the sheets of a comfortable bed after our week's camping out on the bare, hard veldt. Mrs. Bell, a charming old lady, as good as she was handsome, vied with her husband in her efforts to make us welcome; and the next day, being Sunday, the Major most kindly despatched mounted messengers to the few Europeans of the neighbourhood, chiefly traders, to announce the fact of our arrival, and to invite them to the services which were to be held for them. We could at present only attempt English services, not knowing more than a few sentences of Sesuto. We had an early celebration of the

Holy Eucharist at the Residency, at which there were four communicants besides ourselves, one of them being a Zulu woman ("old Wilhelmina") who understood some English and more Dutch and Sesuto, besides her own tongue. I subsequently found that she was the only native Christian in the whole district of Leribe in communion with our own Church. She was a convert from one of our missions in Natal, and was now in service at the Residency. It was pleasant to begin our first celebration of the Divine Mysteries in this heathen country with a native Christian present, and receiving together with us the Bread of Life. The pleasure was, I need not say, an unexpected one, and we took it as an earnest of future blessing upon the work of the Church. All the Europeans at, or near the station, came to Mattins and Evensong, which were held in the forenoon and afternoon in a large tent placed at our disposal for the purpose by Major Bell. After Mattins I gave the people an address, stating the object of our visit. I said that we had come among them at the request of our Bishop, with the intention of establishing a mission of the Church in that part of Basutoland; and I added that I felt sure they would rejoice, not only for their own sake, but also for that of the multitude of heathen around them, that their own Church (for I found that most of them were Churchmen) was at last to be represented in the Lesuto, and that henceforth they were to have a resident pastor of their own. I threw myself unreservedly upon their sympathies, and asked them to assist and strengthen us in our new and arduous undertaking by their alms and their prayers, but above all, by the example of a consistent Christian life. The response to that appeal was most cordial, and from that day to this the Europeans around our mission have, with hardly an exception, aided the work in every way possible.

Next morning, mounted on a couple of the Major's sturdy little Basuto ponies, and accompanied by his eldest son, Mr. Charles Bell, and an interpreter, we rode over to Leribe to pay our visit to the chief. The town of Leribe, which is entirely native, is built on a plateau or broad ledge of rock under the Leribe mountain, which rises sheer above it to the height of about a thousand feet, its bold, well-defined crest being the most prominent object for many miles round. The town is approached by a steep hill, up the rough waggon track of which we clambered vigorously after a short canter across the breezy downs. In a few minutes we were at the inner Khothla, where the chief was waiting to receive us. He had lately built himself a large house of wrought stone, and of European design, which cost him, it is said, more than £2,000; but he preferred his own huts, which, in accordance with native custom, were better built and more spacious than those of the common people. He only used the house on very special occasions, as, for instance, when receiving the Governor, or some high official of the British Government, or of the Orange Free State. Then he would sit in solemn state in his reception room, clad in ordinary English attire, or in some naval or military uniform which he had donned for the occasion, having first been vigorously " tubbed " in warm water, and well washed with the best scented soap by four of his strongest body guards. Notice had been sent to his highness of our intended visit, Molapo always insisting that no white strangers should call upon him without due notice being given of their approach to his domains. We found him very greasy, but very pleasant. He was a huge, fat monster of a man —a human ox—" got up," if not " regardless of expense," at any rate quite *a la Sesuto*. His garments were few in number— simply a kaross and a cincture. The kaross was made of some four and twenty silver jackal skins beautifully sewed together, and had, no doubt, been originally a very handsome one, but it was now as greasy as its wearer. Fat men are said to be good natured, and Molapo did not belie the truth of the saying. He received us with the utmost cordiality, regaled us with his choicest leting, ordered tea to be made for us, and introduced us to a bevy of his wives. He was said to have fifty-five or fifty-six of these, and was paying hut tax upon fifty, so utterly had he relapsed from his first profession of Christianity. His wives were the fattest women I ever beheld. We saw seven of the most favoured of them all squatting together in a semi-circle, drinking copious draughts of tea out of English made basins, for their lord was wealthy, and it pleased him to regale them with this expensive beverage. They looked like so many hippopotami being fattened for exhibition, and I felt sorry that we could not photograph the whole group. Two or three of them had on tiger skin karosses; the others wore nothing but the short leather petticoat of the tribe. Each wore a thick heavy brass collar round her neck, and brass leglets and armlets almost to the knee and the elbow. I looked round upon the crowd of those present. From the chief, on his clay throne, down to the smallest of the small fry playing about at the entrance to the Khothla *all were fat*, the little ones being the fattest of all. I never in my life saw such a collection of fat men, women, and children. There must have been plenty of good nature in that Khothla if the old saying be true.

The chief professed great pleasure at the advent of the *Baruti* of *Ma-Churche*. He had often heard of them—I give the pith of what he said to us—from his father, Moshesh, and from others: now he saw them. He was glad that they were come, and hoped that they would settle in his country and teach his people to speak and write the English language. He was an Englishman, and the Queen was his mother. He would see that the Queen's *Baruti* were protected and treated with respect; and he would send some of his own sons to their school as soon as they were able to build one. A chief liked to have many cows: the more he had the more milk he got, and the better able he was to feed his children. Now he should have three cows, all of them of excellent breed in their way, and yielding an abundance of milk. At first he only had one cow, the French Protestant

Mission. Quite lately, only a month ago, he had acquired another cow, the Roman Catholic Mission; for he had just given permission to M. Gerard to commence a mission at the Khomokoana; and now to-day he was to have a third, and perhaps the best of all; for was not this new cow a present from the Queen of England herself? Now he was happy. He not only had a black cow and a dun one, but to-day a red one also was to enter his kraal.

We took all these compliments for what they were worth, knowing well by experience that a native is nothing if not complimentary.

Then we approached the main point: Where were we to settle?

From conversations I had had with Major Bell and others, as well as from my own observation, I had come to the conclusion that the heights above the junction of the Caledon and the Thlotse, near the village of Mapatsueng, would be one of the best spots at which to commence the mission. We suggested this spot to the chief, and he answered that he was quite willing for us to settle there. He thought our choice a good one, as it was midway between the old-established station of the French Protestants at Manamasoane and the newly-projected mission of the Roman Church at the Khomokoana. If we went there we should not be too far from him, and he would be able to keep all three of his cows in view. He added that before settling there we must get the permission of Major Bell to do so, as he had heard that the Government intended removing their headquarters to that place next year. We were able to assure him that there would be no difficulty in obtaining the Resident's consent; that it had in fact been already given; and that it was the Resident himself, among others, who had suggested the heights above the Thlotse as the most desirable spot on which we could build.

During this conversation there entered a singular individual, a sort of court chamberlain, bearing in his hand a large and handsome metal tea-urn of European design and make. This he placed upon a small, dirty, ricketty table of the commonest deal, which had been previously brought in. Then he proceeded leisurely, and with great gravity, to make tea. Boiling water was brought: tea, sugar, and milk were there in abundance; and soon the steaming contents of the urn were handed round in basins to the chief and ourselves. But the tea-maker! What a curious creature he was! First, he was the only lean man of the whole assembly! Tall, spare, lithe, of handsome figure and well-polished skin, but with a dog-like visage—though pleasantly dog-like, I must own—dignified, and self-possessed as such a functionary should be, he moved about with due and proper gravity, quietly making his preparations, but attentive at the same time to every wink and nod of his master. You ask, how was he clad? Well, gracefully enough, and inexpensively too. Besides his cincture he had nothing on but his wool—the woolly hair of his head which he had allowed to grow to a great length, and then clipped or shaved in the most fantastic fashion. What the pattern was it would be impossible to say. But I am sure that, if one could only have stuck a tail on him, he would have looked for all the world exactly like a clean well-shaved mahogany-coloured human poodle, walking about with befitting dignity upon its hind legs.

Again and again were tea and leting brought round, the inmates of the harem imbibing such copious draughts of the former that the perspiration streamed from them. At last we made our adieus and departed.

Molapo kept his word with us; and only recently it has come to my ears that the day after we left him he sent for Nkouta, the headman of the villages bordering on the Thlotse, and commanded him, under all sorts of grievous pains and penalties, to see that the *Baruti* of *Ma-Churche*, who had come into the country under his special protection, were not in any way molested, and that every one treated them with courtesy and respect.

The next day we rode out with Major Bell and other friends to the scene of our future labours, the Major assigning to us, on behalf of the Government, the usual grant of land for mission purposes, and pointing out the intended site of the Residency, which was at some little distance from our own compound. Trusting that we had been guided aright in our choice of this place as a base of operations for the work of evangelisation, we returned to Leribe, and next morning started for Modder Poort to report progress to Canon Beckett and the Bishop.

The Brotherhood homestead was reached in due time, the diocesan authorities approved of my report, and the Bishop was anxious that we should take up our residence at Thlotse with as little delay as possible. The winter was rapidly coming to an end, and, as spring was the best time for building, we resolved to go at once. We had no tent, and there was neither time nor money to buy one; so we made up our minds to go a-gipsying in the veldt until some sort of shelter could be put up. We hired a large buck-waggon—that is to say, a carrier's bullock-waggon with no tent to it—which was the only large vehicle to be procured on the moment, packed up our goods and chattels, inspanned our bullocks, and set forth. On the 24th August we reached Thlotse, and outspanned on the ground allotted to the mission. The waggon was soon unladen, and returned home at once, leaving Mr. Lacy and myself with our worldly possessions alone in the veldt. It was an anxious moment. Mr. Charles Bell had very kindly engaged a Mosuto named Ntoana, a handy and intelligent man, to build us a round hut, or *rondavel* as the whites usually call it, of native fashion; but little or no progress had been made towards it, the ground being so hard and dry that it was impossible to dig sods; so we resolved to pile up our boxes into three parallel rows, leaving the two openings between them as sleeping places. In these openings we spread our mattresses on the ground, arranged our blankets upon them, and congratulated ourselves upon the possession of a snug and comfortable bed under the canopy of heaven on the breezy heights of the Thlotse. Then we placed our three-legged iron pot, gridiron, frying-pan, and kettle together at a few yards distance, close to some stones which served as a fire-place. Disu and dried grass were soon procured, the fire blazed, and in a few minutes the kettle began to drone, and the frying-pan to send forth its hissing, sputtering sounds, so dear to the heart of the hungry African traveller. Soon a simple meal was prepared and served, seasoned by that best of all sauces, genuine hunger. We declared that nothing could be more charming than such a wholesome, primitive, healthy life in the open veldt; and, indeed, it was so for some time. But we found ere long that it was not altogether without its disadvantages, and we were by no means sorry when, some three months afterwards, it came to an end, and we were able to find a shelter under the roof of our first rondavel.

Next morning Ntoana came to us, bringing his eldest son, a small boy of about ten years of age, whom he wished to consign to my charge. "Monere," said he, "he is your child now. I commit him to your care. From henceforth you are his father. Do what you please with him. He will work for you and obey you, and you will teach and instruct him as you think best." I took the little lad, the first Mosuto I had ever had under my care, and he served me faithfully for many years. We were glad to have him, and he was at once duly installed in the "kitchen," that is to say, among the pots and pans by the fireplace, a position he greatly appreciated. He was intensely ugly, but very good-natured and honest, and always had a pleasant grin upon his broad, fat face. He was, of course, perfectly naked when he came to us, and while we were in the veldt his only garment was a coloured shirt which I managed to procure for him, and which was the admiration and the envy of the many small boys who came all day long to interview him. He soon learnt, under Mr. Lacy's tuition, to clean our simple cooking utensils and boil our kettle, and when not sitting among the pots was generally engaged in seeking and collecting fuel in the veldt round about. He was intensely anxious to learn English, and we taught him to say " Good night, Sir," and " Good morning, Sir," but he mixed up the times, and often roused us at an unearthly hour long before sunrise by peering in at us between our boxes with his black, shiny eyes, and swarthy, grinning face, and shouting out " Gooty nightty, Sah; kittle he cookey." The effect was irresistible, and he joined heartily in our laughter, for the natives have a keen sense of the ridiculous, and dearly love a joke.

We made a time-table for ourselves, dividing and allotting the time as wisely as we could, and we found it a great help. It was good both for ourselves and for the shoals of natives who came all day long to make our acquaintance. It prevented us from wasting many hours in a mere desultory sort of way, and it taught our new friends that there were certain times when we desired to be alone, and must not be disturbed or intruded upon ; though, truth to say, it seemed almost impossible for them to learn this last lesson.

A good deal of our time was spent in selecting grass and reeds for thatching purposes. Supplies of these came in daily, but large quantities of the grass had to be rejected as either too short or too old for thatching. There was of necessity no fixed standard of price, and natives are shrewd hands at bargaining. This is especially the case with the women, and it was they who brought us most of our supplies. They would haggle persistently for hours over a sixpence, and we on our parts, though ready to give a fair, nay, a liberal price for everything we needed, had no intention of being cheated if we could possibly help it. Sometimes it was great fun. One old lady brought, about a month after our arrival, a little milk for sale. We needed it, not having tasted any for some time. So I offered her sixpence for it. It was only a small quantity—not much more than a pint—and the milk season was beginning. Sixpence was therefore a really liberal price for it. But no, our friend demanded a shilling! I resolutely declined to purchase at such a price. "Lady, you wish to eat me," I said, in my broken Sesuto. "By Molapo," said she, "the price is a just one, and a great lord like you ought to be glad of the chance of getting the milk so cheaply." The chaffering went on, I resolutely declining to give way, though I confess I looked at the attractive liquid with longing eyes, for coffee in all its simple plainness for many weeks together is apt to lose something of its attractiveness. But it would never do to start with such an exorbitant price, so I turned away and left her. But she followed me, and insisted on thrusting the vessel containing the tempting liquid under my very nose, that I might smell its contents and see for myself that the milk was fresh and pure. Not to be taken captive in that way, though the temptation was sore, I retaliated by taking out my sixpence and holding it before her eyes, knowing the weakness that natives have (like a good many very superior people) for money. But it availed me nothing. The old lady persisted in the "shilleeng"; and when I again turned away with a shrug and a smile she declared, after bantering me unmercifully for my stinginess before an applauding crowd of sympathisers, that rather than let the white man have the milk for sixpence she would drink it herself. "Drink it," said I; "and peace be with you." And the old thing did drink it before our eyes, amid the laughter of the whole crowd. "Never mind," said I to my disappointed colleague, "we shall see who will give way first." The same farce went on morning by morning for nearly a week, and then the ancient dame surrendered, fain to take the price I had offered. From that day forth she respected me immensely, and as the season advanced brought us each day larger and larger quantities of milk, still only looking for the sixpence; and when one morning she produced a large bowl full and I gave her a shilling instead of the customary coin, she broke out into loud jubilations over her good fortune, praising and extolling my righteousness, beneficence, and wisdom. She is still alive, and still, I regret to say, a heathen; but whenever we meet, and she utters the accustomed "Dumela Monere," there is a twinkle in her eye and a grin on her face which seem to say almost as plainly as the words themselves: "You remember the milk, Monere!"

What with haggling over purchases, chatting with the hundreds of people who came to see us in our gipsy encampment, and paying visits to the villages round the heights, the days quickly passed by. The weather was bright and dry, and this pic-nic life did not hurt us. Though we were more than two months in the veldt, we had rain only once, and that was in the night, when it came down unexpectedly and in torrents—nay, in sheets. We were rolled up in our blankets between the boxes in the soundest of slumbers, when suddenly we were rudely awakened by the trickling of water down our backs. Then we began to realise what was going on over our heads. We led a spongy, sodden existence for a few hours, and then the clouds cleared away, and the sun came out in all his splendour. In a short time we and our bedding were once more warm and dry. Major Bell added to the many kindnesses he had already shown us by the timely loan of a tent for two or three weeks until our huts were ready, and this he did, I feel sure, at great personal inconvenience to himself. So on the whole we got along famously. The greatest inconvenience we experienced was the want of privacy. With all our endeavours we could hardly secure any time for ourselves except at night, and then the moths and the wind together would not permit us to light a candle, and lantern we had none. From dawn to sunset we were absolutely public property. We had to rise in the morning and perform our ablutions, prepare our food, and even say our prayers in the presence of an admiring group of savages. The dust, too, was at times rather troublesome. Sometimes it would whirl about in small clouds, peppering our porridge so effectually as to call up to our minds very forcibly an old and familiar saying with which I have no doubt my readers are well acquainted.

But our first hut was approaching completion, or rather was sufficiently advanced to be habitable, Ntoana having dragged barrel after barrel of water up from the fountain at the bottom of the hill and poured it upon the ground, saturating as far as he was able the spots where he intended to cut the sods he required.

Towards the middle of November we took possession of our hut, though it was not yet properly beamfilled, and possessed neither door nor window. The holes were there, but timber was not to be had in the neighbourhood, and we had to wait for both door and window until wood could be procured from Bethlehem, a Free State town about fifty miles to the north-west of us. But oh, the luxury of even a doorless and windowless *rondavel* after our long sojourn in the bare and naked veldt! The wind might howl at night through the two apertures—and it *did*, though we hung blankets before them—but we were snugly ensconced in our beds, with a roof over our heads, oblivious to rain or storm. By Christmas six of these round huts were finished, or at any rate sufficiently advanced for use. Each of them was twelve feet in diameter, and they comprised a dining-room, store-room, kitchen, and three bedrooms. We had thus a whole suite of apartments, or six detached residences, complete for little more than £60. And these poor rondavels, with certain small additions, were destined to last us nearly nine years, though certainly we had no idea of it when we built them.

Before settling at Thlotse I had engaged a mason, a white man, from Ficksburg, the nearest Free State village, to build us a temporary chapel, school, and mission-room of raw brick. I had only £150 at my disposal to start with, and this had been most generously provided by the congregation of St. Peter's, Eaton Square, London. Without their timely aid we should have been unable to build any place of worship at all. The building we erected was of necessity of the simplest kind, and the smallest possible dimensions. It was an oblong structure, plastered with mud, unceiled, and under a flat, galvanised-iron roof. It was fifty-four feet long, and twelve broad, and was divided into three compartments separated from each other by a thin partition wall. It gave us a chapel twenty feet by twelve, a mission-room twelve feet by twelve, in which I could receive and converse with the numbers of heathen who still poured in daily to interview us, and a school-room the same size as the chapel. Except the cross on its gable, and possibly its small "carpenter's Gothic" windows, there was little or nothing about the exterior of such a building which marked it off as one devoted to religious worship. An accomplished ecclesiologist who came to visit us some time afterwards protested that I had "put up a ginger beer shop," but as he did not offer to procure the funds wherewith to improve it, or still less to erect a more seemly and permanent church, his criticism did not distress me, true though it might be. Anyhow, our poor little "early Sesuto" house of worship was quite as ecclesiastical and "correct" in its style and tone as the great Capetown Cathedral (built, of course, long before the advent of Bishop Gray), which cost so much money that it was said of it that its bricks, like those of the castle, "were cemented together with silver instead of mortar." By the way, speaking of this cathedral, a good story used to be current years ago as to the uniqueness of its architecture. Two tourists from England, on landing at the Cape, intent on seeing all that was to be seen, naturally made their way to the chief church of the place. They paused in astonishment before its portico, and looked up at its tower. In bewilderment one said to the other, "What kind of architecture do you consider this to be?" "Day and Martin," replied his friend. "Day and Martin! What *can* you mean?" "Why, do you not see," rejoined the first, "that the tower is exactly like two of Day and Martin's blacking bottles—a shilling one, with a sixpenny one standing on the top of it?" On entering the sacred edifice they gazed about in greater astonishment than ever. They had never seen such a remarkable church before. Suddenly the gentleman with the knowledge of architecture seemed relieved. He had solved the problem. The church had been built, and rightly so, with a view to the *prevention of idolatry*. Accosting the verger, he asked him " whether any idolatry was ever practised there?" "Certainly not, Sir," replied the astonished guardian of the sacred fane, "Certainly not. But what makes you ask such an extraordinary question?" "I thought not," exclaimed the young Englishman triumphantly. "I thought not. It would be impossible—quite impossible. For "—with a sweep of the eye round the building—" this place is like nothing ' in the heaven above, or in the earth beneath, or in the water under the earth.' "

The interior of S. George's is now very different, but the " two blacking bottles " still remain.

" Beggars must not be choosers," so I had to do the best I could with my £150, which, with a little more added to it by kind friends in the diocese, provided us with a chapel, school, mission-room, and six huts.

A few weeks after our arrival we arranged, with the sanction of the Bishop, a simple mission service in Sesuto, suitable for use among the heathen. Then we taught the children who came to us a Sesuto version of two well-known morning and evening hymns, together with the *Agnus Dei*, likewise in their own tongue. We found a Mosuto who knew a little simple English, and a good deal more Cape Dutch, and him we employed as an interpreter. Thus equipped, we set forth and held our first mission service. This service was begun with the invocation of the Ever Blessed Trinity, and consisted of a short acknowledgment of sin, a hymn, a chapter from one of the Gospels, a discourse upon a portion of this chapter, the *Agnus Dei*, the Good Friday collect for the conversion of the heathen, the Prayer of S. Chrysostom, and the Grace.

As soon as we got into our first hut, Mr. Lacy gathered the children together daily, teaching them to read, write, and sing, and instructing them twice a week in the foundation truths of the Christian Faith. This was, of course, done in the open air, and as the hot weather was approaching, the work soon became very fatiguing under the scorching rays of a burning African sun.

What spare time we could command was devoted either to the study of Sesuto, or to the laying out of a garden. We made some progress with both, but not much at first with the latter, the ground being still very dry, and our spades new and blunt, and there was no means of sharpening them. The knotted roots of the grass (it was all large sour veldt) seemed as hard as nails, and digging through them with our blunt implements was by no means a light task, especially to amateur navvies like ourselves, whose hands soon became blistered. A Boer, who came one day to visit us, consoled us with the assurance that it would be all right soon. We only needed patience and perseverance: the rain would fall in due time; and, meanwhile, we had only lost "the lazy skin" of our hands! So saying, he took my spade, and very obligingly proceeded to dig up a patch of ground for us, doing as much work in half-an-hour—though he confessed it "rather tough"—as I could in well-nigh half-a-day. We laid our friend's exhortation to heart, and in due time the garden and orchard were laid out and planted with fruit trees, vegetables, and flowers; to which we added, as time went on, a few ornamental trees and shrubs. Gardening afforded us a pleasant and healthful relaxation and change from mental occupations; and, moreover, if we were ever to taste vegetables or fruit, it was necessary for us to grow them; besides which, our efforts in this direction acted as examples and incentives to the natives to go and do likewise.

The spot on which we settled is one of the most beautiful in Basutoland. It is situated on the heights above the confluence of the Caledon and the Thlotse. Right in front, to the east stand the Malutis: their bold, lofty, serrated peaks stretching away northwards to the Mont aux Sources, and southwards to Matatiele. There was but one village on the heights when we took possession of our ground: this was the village of Mapatseung, the headman of which was a one-eyed old man named Modibetsana. But though there were few people actually on the heights, there were over a thousand in the small clusters of villages which encircled this mountain ridge, and all these people were heathen. Besides these there were many villages, some large, some small, scattered about in all directions at no great distance from our settlement, and within easy reach of each other; and we therefore felt that we had been guided aright in settling at this particular place—nay, we cherished the hope that Thlotse might become, in course of time, a great centre of Christian life to the whole district. We were just half way between the French Protestant mission at Manamasoane in the north and the newly-formed Roman Catholic station at Khomokoana in the south, and there was ample room for us all. We at Thlotse had before us, almost at our door, many thousands of heathen, all of whom were, as far as we could see, friendly towards us; and many of whom had expressed a wish to "hear about God." Nearly three-fourths of these people were Basutos, the remainder being Matebele, that is to say, Fingoes and Zulus, who were for the most part fugitives—men who had escaped at various times from the tyranny and cruelty of Chaka, Dingaan, and other sanguinary monsters, and had taken refuge in the territory of Moshesh.

The year 1876 was fast drawing to a close, and by Christmas the greater part of our compound was enclosed. We were beginning to feel at home in our huts, and when one day Major Bell's little daughters made us a present of two wee kittens to begin life with, our happiness was complete! Our hut builder, Ntoana, proved to be a very intelligent and trustworthy man, and I was much pleased to observe that he came regularly to our mission services. I had many pleasant talks with him in the evening when the labours of the day were over, and was glad to find that, though he must have been at least thirty years of age, he had not taken a second wife. This looked hopeful; so one day I made bold to say to him that I hoped he would not do so. I besought him not to place such a bar between himself and the service of the Saviour, of Whose redeeming love and power he had now begun to learn. "No, Monere," said he, with a deprecatory shake of the head, "I shall never do so. I should not think of doing such a thing." On my assuring him that that was good news indeed, he replied with something like a suppressed sigh, "No, Monere; indeed, I shall never take a second wife. *What with her bad temper and scolding words, one of them is quite enough; two of them would kill me!*"

What could I reply to that? I felt beaten, and said nothing. Poor Ntoana! He was a faithful fellow, and met his death a few years afterwards in the battle field, pierced by the spears of the rebels while loyally and valiantly defending the property and the interests of his chief.

The new year saw our chapel and school rapidly approaching completion, and on the 23rd of January we were cheered and gladdened by the arrival of the Bishop, who had from the first taken the keenest interest in all that we were doing, and who had now come to dedicate the temporary chapel. His lordship was accompanied by a small party of friends, amongst whom were Sister Emma, the Mother Superior of the recently established diocesan Sisterhood at Bloemfontein, and Miss Trench, a daughter of the Archbishop of Dublin.

On the Feast of the Conversion of S. Paul, 1877—a fitting

day for such a work—the Bishop blessed the Mission buildings, and dedicated the little chapel to the service of Almighty God, by a simple, yet solemn, Service of Benediction. It was a happy day, and one full of hopefulness for the future. A crowd of heathen testified their interest in this first *Mokete* (feast) of the Church, and all the Europeans of the neighbourhood, as well as many from a distance, were present on the occasion. The building thus dedicated was mean and poor, its flat, unceiled iron roof, and its bare, clay-plastered walls, bearing witness to the poverty of the Mission; yet it was nevertheless the sanctuary of the All Holy One, and dear to us all as the first house of prayer and praise set up by the Church in this uttermost and heathen corner of the earth. I have a vivid recollection of the good "Mother" kneeling alone between the services upon the hardly yet dry mud floor, in earnest prayer and supplication to God for the newly-established Mission. She has passed away to her reward, with others who were present with us then; but "their works do follow them," and their memories will long linger as a sweet and abiding influence for good in the hearts of many, not only in Basutoland, but in the whole diocese of Bloemfontein.

The chapel was dedicated to the All Holy and All Merciful Saviour, a dedication Eastern in its origin, and a favourite one in the missions of the Russian Church. The interior of the building was almost as bare and mean as the exterior. A few school forms of deal formed the furniture. The holy table was of the same material, but covered with a plain white silk altar frontal—an offering from a friend in England. The only thing of any beauty or value was a handsome Calvary group which had been given to me when last in England, some years before, by a brother in the Faith engaged in home mission work among the outcasts and practical heathens of London. He thought, and rightly, that such a work of art would not only be a fitting adornment to a mission chapel out in the wilds of Africa, but that it might also be useful as a teaching power to the untutored African—speaking to him even more powerfully than words can do of the love of Jesus. This piece of statuary has been from first to last most valuable to the Mission, and it is now placed above the altar of our permanent church. As soon as it was put up in the chapel crowds of people came to see it. They had never seen such a beautiful "setsŭantso" * before, and were never weary of bringing their friends to look at it, and hearing from our mouths the meaning of it. Many were the exclamations of awe and wonder which fell from their lips, and several of those who thus first saw it have since become disciples of the Crucified. They never failed to enquire what the "assagai" wound in the side meant; and one day a man stepped forward and asked me, "Monere, what did *That Man* do that they thus nailed him to the wood, and stabbed him in the side with the *lerumo?* Was he a *very bad* man? Was he a *robber* or a *murderer?*"

His wonder was great when I told him the story of the Cross. He looked up in awe and reverence, and quietly left the chapel, pondering doubtless on what he had heard.

I give this as a sample of the utter ignorance of many of the Basutos. They had never so much as heard of the Lord Jesus Christ or of His Salvation. No doubt many of those who live near mission stations have learnt something of Christianity, and have some knowledge of Christ, but in our northern district, and especially among the mountaineers, the darkness was deep, and the ignorance dense. It was among such a population that we had been called to unfurl the banner of the Cross, and build up in our humble way the Kingdom of God.

---

* Representation, picture, image, parable.

CHAPTER VI.

LENGTHENING THE CORDS.

The First Convert—Arrival of the Rev. F. Balfour—A Visitor from England—Application of Joel for a Missionary—Joel and his People—Sekubu—Mosola and Maoeng—Building Operations—A True Friend—"Not a Mealie"—Modibetsana's Money—Fat Daniel.

GOD gave us our first convert soon after our arrival, and before we had thoroughly settled down to the work. His heart was touched at the first preaching of the Gospel of Christ, and grace conquered him. He was a bright, manly young fellow, belonging to the Native Mounted Police, of whom there was a detachment close to us, all of them heathen. He bore an excellent character in the force, and was respected and trusted by his officers. Born and brought up in the mountains, living all his life among heathen relations, and knowing nothing of Christianity, he had left his home to take service with the Queen of England, his "mother," as the natives call her, little dreaming that very soon he was to enter a higher service still—the service of the King of Kings. As far as man can judge, he gave himself to his Lord and Saviour with all his heart, and he has been faithful ever since. Would that all our converts had been equally earnest and sincere! He was the first-fruits of the Mission—given to us as an earnest of the harvest to come—and he has always been one of the best and most consistent of our Christians, never having given the Mission the least trouble during the fourteen years I have known him. As a tribute to his fidelity and integrity, I may perhaps mention the fact that, whenever the officials of the district wished to send a trustworthy man to the nearest bank (in a Free State town) to obtain cash for a Government draft or note, he was the orderly invariably singled out for the purpose ; and I have often met him on the road riding home from Bethlehem or Ladybrand with a large leathern satchel at his back, packed almost to bursting with silver coins. A cheery " Dumela " would be exchanged between us, a joke cracked at his expense as to the bigness and weightiness of his burden, and with a pleasant " Sala hauthle, Monere," he would ride on alone ; I meanwhile musing upon the honesty of my black brother, and the absolute security of the country, anything approaching to highway robbery being unknown in it. May God give him grace to continue " Christ's faithful soldier and servant unto his life's end."

The Bishop had not long left us when a new labourer in the mission field came to us, with the intention of devoting himself to work in the Lesuto. This was the Rev. Francis R. T. Balfour, a young priest, who had but recently arrived from England, and who desired, with the sanction of the Bishop, to attach himself to the staff at S. Saviour's. A man of culture and refinement, genial and sweet in disposition, and full of ardour and devotion, his presence was like a gleam of sunshine in our midst. He had left his " ancestral halls " and his delightful family circle in Ireland to cast in his lot with us, and live in a rude hut of sods and hard-baked mud in the wilds of Basutoland ; and though in after years he was called to other fields of work in the vast diocese of Bloemfontein, he and his have never ceased to take the keenest interest in his " maiden " mission, and to aid it in every way in their power. He speedily acquired a fair knowledge of Sesuto, and took as his special work the evangelization of the heathen people in the villages round the heights and over the Thlotse, visiting them daily, either on horseback or on foot, and sitting down and chatting with them in their own huts and kraals. Such spare hours as he could command were devoted to tree planting in the Mission compound, a work of which he was very fond, and in which he found his principal recreation. He was assisted in this by his brother, Mr. Blagney Balfour, a layman, who came to us in March, and was desirous of remaining some time in the country, with a view of studying the Church's method of mission work, as well as the characteristics of the native tribes among whom the Kingdom of God was being set up.

In April Mr. Blagney Balfour wrote a letter to some friends in England which was published soon afterwards in a missionary magazine; and from this letter I give the following extracts, as showing his first impressions of the work at Thlotse, and also of needs which were even then becoming apparent :—

"Thlotse Heights, April 6th, 1877."

"I have now been a month as a visitor at this station, and have seen enough to make me believe that a real work is going on which only wants time to grow. . . . Basutoland affords the most obvious and widest field for missionary work in the whole diocese. It is is expressly reserved by Government for *natives*. White people are obliged *to ask leave* to settle here. . . .

"If people ask what we want, I may say that we want as much money as we can get. It is wanted for three main objects :—

"1. To build a mission house. Huts are very comfortable in summer, but they have no chimneys, and will no doubt be cold in winter on a spot some 6,000 feet above the level of the sea. Besides, they are not durable, and can only be regarded as a makeshift.

"2. *Church.*—The congregation will, no doubt, under God's blessing, increase. . . . Natives come here from all parts; many (with faces painted with red clay) come to have a *look* at the church. This gives an opportunity of inviting them to come on Sunday to *pray*.

"3. *Schools.*—There are some twenty boys ready to come to an Industrial School, where they would be taken as boarders, and taught trades. A girls' Industrial School might also be started if money could be obtained for building."

The June of this year marked a forward step in the history of the Mission. In that month Joel Molapo, a chief hitherto unknown to us except by name, made an application to us, through Major Bell, to provide his people with a "Teacher."

He was the eldest son of Molapo, but not by his great wife, and though not a chief of the front rank was a man of power and influence in the northern portion of the district. Mr. Francis Balfour and I rode up to Buta-Bute (Moshesh's first stronghold, it will be remembered), at the foot of which Joel had built his village, in accordance with the wishes of his father. We had an interview of some length with the young chief, the result of which was that we felt it our duty to report his application to the Bishop. Some of the traders who knew him well warned us that he was not altogether a reliable person. He was said to be a man who gave himself airs; besides which he had the reputation of being quarrelsome, hot-tempered, and ambitious. Still, as he had invited us to come into his country, had promised us protection, and ardently desired that his people might be instructed in all that the white man had to teach, we could not refuse to entertain his request for a white teacher. He had, moreover, expressly given us full and free permission to preach the Gospel to all in his territory who might come within our influence, and this was an additional reason why we considered ourselves bound to make known his wishes to the chief pastor of the diocese. Joel and his people were thoroughly heathen, and were as yet untouched by any Christian agency, and this seemed all the more reason why the Church should, if possible, respond, and respond at once, to the call that had been made to us.

The Bishop replied that "such a door being thus opened by the Great Head of the Church," it would be "wrong of us to close it, and not attempt to enter"; and he therefore thought that we were bound to take advantage of it, and to commence a mission at or near Buta-Bute as soon as possible.

He suggested that Mr. Balfour might undertake this new and unexpected work, aided by the services of a young lay catechist, Mr. T. R. Grimsley, then working in another part of the diocese.

Mr. Balfour at once responded to the Bishop's wishes,

generously offering not only to work at Buta-Bute without stipend, as he had been doing at Thlotse, but also guaranteeing the support of the catechist, and promising to obtain from friends in England the money necessary for building purposes. He and I rode up to Leribe to interview Molapo on the subject of Joel's proposal, it being necessary to obtain the old chief's consent to the establishment of the Mission before any definite move could be made towards acting upon Joel's invitation. We found the great chief as fat and good humoured as ever. He received us graciously; was pleased to hear that his son wished to have a "Teacher;" and gave his formal consent to our settling in the northern part of his country. A few days afterwards he and Joel together assigned to us a suitable piece of ground on which to build and commence the Mission. Preparations for departure from Thlotse were soon made, and a week afterwards Mr. Balfour and his catechist were encamped at Sekubu—the name of the village nearest their ground—busily engaged in hut building.

The site of this new Mission is a very fine one. It is at the foot of a high ridge jutting out from a leading spur of the Malutis, at the back of which are several interesting Bushman caves; and the view from the crest of the ridge is one of the wildest and most magnificent to be found anywhere in the world. At any rate, such is the opinion of those travellers who have seen it. A number of scattered kraals and villages are spread all round, the inhabitants of which are some of the rudest, most savage, and most thoroughly heathen in the whole of Basutoland.

Within three months several rondavels were finished, and the foundations of a small, but substantial church of stone put in. A peach orchard was laid out, enclosed with a sod wall, and planted with young trees; and, in fact, the "English Teachers of Ma-Churche" were fast settling themselves down and feeling at home in their new field of labour. They soon made the acquaintance of the people, who for the most part gave them a ready welcome, and seemed pleased to think that missionaries had come to settle so near them. The rain doctor of the place, a grimy-looking individual named Mosola, with three wives, brought down his eldest boy to Mr. Balfour a day or two after his arrival, and desired that the lad might remain at the Mission to be trained by the missionaries as they thought best. Maoeng (that was the boy's name) was a gaunt creature, all arms and legs, and as grimy as his father—in fact, he would have made an admirable scarecrow in an English cornfield. He greatly enjoyed his new life, and was usually to be found squatting before the fire with his eyes fixed upon the coffee-kettle, and surrounded by a group of boys of his own age patiently waiting for a small share of the precious beverage which the dearly loved vessel contained, for the native is yet to be found who does not appreciate coffee.

Mr. Balfour had fortunately succeeded in securing the services of a clever American, living not far off on the borders of the Free State, who "knew a great many trades, and could turn his hand to anything." This man engaged to build a church, and a school room at a little distance from it, for a very moderate sum, and he carried out his contract faithfully. Two of the rondavels were placed at his disposal, and shortly afterwards he arrived with his wife and family. The wife was a good natured Dutch woman from the Cape, a good cook, with a passionate love of her art. She was particularly addicted to making "cookies" (cakes), and contrived to have about once a fortnight a "born day," as she expressed it in her broken English. She had a prodigious number of relatives and kinsfolk, and remembered most religiously the birthdays of all of them. There was a perpetual production of "cookies" and tarts going forward, much to the satisfaction, no doubt, of the hungry brethren, who duly appreciated her shining talents as a pastry-cook and confectioner. How she managed to get the flour, currants, and other ingredients necessary to the production of such dainties I do not in the least know—but she did; and when a third missionary appeared in the person of Mr. Woodman, who had just been ordained to the mission, her number of "born days" began even to increase, and the "cookies" increased with them. She had a special veneration and affection for the head of the mission party, and used to say of him, "Mr. Balfort, he very good man. Yes, he very good man indeed. He eat plenty, plenty cookies, and he say plenty, plenty prayers."

In preparing designs and plans for the church and school, as well as in all practical matters connected with the mission, Mr. Balfour was greatly aided by the advice and experience of the leading trader of the district, Mr. Alfred Ernest Richards. This gentleman, whose headquarters were at Leribe, most kindly acted as "Clerk of the Works," and spared neither time nor trouble in superintending the building operations; making also many valuable suggestions, which were the outcome of his own personal experience in the country. The result was that the Epiphany Mission—for such was the dedication of the church at Sekubu—soon possessed neat-looking and thoroughly substantial buildings, superior, in durability at least, to any others then in the diocese. And here let me say that Mr. Richards has been a true friend to the Church ever since we have known him. He has been the standing churchwarden of S. Saviour's for many years past: his hospitable house has ever been open to the workers in our missions, and his sympathy and aid in times of trial and perplexity have never been invoked in vain. Were all English colonists imbued with his spirit there would be no fear of the black man learning the vices of civilization instead of its virtues.

Here we must leave Sekubu, merely adding that when, a short time afterwards, Mr. Balfour was called to labour elsewhere in the diocese, Mr. Woodman succeeded him, and ably carried on the work of evangelization thus begun. In his labours among the people of the north his hands were greatly strengthened and sustained by his sister, Miss Woodman, who devoted herself entirely to the work of the mission until the outbreak of the rebellion in 1880.

In preaching to the heathen, and in our conversations with them, we found that, at first, the men were more ready to hear and receive the Word of God than the women. I ought, perhaps, rather to say *the young men;* for the older ones, who were mostly polygamists, were, for the most part, very stolid, and turned a deaf ear to our message. The women seemed afraid to listen to us; partly, no doubt, from their innate conservatism, and partly because they did not know anything of this new "thuto" (teaching) of Christ or its teachers. But, after the lapse of a few years, the contrary became the case: the women, finding out that Christianity was their truest friend, and its teaching such as would raise and ennoble them, began to give ear to the truths of the Gospel, while the men held aloof from it. Yet the ingrained heathenism of the women was not quickly or easily overcome. They saw clearly enough—as clearly as the men—that in embracing the faith of Christ they would have to come out, not only from their old superstitions, but from other and nameless degradations of heathenism, and rise to a higher and a purer life; and this was distasteful and irksome to them. They preferred the beer-drinking and other sensual habits and pleasures in which they had grown up, and shrank from the discipline of the Cross of Christ. "I am not a mealie," said one such one day to a Christian friend, who was endeavouring to persuade her to attend a Christian service, and listen to the new teaching. "I am not a mealie, to be wetted first and bruised afterwards." A remarkable answer, truly, for a heathen woman to make, and one that showed quite clearly that she had grasped the import of the Gospel message. For in South Africa it is the custom among the Boers, and many of the natives also, to wet the maize, and then bruise it in a large wooden mortar before boiling and preparing it for the table, and the woman was well acquainted with this custom. Hence the force and reality of her reply. The " wetting " referred, of course, to Holy Baptism; the " bruising " to the discipline of the Cross—that " crucifying of the flesh, with its affections and lusts," so absolutely necessary to progress in the spiritual life.

Among the people with whom we were brought into contact there were, as may be supposed, many " queer characters."

I will give one or two samples of them.

There was a funny, one-eyed old man, who was a miser. His name was Modibetsana, and he was, as the reader may perhaps remember, the headman of the village of Mapatsueng—the village already mentioned as the nearest to our station. The old fellow, who wore a fur cap, and pottered and tottered about with a long staff in his hand, came to me one morning in great trouble.

" Monere," he said, " a dreadful thing has happened to me. Last night my hut was burnt down through the carelessness of the children playing with the fire, and everything I had in the world was destroyed or ruined."

Then he, of course, asked me to help him. He begged for a blanket or two and a pot, or the wherewithal to purchase them at the store.

I knew that his story was true, but suspected that he was not so poor as he pretended. He was reputed to be a miser, who had laid up a secret hoard of coins in some private corner of his hut.

So I asked him what had become of his money.

" Money ? " said he, " I have no money; I never had any."

" Brother," said I, " that will not do. I know better. I am sure you had some. Tell me what has become of it. You must have saved it from the flames."

" Well, Monere," he replied, " you are my brother, and my father too, so I will tell you. I really did have some money: only a little—just a very little."

"Oh!" said I.

"Well, yes, Monere, it was a great lot: *a fortune* for a poor old man like me to lose. It was *two pounds*—two golden sovereigns with the Queen's likeness stamped upon them; and I kept them rolled up in a *lappie* (old piece of rag), and hidden away in a corner where no one could find them."

"Well?" I rejoined, "What has become of them? Where are they?"

"Monere," said he, "I do not know where they are. That is a mystery to me. I only know that they are nowhere to be found. I have looked everywhere, and I can find neither the sovereigns nor the rag they were wrapped in."

"But," said I, "the money must be where you left it, unless it was stolen. The fire was not fierce enough to melt it."

"Now," rejoined the old man, "I will tell my father the real truth. *The money has gone up to heaven.*

"Gone up to heaven! my brother. What *can* you mean?"

"I saw it go up," said he, "*It went up with the smoke.* The fire melted it, and it went up into the sky, pouff, pouff, pouff, like shining smoke, higher and higher, till I could see it no more."

The old man firmly believed his own statement, and nothing that I could say could disabuse him of his impression. The money was never found, and I have no doubt that it was abstracted during the conflagration by one of his many sons, none of whom were of much reputation for their honesty. But Modibetsana believed that it had been taken from him by God as a punishment for his undue love of it.

Another "character" was a Zulu, whom everyone called "Fat Daniel." He was not a true, blue-blooded Zulu, but belonged to one of the fish eating tribes. Most natives do not eat fish. They call it water snake, and consider it unwholesome.

How "Daniel" got his name I do not know. He seems

never to have had any other, though he was a rampant heathen, and had certainly never been baptised. Fat he certainly was, and very black too. When his face was well anointed with pig-fat and thoroughly polished up, as it was on great occasions, he always reminded me of a sleek, sly, comfortable looking tom cat; black, of course, and demure in demeanour; but always ready nevertheless for any emergency.

He had in his youth learnt in Natal to speak a little English, probably from a west country Englishman, for his English, such as it was, was pronounced with a strong "Zummerzetsheer" accent. He had, of course, a numerous progeny, and his eldest son, Voerman (a Dutch name), was a faithful copy of his father except in the one item of portliness of person. Father and son used to quarrel one day, and kiss and make friends the next. As neither of them was renowned for his veracity, it was sometimes difficult when they quarrelled to get at the truth, and I was now and then sorely put to it when they both appealed to me to settle their disputes, and decide which was in fault. It was said of them that they did speak the truth sometimes; but that was by accident.

One day there was a furious quarrel between them, which resulted in the son summoning his father before the court of the Commissioner of the district for the payment of the sum of four shillings and threepence, which Voerman declared the old man owed him.

The case was gone into, and the debt clearly proved, and Fat Daniel could not deny it.

"Has the defendant any questions to ask before I give judgment?" asked the Commissioner.

"Yez, Wosshop," answered Daniel.

"Well, then," said the Commissioner, "ask them at once."

"Yez, Wosshop," was the rejoinder, "Yez; I wants to ahks that man there"—pointing to his son—"I wants to ahks him *what I bornd him for?*"

CHAPTER VII.

Loss and Gain.

1877.

General Progress—Ficksburg—Visit of Mrs. Webb—Death of Mr. Lacy—His Character—A Hurricane—Personal—Women and Girls cared for—Hopeful Outlook.

The year 1877 was a chequered one, full of light and shadow to the Mission. We began it, as I have said, full of hope for the future. Our temporary buildings were almost complete, and the chapel had been solemnly set apart to the service of God by our chief pastor.

On Easter Eve we baptized our first little batch of converts, four in number: three Basutos and a Zulu. The chapel was already too small for the congregations of enquirers and heathen who frequented more or less regularly the Sunday services. So in June we pulled down the partition wall between the mission room and the chapel, thereby enlarging the latter by twelve feet; and in lieu of the former we built an oblong hut of raw brick and sods, which served for study and reception room.

Mr. Balfour left us for Sekubu at the end of July, and up to the time of his departure S. Saviour's had been responsible for fortnightly Sunday services at Ficksburg. This place was our nearest Free State village, and is prettily situated under the shadow of a spur of the Platbergen, close to the banks of the Caledon. These services were in English, and were well attended by the handful of English speaking people in the place; and once a month, when the farmers came in from the neighbouring homesteads, the church was inconveniently crowded. The church was, in truth, a very humble building. It was really nothing more than two rooms of a not very large cottage knocked into one, and had been purchased, and fitted up mainly through the efforts of Canon Beckett, who, as Rural Dean of that part of the diocese, was responsible for the spiritual oversight of Ficksburg, and did his utmost to provide the scattered members of the Church with the ministrations of religion.

As the work of S. Saviour's began to grow, we found it almost impossible to keep up these fortnightly visits to the Free State without injury to our own proper duties, and accordingly, when Mr. Woodman joined Mr. Balfour at Sekubu, it was arranged that these two brethren should make themselves responsible for visitations and services both at Ficksburg and along the western bank of the Caledon; and this arrangement continued for some years, until the increase of the staff at Modder Poort, under Father Douglas, enabled the brotherhood to take over the entire charge of the Ficksburg district.

In September we were cheered by a visit from Mrs. Webb and her two little boys. They had come to Basutoland for a short holiday, and took to their rough, Robinson Crusoe like life in our round huts very kindly. Mrs. Webb, always gentle and sympathetic, and full of devotion to the mission cause, had suffered of late from the extreme heat and drought of Bloemfontein, and the change to the green slopes and mountain glens of Basutoland was grateful to her. Moreover, Thlotse now boasted of a skilful and accomplished medical man in the person of Dr. Taylor, who had recently been appointed medical officer of the Leribe district by the British Government, and had taken up his residence on the heights between the Mission Compound and that of the Residency. Mrs. Webb and her children stayed with us until the first week in November, when she returned to Bloemfontein, Mr. Lacy riding with them on the way as far as Ficksburg.

The drift on the Caledon at Ficksburg was in those days a break-neck place (it is bad enough even now), and the river was known to be treacherous; but the party crossed it in safety, and next morning Mr. Lacy started on his return journey. But during the night there had been a good deal of rain near the sources of the river, and by the time he arrived on its banks it had considerably increased in depth. At such times it was barely if at all fordable, and, moreover, the current ran swiftly, and was very strong. But Mr. Lacy did not realize the danger. He rode into the treacherous stream, and was seen no more. This was on the 9th of November. Some white men, working in the fields on the banks of the river, had seen him descend into the drift, and about two hours afterwards they noticed a horse standing, saddled and bridled, without its master on a little reach about half a mile distant down the stream. They hurried to the spot, and found it to be the horse of our poor young friend, who was evidently drowned. How it happened no one could tell. I think he must have lost his seat when the pony began to swim; and as there was no one near to help him, he was probably whirled onwards to his death by the rushing torrent. The horse, more fortunate, after being carried some distance down the stream, managed at last to swim out to the reach, and remained there patiently waiting for his master, until noticed by the labourers on the farm above.

The sad tidings did not reach us until late in the afternoon, and meanwhile the men who noticed the pony had been searching diligently, but in vain, for the body. Hastily our horses were got in from the veldt and saddled, and Dr. Taylor, Mr. Charles Bell, and myself, accompanied by some of the Native Mounted Police, reached the scene of the misadventure just before dusk. The men were still searching for the body, but as yet no trace of its whereabouts could be found. The river was still rising very rapidly, and nothing more could be done that night; so all that we could do was to return sorrowfully home. Next day, and for several days afterwards, the good Ficksburg people and their neighbours continued their efforts. The Caledon had now begun to run down, which made the search easier, and on the fifth

WILLIAM LACY
(When a Chorister in London).

day after the accident the body was found. It was discovered in the overhanging branches of a willow tree about a mile below the drift, having been thus caught, and its onward progress arrested, while the tree was still under water. It was very much bruised and disfigured, and partly decomposed, but it was nevertheless taken to the mission station and buried there, making the first grave in the but recently enclosed cemetery.

Mr. Lacy's death was a great blow to the Mission. He was a young man of much promise, and had given his whole life to the work. He came to the diocese when only sixteen years of age, having been sent out to Modder Poort by an English friend of Canon Beckett's (the Rev. C. Gutch, of London), who had educated and trained him from boyhood, and carefully fostered the missionary spirit which he displayed. He possessed exactly the qualifications necessary in a successful mission worker: a powerful physique, robust health, a receptive mind, an aptitude for learning foreign languages, a good baritone voice, a love of school work and of children, plenty of patience, a fair amount of common sense, and a willingness to " endure hardness as the soldier of Christ." At the time of his death he was reading for Holy Orders, expecting to be ordained to the Mission in the following year. He seemed to be specially fitted for the work he had entered upon—quite the right man in the right place—and now, in the mysterious working of Providence, he was suddenly snatched away just at the moment that he was most needed. So it has often been in the history of the Church, and we must be content to wait for the explanation of the "why" and the "wherefore" of God's dealings with His people until the great day of the unveiling of all things, when all will be made clear, and when we shall see as well as know that

"All that God does, it is well done."

I had known my young comrade for six years, the last two of which we had spent side by side, first at Thaba 'Nchu, and then at Thlotse. Having been thus intimately associated with him, I can testify to his goodness, and I have no hesitation in saying that he was one of the purest minded and most devoted young men that I have ever known. To the purity of a child was in his case added the strength and endurance of a man. His special work at S. Saviour's was that of the school, to build up which he worked with unwearied patience and perseverance; and his bright, playful manner and loving disposition endeared him to all who came into contact with him. He was by birth a Londoner, and used often to amuse us by his Cockney way of looking at things. I remember that when he first caught sight of the Malutis, and saw them in all their glory—their lofty peaks lighted up into the most gorgeous colours by the glow of the setting sun—he exclaimed in his simple, playful way, "How beautiful they are! They remind me of those lovely silk dresses arranged side by side on stands, in their flowing folds, at Peter Robinson's in Oxford Street!" Surely no one but a Cockney could have been guilty of perpetrating such a simile!

Peace be with thee, guileless one, so early called away to thy reward! In thy short life thou hast "fulfilled a long time," * and taught us by thy sweet and pure example how best to labour in the Master's vineyard, with a single eye to the Master's glory, and the salvation of the souls so dearly purchased by His most Precious Blood.

A few days after Mr. Lacy's funeral there was a terrific hurricane, which did much damage to all kinds of buildings in many parts of the country. The little chapel did not escape its violence. It was unroofed, the rafters broken in pieces, and the sheets of galvanised iron rolled up like so much paper, and whirled away to a considerable distance in the veldt. Fortunately no one was hurt, it being night when the storm was at its height and the mischief done. In the morning we found the timbers strewn about in splinters, and the poor building did look such a

---

* Wisdom of Solomon iv. 13.

wreck! I had feared from the first that such a roof would not stand the force of our north-westers. These winds usually set in from the Kalahari Desert, blowing up clouds of dust, and accumulating in force on their onward sweep until finally they spend their fury at the base of the Drakensbergen. But it is only occasionally—say, once in three or four years—that they put forth all their strength. I had hoped that the roof might stand until we were able to put up a stronger one, but it was gone now past repair. There was nothing for it but to provide a new one, and that as soon as possible. And how was that to be done? Such a roof as the building required would cost at least £120, and as the diocesan funds were low we could expect no help from that quarter. But our people came bravely to the rescue. Led by our devoted friend, Mr. Richards, they all came forward—Europeans and native Christians—and speedily raised a sufficient sum to enable us to put up a strongly-tied and substantial pitched roof of the best galvanised iron, which has stood firmly, and resisted all attacks of wind and storm from that day to this. Meanwhile, we held our daily services and classes in one of the huts, and the school and Sunday services in the open air in a corner of the compound.

At the end of November I married, and my wife, on her arrival at Thlotse, began at once to interest herself in the welfare of the native women and girls. No woman's influence had hitherto been brought to bear upon them; and now that they saw a Christian gentlewoman visiting them in their homes, sympathising with them in their difficulties, and rejoicing with them in their joys, their hearts went out to her at once. A sewing class was formed for the young girls, at which they learned to make simple cotton dresses and other garments for themselves, and they made good progress in the work. Then, too, our boy boarders were cared for as only a woman can care for them, and these small savages promptly responded to the care and guidance bestowed upon them. In a few months their rough and repulsive

I

habits were softened down, and they became amenable to discipline and cleanly in their persons. In a word, they were tamed.

At the end of 1877 all looked hopeful. Catechumens came in, the school (now conducted mainly by myself until a successor to Mr. Lacy should arrive from England) increased in numbers, the services were hearty and well attended, the women and girls cared for, and the chapel thoroughly repaired and strengthened with its new and firmly-fastened roof. Seed was being sowed which, please God, would spring up and bear abundant fruit in time to come.

CHAPTER VIII.

Via Crucis.

1878.

Easter — Native Singing — Native Sense of Beauty — Atmospheric Phenomena — Another Visit from Mr. Blayney Balfour — Proposal for a Native Training College — Death of Mrs. Widdicombe.

Easter 1878 marked a new advance. A little band of converts had been gathered together, among whom were several boys with good voices, and these were formed for the first time into a choir. That Easter Eve service was a very bright one, and the boys and men—there were ten of the former and two of the latter—looked really nice in their cassocks and surplices, and sang the Sesuto Evensong very heartily, and in good time and tune. Natives always do sing heartily—so heartily that they often get carried away by excitement—and then, if they are not checked, they will go on to shout, scream, and even *yell* as only savages can. Most of them have good voices, but they easily flatten, especially in chanting. Hence they require to be always well led, and that if possible by a European with a good baritone voice, if the proper pitch is to be duly sustained for any length of time. I have noticed that very few good tenors are to be found amongst them; but really good, deep, rich basses are by no means uncommon. Among the women the contraltos, too, are as a rule superior to the sopranos. Perhaps this may be partly accounted for by their language, which is emphatically a *chest* one, the broad, resonant A and E being of frequent occurrence in it. Men, women, and children easily learn to sing simple melodies and pieces in the tonic sol-fa notation, but they rarely succeed in rendering accidentals with any degree of nicety. They are passionately fond of hymn tunes, especially the more solid compositions in " Hymns Ancient and Modern," and " pick them up " as quickly as English people; indeed, it is now quite a common thing to hear the Christian herd-boys in the valleys round the heights singing in two parts many of the standard hymn tunes in our English hymnals. Some of these—such, for instance, as Sullivan's " Onward, Christian Soldiers "—are special favourites, and are taken up with a swing and verve which would astonish a stranger, more especially were he told that the singers were only a few years ago barbarians with but the faintest and most rudimentary ideas of music, and with no conception whatever of European compositions.

The native in his natural state has no appreciation of the beautiful in nature. I was going to add in art likewise; but perhaps that would hardly be fair, considering the immense pains the young girls take in the adornment of their persons with beads and bangles. These braveries are often arranged with a certain natural grace, and great taste is sometimes exhibited in the selection of the colours of the beads which are used for collars and other personal ornaments; but of the beauties of nature, as we are accustomed to understand the term, they seem to have no conception. " A thing of beauty " is not to the native " a joy for ever."

When we first began to decorate the church at Christmas and Easter our people could not comprehend what we were doing, or why we were doing it. But gradually the sense of beauty, which is latent in every man, was called out in them, and this was, of course, especially marked in the case of the converts. We have planted from time to time in the mission garden not only many varieties of European and African flowers, but also a number of flowering trees and shrubs, most of which are unknown in the Lesuto. Heathen natives often come to feast their eyes upon these strange and foreign productions, and, after contemplating them for some time in silence, they invariably break out with " Monere, what is this tree good for? Is its fruit *very* delicious to the taste?" I answer that it does not bear any fruit. "Then it must be a medicine tree? Is its medicine very potent? Will it cure *many* kinds of disease?" I answer again, "No, it is not a medicine tree. As far as I know, it produces nothing that can be used as medicine." "Baesu!" is the exclamation; "why then do you plant it? What is the use of it? It must be good for something." I reply that it is a beautiful tree to look at, and that it bears beautiful flowers. We planted it, I say, for *khabiso*—ornament. For " *khabiso feela* "—" ornament only?"—say they. " Yes, for ornament only. It gladdens our eyes, and makes us think of the goodness and beauty of God."

A grunt of doubtful approbation is the answer, which, put into plain words, would be interpreted thus:—" What an extraordinary being the white man is! He actually expends time, labour, and money upon a tree which is of no earthly use to him! It is a barren cow; it yields him no milk; a useless cumberer of the earth, for it gives him no medicine. It does not even supply him with his tobacco, and perhaps its leaves would poison him if he attempted to smoke them. Prodigious! Who ever heard of a human being planting a tree merely to look at! Monere says he has not even planted it for fuel: it grows there, this curious tree, merely to be looked at! Verily, the white man is an inscrutable being. We thought him wise, but he seems to be only a simpleton after all!"

Yet they go away and ponder over it, and in the end come to the conclusion that, no doubt, there must be something in it. As for the Christians, they soon learn to appreciate beauty, and many of them come from time to time to ask for rootlets or cuttings of flowers, especially of bold or showy ones, which they carefully plant in their *serapa*, near their huts, and learn to value as time goes on. Nearly all the converts now take the greatest interest in church decoration, some of them regularly sending us the produce of their flower-beds for the purpose.

They are great admirers of colour, and greatly prize the oleographs and coloured prints which form the supplements to the *Illustrated London News* and the *Graphic*, and which we distribute to them when the annual mission box from friends at home yields up its treasures. They nail up the prints on the walls of their huts, and the rondavels of some of our Christians are almost papered with them. Of course, we do all we can to foster the sense of beauty among the people, but we do not forget to supply them with the useful as well as the beautiful. Every year we give away large numbers of young peach and other fruit-trees, besides cuttings and seeds of flowers and shrubs.

The year 1878 was celebrated for its meteors. Magnificent meteoric displays are often seen in Basutoland, especially in the months of July and November. For hours together the sky is lit up at night by an almost continuous succession of the most brilliant rockets—for so they seem to be—varied at intervals by *showers* of shooting stars. These aerolites fall in great numbers in the mountains, and I well remember being awakened one night in the July of this year by the sound of a violent explosion—a tremendous crash—in the Malutis right in front of our station. I rushed out of the hut just in time to witness a most beautiful sight. The heavens were ablaze with meteors, one of which had just fallen upon a huge crag, thus causing the report we had heard. Almost every person in the place was roused by the concussion, and some of the women ran about outside their huts screaming with fright; when suddenly the voice of the native sentry rang out clear and full from the watch-tower in the distance, " All's *Wool!* "

It was probably the only English he knew, and he was determined to make the most of it. The effect was irresistible.

I remember also another and still more remarkable instance of these natural pyrotechnic displays. It happened some years afterwards, and was witnessed by Mr. Champernowne, one of my colleagues, as well as myself, as we were riding together to the village of Ficksburg. It took place not at night, but in the middle of the day. It wanted but a few minutes to twelve o'clock; the sky was without a cloud, and the sun blazing down upon us in all his noonday splendour: in fact, the day was a thoroughly African one. As we were riding along on the great flat between the Khomokoana and the Caledon, our attention was suddenly arrested by an unusual light in the sky above us. We reined in our horses and stood still to look upon the most astonishing sight we had ever beheld. The sun was at its zenith to the north of us, and about midway between it and the Malutis there appeared a succession of rapid coruscations of dazzling brightness; ribands of fire came into view, were unrolled, shaken out, and consumed like burning scrolls; bands of light were seen for a moment, and then lost to the eye; chains of flames—as of glowing, molten gold in a furnace—burst upon the vision, were swallowed up, and disappeared from sight. The brilliancy of this wonderful display quite obscured the light of the noonday sun; an *African* sun, too, be it remembered. It lasted several seconds; how many I cannot say; for we were so overwhelmed with astonishment that we forgot to take out our watches and count them. We remained for some minutes riveted to the spot in sheer amazement, reminding each other of what Josephus relates concerning the portents that appeared over Jerusalem before its final destruction. After such a sight as we had then witnessed we could easily believe the testimony of the historian without having recourse to miracle in explanation of it.

On arriving at Ficksburg we found that all the people in the streets at the time saw the same remarkable display, and next day we heard that just after we had witnessed it several large fragments of aerolites had fallen in the mountains behind Sekubu, about forty miles distant. I have often in Africa seen many remarkable natural phenomena, but none to equal in splendour or magnificence the spectacle which on that occasion was presented to our view.

In the Easter-tide of this year we received a second visit from Mr. Blayney Balfour, who, after leaving us the year before, had volunteered to fill a gap at Bloemfontein, by taking the tutorship of some natives there, who were desirous of being trained for Church work. He came to us now for a period of three or four months before returning to England, and during this time was good enough to help us both in our services and schools. The evening school for the men was a work which specially commended itself to him, and the patience with which he plodded away, night after night, in teaching a number of half-witted and half-naked savages to master b, $\bar{a}$—$b\bar{a}$, and spell out the simplest words of their own language, was in itself a valuable lesson in mission work. Now and then he and his sable pupils rose to higher flights. Some of the men, chiefly those of the Native Mounted Police, wished to learn English, the most difficult of all tongues to the native. He can generally manage to " pick up " Cape Dutch in some sort of way if he makes a real, honest attempt to do so, but English is at once his hope and his despair.

To see half-a-dozen of these stalwart sons of Africa resolutely attacking the short, monosyllabic sentences in Nelson's " Step by Step ;" to hear them shouting out with intense earnestness and gravity, " De okkies gan nod go indo de bokkies," was too much for mortal man! The teacher would smile softly to himself; and the class, catching the expression of his face, would burst out into a violent explosion of laughter. But nothing daunted, the next man would gird himself to the attack, determined to do or die. Spearing his enemy in the battle-field was a light thing to him, but demonstrating to his fellow-men that " the ox cannot go into the box" was a painful and all but impossible task to both brain and tongue. " *Gan* de okkies go indo de bokkies?" he would indignantly demand, with screwed-up mouth, contorted visage, and eyeballs staring out of their sockets. Then, with a violent shake of the head which suggested a terrier and a rat, he would return to the attack and exclaim triumphantly, " *Naw*, de okkies gan *nod* go indo de bokkies."

The effort was prodigious. The pent-up feelings would find relief in a deep and prolonged sigh, the face would be bathed in a profuse perspiration, and a general roar of laughter all round would for the moment end the scene.

Yes, night-school with raw natives was often great fun. To a refined, cultivated layman, fresh from an English university, this must have been a novel experience indeed! Our friend entered into it with ardour, and I have no doubt often smiles when he looks back upon that brief but brilliant African experience.

The two years I had been in the country had taught me more and more plainly that if the Mission was to prosper and do its appointed work, it would ere long be absolutely necessary to train up the native converts to take a large share in it themselves. But so much had to be thought of for the Europeans in the diocese, if they were not to be lost altogether to the Church; so many institutions had to be set on foot for the education of their sons and daughters, that it had been impossible for the Bishop to establish anything like a training institution for our converts, either at S. Saviour's or elsewhere in the diocese.

Hence we were without any means of educating and preparing such converts as might show a vocation for work among their fellow-countrymen as evangelists, catechists, or schoolmasters. We had absolutely no machinery for the purpose, and yet the need was great and pressing, and increasing day by day. It could, indeed, be partially supplied by sending such young men as might show an aptitude for the work of evangelization to the training colleges at Grahamstown or Capetown, but this was an expensive and cumbrous proceeding, and we mission clergy all felt that our diocese ought to have a training institution of its own.

I ventured to write to the Bishop to set this need before him, and received a most sympathetic reply. In truth, his lordship was as keenly alive to the situation as any of his mission clergy could be, and promised to aid me in any way that lay in his power should I be able to propound some workable scheme, whereby an institution for the training of native catechists could be established, the outcome of which might be, as time went on, if God so willed it, a native ministry—the greatest need of all. But he was unable to promise any pecuniary help, the diocese being already heavily freighted with the important works that had been set on foot in Bloemfontein for the Europeans.

Then I sounded the Government, knowing their liberality to schools and other educational agencies for the native races. The Basutoland executive were willing to make an annual grant towards the support and education of native students in a training college, provided that suitable buildings could be erected, a competent teacher appointed, and the secular studies such as met the requirements of the Educational Department. This seemed hopeful, and was indeed all that could be reasonably expected. But where was the money to come from? Students we could get; I had no doubt of that. But how were a " suitable building " and a " competent teacher " to be provided?

I took counsel with my brethren at Sekubu. Mr. Balfour and Mr. Woodman came down to S. Saviour's, and after an early celebration of the Holy Communion and united prayer for guidance, all three of us went down after breakfast to the banks of the Thlotse, and there talked the problem out. A scheme was propounded which will be explained hereafter, by means of which a native training college was to be established at Thlotse, with the sanction and approval of the Bishop, and the education and training of a limited number of lads secured.

But God in His Providence ordered it otherwise. Through unforeseen and unexpected circumstances our plans came to nought, and the desired institution is still a thing of the future, though, as may be imagined, the necessity for it is tenfold greater now than it was in 1878. I am not, however, without hope that in the near future this long felt want may be supplied, the present Bishop of the diocese being as anxious as his predecessor to wipe away such a long standing reproach from the Church.

The immediate cause of the frustration of our hopes was an event as sudden and unlooked for as it was calamitous and full of sorrow.

On the morning of the 9th November, the anniversary of Mr. Lacy's death, Mrs. Widdicombe was taken to her eternal rest, after giving birth to a little daughter.

Even at this distance of time I hardly dare to trust myself to write of it; nor would it be desirable, either for my readers or myself, that such a personal bereavement should be intruded upon their notice more than is absolutely necessary to the purposes of this narrative.

Of the event itself I will only say that all that medical skill could do was done, but that it availed nothing. A few minutes, and all was over. The light of my eyes had gone from me, never more to return. The blow stunned me by its awful suddenness. There was not in it even the short respite given to the prophet : " Son of man, behold, I take away from thee the desire of thine eyes with a stroke . . . . So I spake unto the people in the morning : and at even my wife died."*

But the All Merciful One showed mercy upon me in that hour of desolation, or I should utterly have fainted. My dear brother priest, Mr. Balfour, came and stayed at S. Saviour's as long as was possible, and both by word and deed did all that man could do to comfort and sustain ; and the little orphaned babe found a mother in tender-hearted, sympathising Mrs. Bell, whose continued care and kindness I shall never be able to repay.

Of the lamentations of the people at the loss of the "mother" who had endeared herself to them I will say nothing. It will be better imagined than described.

But I may perhaps be permitted to print the following extracts from two letters that were written at the time, and published soon afterwards, in the " Bloemfontein Quarterly Paper." The first is from one written by the Bishop.

" You will all mourn with me over the sad tidings of Mrs. Widdicombe's death. So much of the work at her husband's mission station seemed to depend upon her presence and personal help, and she had thrown herself so entirely into it, winning the hearts of the native women and girls in a wonderful way. She had previously, as you know, done a good and faithful work at S. Michael's Home for four years. God called her away on the anniversary of the date of Mr. Lacy's death, to pray for the Mission in Paradise ; surely not meaning otherwise than to put His blessing upon the work ; giving it the promise of victory by the ' corn of wheat ' so falling into the ground and dying, and therefore not abiding alone."

The other is from a letter by the Rev. Francis Balfour.

" I cannot believe that God should have taken away two such pure, devoted, self-denying, active lives so soon after the beginning of Church work

---

* Ezekiel xxiv. 16, 18.

here, without intending to send some great blessing down some day upon us. He may be angry with us as a body for having neglected this work so long. He may wish to test our faith, and the mettle we are made of. He may wish to see if Christians who hitherto have helped us will persevere in spite of these afflictions. I cannot tell, but of this I feel quite confident, that the corns of wheat which have fallen into the ground and died will bear much fruit, and that the united prayers of these devoted souls will receive their promised answer from the throne above."

For a time it seemed impossible that I could stay on at Thlotse. The bright hopes of years had been quenched in a moment: the happiness of life blotted out.

. . . . .

"But it is written: The eternal God is thy refuge, and underneath are the everlasting arms."* God in His mercy gave me grace to take this comfort to my soul, and to say—fearfully it might be, and perhaps falteringly—yet not, I hope, without something of truth and reality, "Not my will, but Thine, be done."

>Though, like the wanderer,
>   The sun gone down,
>Darkness comes over me,
>   My rest a stone,
>Yet in my dreams I'd be
>Nearer, my God, to Thee,
>   Nearer to Thee.

>Then, with my waking thoughts
>   Bright with Thy praise,
>Out of my stony griefs
>   Beth-el I'll raise;
>So by my woes to be
>Nearer, my God, to Thee,
>   Nearer to Thee.

---

* Deuteronomy xxxiii. 27.

CHAPTER IX.

NEW WORKERS.

1879-80.

Isantlana—Arrival of New Workers—New Compound—Laying the Foundation Stone of the Training College—The Morosi Campaign—An Important Pitso—Second Visit of the Bishop—Letters Describing the Work of the Mission.

JANUARY, 1879, saw the advance of a large British force into Zululand under Lord Chelmsford, and on the 24th of that month a report reached us through native runners that "all the soldiers of the Queen of England had been cut to pieces by the Zulus at Isandhlwana," or, as the Basutos pronounce it, Isantlana. We were amazed as well as horrified at the report; the more so that no such news had reached us through any white source, though we ought to have known that the native intelligence department is usually wonderfully well-managed and efficient. Indeed, considering the multifarious appliances of European armies, it is astonishing how the African contrives to hold his own in this respect, often successfully competing with the white man in the rapid transmission of news, notwithstanding all the superior advantages of the latter. A few days afterwards the tidings, as sad as they were astounding, were almost literally confirmed by a Free State newspaper.

Isantlana was only three days' journey from us by the short cuts through the mountains, though I had never heard of the place before. Dreadful as the news was, we had no reason to fear that it might have a disquieting effect upon the Basutos. The Zulu monarchs, from Chaka onwards, had been such tyrants, and their hands so often imbrued with blood, that they were hated as well as feared by our people; and numbers of Zulu refugees had from time to time, as the reader knows, found shelter in the Lesuto, especially in our own district of Leribe. Furthermore, the Government officials had in detention at the Thlotse magistracy at that very time four of Cetywayo's secret ambassadors to the Basuto chiefs, who had been sent by their master to endeavour to persuade them to join with him in resisting the British power. But these emissaries never succeeded in getting further south than Thlotse, Molapo having privately informed Major Bell of their arrival at Leribe and of the object of it, advising him to detain them as persons dangerous to the peace of the tribe. This the Major accordingly did, promptly but quietly, while they were on their way to Letsie, suspecting nothing, and hopeful of the success of their mission. They were detained for some months at the magistracy, kindly treated, and, when the danger was over, after the victory at Ulundi, set free. They were in no hurry to depart, and one of them elected to stay permanently at Thlotse rather than return to a home convulsed, as Zululand then was, with anarchy and bloodshed.

Even had Cetywayo's messengers succeeded in reaching Matsieng and getting the ear of the Paramount Chief, it is very unlikely that he would have listened favourably to their master's message. He was too old a fox to be caught in such a trap as that, and if the truth were told, rejoiced in his inmost heart at the prospect of the Zulu king being humbled and reduced to submission by the power of England. But the news of the disaster at Isantlana astounded the Basutos, as well it might. Humanly speaking such a catastrophe ought never to have happened, and, judging from experience, it could not have taken place if only the waggons had been *lagered* in the usual Boer fashion. The fact that they were not, and that by their recklessness or their neglect the English commanders allowed their soldiers to be cut to pieces, astonished the Basutos in the highest degree, and tended to lower the prestige of the British army in their eyes.

In Lent two new workers arrived from England. These were the Rev. R. K. Champernowne, recently ordained to the priesthood, and his sister, Miss M. E. Champernowne. They had come out to the Mission as permanent workers, free of charge in any way to the diocese, and full of devotion to the good cause. Not long afterwards I had the additional pleasure of welcoming another worker, Mr. M. A. Reading, who came to us from S. Boniface College, Warminster, as a candidate for Holy Orders. Mr. Reading naturally took the place of my first catechist, Mr. Lacy, making the school his special work, and assisting in the services, especially on Sundays, as far as possible.

Mr. Champernowne had come out as chaplain to the projected native training college, and his sister had volunteered to accompany him as housekeeper and matron of the institution; but as our original plans could no longer be carried out in their entirety, a modification of them had become a necessity should the attempt be made to set the training college on foot. Accordingly we all took counsel together, and the result of our deliberations was that Mr. Champernowne was to endeavour to raise funds for the college; and that, should the proposed institution ever become an accomplished fact, he and his sister together were to take the entire charge and management of it. Meanwhile, he was to be licensed as an assistant curate at S. Saviour's, and I, as head of the Mission, was to apply to the Government for a small grant of land for the projected institution. This I forthwith did, with the result that a new compound not far off on the southern slope of the heights was generously made over to us for the purpose.

Some of Mr. Champernowne's English friends eagerly caught at the idea of a native training institution, and did their utmost to collect money for building purposes; and in July the ground was enclosed and laid out, and plans procured for a suitable building. The Bishop, it is needless to say, entered warmly into the proposal, only too glad to see a prospect of our idea being carried out; and in September the foundation stone of the new institution was laid by Mrs. Bell, who had now become quite a "mother in Israel." Many natives were present on the occasion, and the clergy and choir went in procession to the compound, singing Sesuto hymns on the way. A brightly rendered and appropriate service followed, and, after the stone was duly laid, Major Bell, in his official capacity of Resident, addressed the natives, especially *the men*, pointing out to them the utility and value of the institution now being founded, and telling them that it was being built for the benefit of themselves and their children. They might not be able now at once to see its advantages, but if they listened to the teachers that had been sent to them they would become wiser and better men, and would rejoice that such a school of training, instruction, and discipline had been founded in their midst. He hoped that this school might be the means of leading many of their sons to higher things, and of training them in habits of industry, sobriety, and those other virtues necessary for the work to which they might be called.

Alas, that these hopes never became a reality! The building which was begun with such high expectations was destined, as we shall see, never to be completed.

The Basutos had now enjoyed under British protection more than ten years of peace and prosperity. The protection of the British crown had not only secured to them an immunity from the attacks of foreign foes, but had also enabled them to live at peace among themselves. Cattle raiding had ceased, crime had diminished, Christianity was making way in the country, education was extending, industrial pursuits were regarded with favour, new land was being brought under the plough or the mattock year by year, when suddenly a small cloud arose in the south which proved to be the precursor of a violent storm which was to rage throughout and ravage the whole country.

It will be remembered that about half a century before Moshesh had conquered the Baphuti, a tribe living in the Quiteng district, at the south-eastern corner of the Lesuto; and that they and their chief, Morosi, became henceforth the subjects of the "Chief of the Mountain." These Baphuti were reported to be growing restive, and giving the Government officials a good deal of trouble. Morosi was now a very old man, and was practically in the hands of his son Dodo, a turbulent individual who was perpetually seeking opportunities to "ikhansa"; that is to "vapour" or "show off," as the natives say. This conduct culminated one day in the early part of the year (1879) by his openly defying his magistrate. This, of course, could not be tolerated, and the obnoxious chief, together with some of his principal aiders and abettors, was fined and imprisoned. But the imprisonment was not rigorous, and the prison was a very different structure from that which an Englishman usually understands by the name. It was a mere rickety "shanty," and Dodo had little or no difficulty in making his escape from it. Indeed, it was currently asserted, with I know not what amount of truth, that he and his friends had escaped rather *with* the gaol than *from* it—carrying away their place of detention bodily with them!

The Baphuti, now in open revolt, fled to their stronghold, "Morosi's Mountain," one of the flat-topped hills of the country, and the Colonial Government called upon the Basutos, through Col. Griffith, the Governor's Agent at Maseru, to take up arms against them, and reduce them to submission. The Basuto chiefs promptly responded to the call, and in April Morosi's stronghold was stormed, but without success, by a combined force of Colonial troops and Basuto levies.

Then followed a weary siege, which lasted till November, when those of the Baphuti who still remained upon the mountain were finally starved out, and the stronghold taken. Morosi was killed in the last fight on the top of the mountain; but Dodo and some others escaped to the inner fastnesses of the Quiteng.

Previous to the capture of this stronghold, a Pitso of great importance was held at Maseru on October 16th, at which Mr. Sprigg (now Sir Gordon Sprigg), the Premier of the Cape Ministry, was present. A Disarmament Act had recently been passed by the Cape Parliament, and it was proposed that its provisions should be extended to Basutoland, and made binding upon the Basuto people, who were now under the direct rule of the Colonial Government. The Premier's message was a very unwelcome one to both chiefs and people, and led to results which in all probability were little anticipated either by the Governor or his Ministers. No definite action on the part of the Government immediately followed the Pitso, and meanwhile the year 1879 drew to a close.

In the April of the next year we and our people were cheered and strengthened by a second visit from our chief pastor. The Bishop came to us on Saturday, April 24th, attended by Canon Crisp as Rural Dean and Chaplain. Canon Crisp wrote an account of their visit, which afterwards appeared in the pages of the Quarterly Paper of the diocese, and from it I take the following extracts as tending to show the impression which S. Saviour's made upon an able and experienced mission priest :—

"Thlotse is such a charming station. It is the seat of a magistracy, and is situate on a plain at the top of a hill. On the east one gets a grand view of the Malutis, with their picturesque peaks and constant variations of light and shade. In the valley below the Thlotse river runs amid fields of maize and millet to its junction with the Caledon, about half a mile off. Mr. Widdicombe's school-chapel of S. Saviour's, at the south-eastern corner of the oblong piece of ground allotted to the Mission, looks into his garden, which, though little more than three years old, abounds with young trees, choice roses, and other flowers and shrubs. The bell rang for Evensong soon after we arrived. It was sung very heartily by the native choir in Sesuto, and when it was over we adjourned to Mr. Champernowne's compound for supper, Mr. Widdicombe staying behind to prepare the Christians for the morrow's Communion.

"On Sunday morning (4th after Easter) the Bishop celebrated the Holy Communion in the little mission chapel. The service was choral, and one feature in it was very delightful; both Europeans and natives joined in it as one people. The service was in English, except the Gospel and the Confession, which were read in both languages, while the hymns used were Sesuto; but the little dark-skinned choristers were quite *au fait* with the English parts, and sang out the Kyrie, or said the Creed, as well as if they had been in Sesuto.

"At 9.30 a short form of Matins was sung in Sesuto, after which the Bishop preached to the people by means of an interpreter. The whole country around the station is densely crowded, and with few exceptions the people are heathen. The work is indeed an uphill one, needing the utmost patience and courage. All that can be done at present is a quiet laying of foundations, and this is what is being done in a very thorough way at S. Saviour's. The natives are being regularly visited at their villages; the schools are punctually assembled and most diligently taught; classes for the instruction of the converts are held; translations are being prepared; the daily services are carefully rendered; and in this way, while the life of the Church is brought constantly before the people, an earnest preparation is being made for the future.

"The Service was followed at eleven by English Matins with the Litany, and a sermon from the Bishop. The European work at Thlotse is a very striking and admirable one. The large trade in grain has attracted many traders, and these, with the Government officials, form a considerable community. Many of the first named were, before their residence in Basutoland, members of one or another form of dissent. The patient work of the Church among them is bringing these one by one within her fold. One marks at Thlotse, with great thankfulness, an absence of that lethargy which too often characterizes Churchmen living in scattered numbers. . It is most cheering to see the European members of the congregation riding in from distances of ten and twelve miles to the Sunday services.

"In the afternoon Evensong was sung in Sesuto, and a sermon preached especially to the Christians. English Evensong with a sermon closed a busy, happy day."

On the Monday there were two Confirmations held, one in Sesuto, and the other in English. At these services eight native converts and eleven Europeans received the Apostolic rite, the services being heartily rendered, and the chapel crowded to the doors.

"I have spoken of the mission garden; but there is another little garden without a mention of which no notice of Thlotse would be complete. Half way between S. Saviour's and Mr. Champernowne's is the enclosure of the two graves which mark the resting-place of the dear ones whose memory seems to cast a constant blessing over the Mission and all its surroundings. There lies the dear, pure-minded lad whose brave young heart was such a blessing to the priest he served in the very first days of the work, and whose name even now brings a glad look into the face of every native who knew and loved him. And by his side lies the gentle lady, taken away ere her first year had come to an end, but not before her influence had been felt on all around, and the native women had come to look upon her as a mother."

A portion of a letter from Mr. Reading, describing his daily work in the school, may fitly close this chapter.

"S. Saviour's, Thlotse Heights, 19th June, 1880.

"The children are very fond of reading. I think they like poetry more than prose. I suppose one may account for this, since they have musical ears, and therefore quickly detect the rhythm. There is with them an eagerness to read. They have a keen sense of the comical, and quickly notice anything in the way of a joke. Small things seem to try their risible faculties most. If a fly alights upon their book it is a great matter; they seem to imagine that the little creature is trying to read, and finds it a puzzler! A spider hanging from its web is too much for them; they cannot think how it manages to stick to the fine thread; and, when it ascends, a host of absurd ideas seem to pass through their brains. They cannot govern themselves in the least. If a thing strikes them as funny they make it a matter of conscience to laugh, and laugh they will.

"At the end of the reading lesson some little time is spent in translating. They are very fond of this also. Perhaps one boy may give a rendering which in the opinion of another is not altogether classical, and then follows a tug of war. I always allow, in moderation, a free discussion about any word which is called into question. This not only helps them to think, but it brings their English into play, makes them examine their own language, and teaches them how to reason with each other without losing their tempers.

They, of course, find it more difficult to translate Sesuto into English than the contrary.

"Trying to get them to define things is no easy task. They cannot think why they should be asked to define a certain thing. In their minds it is quite clear that the thing in question is *what it is* simply. A slate is a slate, sugar is sugar, and so on; though one small boy ventured the other day, when pressed, to say that a waggon was 'a case going on legs.' A still smaller youth vouchsafed the information that 'a horse was a big thing, bigger than a goat, like a horse.' A third, an older lad, made it his duty to enlighten his younger friends by telling them that 'bread was sticky stuff with water.'

"The sea, which of course they have never seen, is the greatest mystery to them: and when they have got some glimmering idea of what a ship is, the question immediately arises in their minds: 'How can a ship find its way?' One suggested that there were roads in the sea; another that ships were stationed in different parts of the sea to point the way to travellers. However, they do not seem surprised at *anything* done by the white man. They imagine that there is no limit to his power and to his wonders."

So much for the mind of the youthful Mosuto.

CHAPTER X.

The Rebellion, 1880.

The Disarmament Act—Attempt to Enforce it upon the Basutos—Death of Molapo—Molapo and Moroka—Attitude of the Missionaries—The British Power Discredited—Unpreparedness of the Government—Losses of Traders—Letsie and Masupha—State of the Leribe District—Jonathan and Joel—Masupha and Tukunya—Defensive Force at Thlotse—Threatening Messages—First Attack upon Thlotse—Jonathan Eaten up—The French Protestant Christians at Manamasoane—Siege and Relief of Thlotse—ekubu—Christmas.

The Disarmament Act, passed by the Cape Parliament no doubt with the best intentions, had been already enforced in the Transkei and other extra Colonial territories; and, as the Fingoes, the most loyal tribe in South Africa, had been called upon to submit to it—an ungracious proceeding as all must admit—it was felt by the Government that its provisions should be extended to Basutoland. It is somewhat difficult to speak of the action of the Governor of the Cape Colony, Sir Bartle Frere, and his responsible advisers at this crisis without trenching upon politics, but in view of the results of that action the attempt must be made.

Looked at in the abstract, the determination of the Government was, it seems to me, defensible. The native tribes had everywhere increased, and were still fast increasing in numbers; and it was undoubtedly unwise, and possibly dangerous to the peace of South Africa, that hundreds of thousands of savages or semi-savages should be allowed to possess fire-arms to an unlimited extent. There had been enough, nay, alas! too much of war and bloodshed in the past, especially on the borders of the Cape Colony, and the Government thought that, now that the Kafir tribes had been reduced to submission, the time had come when the natives generally should be deprived of the means of making war, either upon the white man or upon one another. "Let us draw their teeth," was the cry, "and they will be no longer able to bite."

The terms of the Act were stringent. Not only the much coveted and dearly-loved gun was proscribed, but even the assagai was to be given up. No weapons whatever of a warlike character were to be permitted in the territories where the Act was in force. On the other hand, fair and full compensation was to be granted for everything of which the owners might be deprived. A commission was appointed for each district, consisting of the Magistrate or Resident, the local chief or headman, and the principal trader; and this commission was authorised and instructed to assess each man's weapons at a fair and just value, the weapons being deposited at each magisterial court house for that purpose.

But, in applying the Act to the Basutos, the Government, it

would seem, had not taken into sufficient consideration two important facts, which, had they done so, might—perhaps ought to—have had the effect of staying their action.

There was, first, the well-known fact that the Basutos had become possessed of firearms largely, if not indeed mainly, *through the action of the Government authorities themselves.* Large numbers of Basutos had been induced to go down in to the eastern districts of the Colony to work as navvies in laying out the new lines of railway, the inducement held out to them being payment, either in the shape of money *or of a gun.* Now the railways in the Cape Colony are all of them, it must be remembered, public property, and regarded as a department of the Government service; and although it is true that they were constructed by private contractors, yet the Government permitted these contractors to entice large numbers of natives to leave their own territories and work on the lines on the terms I have mentioned. And this was the case, not only on the railway works in the Cape Colony, but also in the diamond mines at Kimberley. In both these cases the Government had systematically winked at "free trade in guns for the natives," in order that the labour market might be adequately supplied. They had done this, too, against the repeated protests of the Government of the Orange Free State, through which territory most of these natives had to pass in order to return to their homes when their period of service had expired. It was of no purpose to allege, as the present ministry did, that these were the actions of their predecessors in office. The *fact* remained the same, and ought surely to have been taken into due consideration before proceeding to extremities.

The other important fact was that only a few months before the Basutos had been called upon by this same Cape ministry, and had at once responded to the call, to take their part in punishing and reducing to order a fraction of their own tribe—for Morosi and his people had become to all intents and purposes Basutos.

But these important factors in the consideration of the question were both ignored. In view of them the Government might surely have held its hand, and taken a middle course. It might, for instance, have been content with issuing an annual gun license, the amount of which, if not excessive, would have been cheerfully paid by the people. This course was, indeed, suggested to them by a deputation of chiefs, who were sent down to Capetown by the whole tribe to represent to the Government the extreme unpopularity of the Disarmament Act, and the danger of attempting to enforce it. But it was all in vain. The fiat had gone forth: "Let the Basutos be disarmed"; and disarmed they were to be—at least so thought the Cape Government.

On the other hand, it must not be forgotten that the Basutos had been saved from national extinction by the British Government only twelve years before, and that Moshesh to his dying hour had never ceased to exhort his people to "remain in the cave" which the Queen of England had provided for them, and never on any pretence to leave it. Moreover, their position as a nation was now absolutely secure, and they had therefore no need of weapons and no use for them. Enemies they had none: the Free State would never dream of declaring war against them as long as Basutoland was British territory, and the neighbouring tribes of Kafirs and Zulus were powerless to do them harm. Nor did they need firearms for the purposes of the chase, for, except in the innermost recesses of the mountains, there were no wild animals left to kill. Their grievance was therefore only a sentimental one, but it was not the less in their eyes a real one; for sentiment is often a most powerful factor in the affairs of men, and no wise or far-seeing statesman would consent to ignore its influence.

Unfortunately for us in the north of the country, Molapo, our chief, died at this time, on the 28th of June, the very heart of the crisis. Had he lived, events might perhaps have turned out differently; for it was well known that he would never have consented to an appeal to arms against the Government; and that he had up to the last counselled his sons and his people generally to obey the new law at whatever cost to their own wishes, and trust themselves implicitly in the hands of the Governor and his ministers. But he died when his counsel and influence were most needed, his end having no doubt been hastened by his own follies and vices.

I may here mention that only two months before, on the 8th April, another important chief, Moroka, the ruler of the Barolongs at Thaba 'Nchu, had passed away after a long, and on the whole prosperous, lease of power. A few days after the death of Molapo the shock of an earthquake was distinctly felt in Basutoland—an unusual occurrence in this part of the Continent of Africa. It was not severe, and was happily unaccompanied by any damage; but it was loud enough and awe-inspiring enough to make the Basutos exclaim, "See, the earth trembles! To-day the two great chiefs who have lately passed away from it are greeting one another in the world of spirits." This was the exclamation of the heathen, and is an emphatic testimony to their belief in the invisible realm of spirits.

"But what was the attitude of the missionaries at this juncture?" the reader may ask. "Did they use their influence in the direction of submission to the law, or did they counsel the people to withstand and oppose it?" Important questions, which have been often asked before, and which I will try to answer as truly and impartially as I can.

As has been already stated, the largest and most influential Christian body in the country was that of the French Protestant Mission. The great majority of the mission workers of that Mission regarded the policy of the Government as one of intolerable oppression, and some of the most influential among them did not shrink from openly stigmatizing it as unwarrantable, dangerous, and tyrannical. That they acted conscientiously I am quite sure; and it must not be forgotten that, as a body, they had been fifty years in the country, and had, perhaps of necessity, been at times largely identified with the political fortunes of the tribe. Moreover, they were Frenchmen, and, naturally enough, Republicans. They were hostile to the Disarmament Act; and their hostility, as soon as it became publicly known and expressed, added fuel to the flame already being kindled throughout the country. They did little or nothing to restrain the more violent among the chiefs, who were beginning to threaten resistance should the new law be carried out. Perhaps they thought that the bold front the majority of the nation presented might have the effect of staying the action of the Government. At any rate, it was only when they saw the great mass of the people, and among them their own Christian converts, carried away and standing on the very brink of the precipice, that they sought to restrain them from open rebellion. They began then to realize the danger; but it was too late.

The Cape ministers were obstinately bent upon enforcing their policy, and the Basutos as obstinately bent upon resisting it. The time for moderate counsels or compromise was past. The chiefs, especially the younger ones, were thirsting for the fight; swaggering to and fro, and boasting what they would do to the "Makhōa" (whites) who threatened to deprive them of their beloved gun; babbling about the "defeat" of the English at Berea, and proclaiming that the time had come when they were to wet their spears once more. In vain now did the missionaries exhort their disciples to submission. The man who declared his intention to obey the law and give up his weapons at the bidding of the magistrates was stigmatized as a traitor to his country, boycotted, and threatened with being altogether eaten up should he persist in carrying out his intention. A few of the French Protestant converts, to their honour be it said, listened to the injunctions of their teachers, but the great majority openly allied themselves to the dominant party (who were, of course, heathen), reproaching their pastors for their faithlessness to the "national cause" as they did so. The French Missionaries had, with the best intentions, endeavoured to "swop horses in the middle of the stream," and had, as was to be expected, failed.

Nevertheless, the knowledge that these good men sympathized in their hearts with the insurgent party saved their missions from destruction, and secured to them also an immunity from personal danger during the campaign that followed. During that terrible time they, together with a few of the anti-English Boers of the Free State, were the only Europeans who could move about freely and unmolested in the country. Though their mission work was of necessity paralysed for the time, and their schools closed, their buildings remained untouched, no damage whatever being done to them by the rebels, and only a very few of their out stations being injured (inadvertently, it was alleged) by the forces of the Government.

The Roman Catholics, also French, adopted, as far as possible, an attitude of neutrality. They were a much smaller body than the Protestants, and possessed but little political or social power or influence. Moreover, they gratefully appreciated the peace and prosperity which had been secured to the country through its incorporation into the British Empire, and the freedom they themselves enjoyed under the British flag. This feeling of gratitude to England for her intervention in the past, tempered, perhaps, by their known anti-republican sentiments, restrained them from making any public utterance against the policy of the Government; though doubtless, like every other European in the territory, they deplored the want of wisdom and consideration manifested by the Cape ministry. Their converts were apparently left to join whichever party they pleased, and, naturally enough, nearly all of them united themselves to the insurgent leaders. No doubt the presence of these

Roman Catholic Christians in the rebel camp saved the mission stations of the Roman Church from destruction, and the missionaries themselves from personal molestation, though the clergy were for several months unable to leave their stations, or enjoy the personal freedom possessed by their Protestant brethren.

But a very different fate awaited our own missions.

Acting on the advice of their Bishop, the clergy of the English Church had rigidly refrained from taking any part in politics; but now they were brought face to face with a question which demanded a plain answer, "Yes," or "No," from them, so long as they remained in the Lesuto and laboured there in the cause of Christ. There was no evading the question. They were beset daily by numbers of natives—not only by their Christian converts, but by a far larger number of heathen—who came to them with the same question upon their lips: "Monere, what am I to do? Am I to obey the *muso* " (Government) "and give up my gun, or am I to fight?" To all of whom the same answer was returned: "Remain in the cave secured to you by England, according to your own great chief's advice. Trust the Queen, your mother. Obey the law, though it be a hard one. Give up your weapons, and do not fight."

"Trust the Queen of England," was the pith of our advice. "Depend upon it she will not see you wronged. The Governor who has promulgated this new law and the ministers who have advised him to do so are all the counsellors and servants of the Queen. You will be paid for your guns, and perhaps if the Government see that you do not refuse to obey the law—harsh though the law be—they may learn to trust you more, and in a few years permit you to repurchase the arms they now ask you to surrender. It is madness to fight; the Government are strong and you are weak. And do not forget that it was a Governor of the Cape who saved you, when as a nation you were about to perish. Therefore, trust the Queen and her Governor, and all will in the end come right."

Alas for the poor men who took our advice! They were promptly eaten up, and lost everything at the very first outbreak of the rebellion. All of them without exception were called upon to suffer in the cause of loyalty and obedience. More than a year afterwards, when the rebellion was over, the Government promised them compensation for their losses; but to the disgrace of the British name be it said, this promise, publicly made and reiterated, was never more than partially fulfilled. To this day none of the loyals of the north—and they were by far the greater number—have ever received more than two-thirds of the amount officially acknowledged as due to them.

Yet it was difficult, if not impossible, for us as Christian missionaries to give any other advice. At any rate we thought so. And looking back upon that confused scene of ten years ago, I for one refuse to believe that we could have acted otherwise.

Though the path of obedience entailed upon the loyal Basutos, not only at the time but for years afterwards, the loss of worldly goods, the hatred of their fellow-countrymen, and the contemptuous cynicism of some who ought to have known better, but who were not ashamed to stigmatize them as "frauds"—"a set of Kafirs who had given up their guns for the sake of bread and butter"—yet, as we shall see, they won their way out of their difficulties by their own endurance and bravery, and eventually compelled the admiration of these very detractors. There is, I imagine, hardly anyone now in South Africa who does not think that the loyal Basutos were very badly treated, or who refuses to acknowledge that, whatever their loyalty to the Cape Government and the British flag brought to them, it did not bring much in the way of "bread and butter."

By way of setting an example, and emphasizing their advice by their actions, our missionaries were among the first to obey the Proclamation and give up their weapons. For myself I had none to give up. I had gone into the country with neither shot gun, nor rifle, and the tomahawk and assagai were beyond me.

All that I owned in the way of "weapons" was a pen knife and a pair of scissors, which, stringent as were its provisions, the Proclamation had happily overlooked, and I therefore retained a peaceful possession of them.

It was, of course, quickly known among the Basutos what line the missionaries of "Ma-Churche" had taken on this burning question. Indeed, some of those who had come to us for advice were nothing less than emissaries from the more turbulent chiefs, who had already made up their minds to fight, but who wished to sound us in order to hear, if possible, from our lips some justification for their line of action. Failing to get this, their vengeance fell upon us. Had "Ma-Churche" declared for the Government? Well, then, "Ma-Churche" must be eaten up. Moreover, the English Church was, as we know, "the Queen's Church;" and that was now no longer a recommendation and passport to favour, but the reverse. And thus our missions were singled out for destruction.

The Church had at the time three Missions in Basutoland: one in the south at Mohale's Hoek, under the charge of the Rev. E. W. Stenson; a second, as the reader already knows, at Sekubu, in the extreme north, where the Rev. T. Woodman and his sister were working; and my own at Thlotse Heights.

Of these the first was speedily destroyed: the mission buildings being rased to the ground, and the very foundation-stone of the church dug up by the rebels for the sake of the coins known to be enclosed in it. It was not until several years afterwards that this Mission could be resumed, the converts being meanwhile scattered to the winds, some few of them trekking northwards and attaching themselves to my own mission as soon as the way was open for them to do so.

At Sekubu the buildings were rifled of their contents, and the huts burnt. The church and the school being stone structures escaped the flames, and were used as cattle kraals and stables. A year afterwards, when Mr. Woodman ventured, with the sanction of the chief, to return to the station and again take possession of them, they were found to be in a most filthy condition—the House of God especially so. The rebels had appropriated not only the clothing, bedding, and furniture of the missionaries, but also everything they found in the church. They wrapped the altar frontals (handsome gifts from friends in England) round their greasy ochre-daubed bodies, and strutted about in them with great glee. Poor fellows, they were such utter barbarians, and so steeped in ignorance and superstition, that one could hardly be angry with them. They had no idea of reverence for the house of God, or for holy things. How should they? And they believed that they were fighting for liberty and freedom against the tyranny of the white man.

It is needless to add that neither of these Missions has ever obtained a farthing's compensation from the Government for the losses thus sustained.

How it fared with Thlotse we shall see.

Up to the time of the outbreak the British power in Basutoland had rested upon prestige. The Basutos had seen in 1868 a handful of white police take possession of their country—in answer to their prayer—in the name of the Queen of England. They had witnessed the magical effect of the presence of this little force upon the Boer commandos, and they drew their own conclusions. If the Governor of the Cape, by merely publishing his commands upon a piece of paper, and sending a small detachment of mounted men into Basutoland, could at once compel the Free State armies to retire from the country they had conquered at so great sacrifice, and so much cost, after years of conflict, without doubt the power of England must be great. For years they reposed upon this greatness, feeling secure in the cave which Moshesh had provided for them, and yielding an unquestioning compliance to the wishes of their magistrates. But, unhappily, the Zulu war had broken down that prestige, and a new generation, which knew nothing of past dangers and distresses, was fast attaining to manhood. All that they saw was that the British arms were not invincible, and that the British power was—so it seemed to them—on the wane. Isantlana had made a profound impression upon them. It was true that the Queen's soldiers had retrieved their fallen fortunes at Ulundi, and taken the Zulu king a prisoner, yet they had shortly afterwards retired from Zululand altogether. Was not this a plain proof that the Queen of England had no more soldiers left wherewith to fight the Zulus or control them? She had none; and therefore it was that she set up the thirteen kinglets in the country, knowing well that they would begin to bite and devour one another, while she had to stand aloof, powerless to interfere between them.

That was the way the young Basuto chiefs interpreted the position. We may smile at them for their innocence, but, placed in like circumstances, should we not have drawn the same inference? And we must not forget that these observations were apparently confirmed by what was taking place in the Transvaal. England had annexed that country, but she did not seem able to hold it. Her soldiers there were few in number, and the Boers were evidently bent upon shaking themselves free from her yoke. Added to all this, there was another fact which appealed powerfully to the Basutos. When Morosi and his son were disobedient to their magistrate, did the Queen's soldiers come up at once and punish them? No; the Basutos themselves were asked to reduce them to submission; and it was not until some months afterwards that a white force, and that only a small one, was placed in the field. "Where were the red coats? Why did not the Queen send them when they were wanted? Because there were none left. The Zulus and their other enemies had slain them all. The 'thin red line' existed no more."

Certainly, at such a time as this the Cape Government should have been very chary of enforcing a Disarmament Act upon the Basutos, whatever might be its merits or advantages, real or imaginary. Or if they had become convinced that it was necessary to the peace and welfare of South Africa to enforce such an Act, had they counted the cost of doing so? Were they prepared, if necessary, to enforce the law at the point of the bayonet? They had been warned enough on the subject. They knew how distasteful their policy was to the people; and they knew also that their own officials, as well as the traders and the missionaries—in fact, everyone in the country—united in representing to them the danger that confronted them. Had they any force at their back wherewith to withstand a general rising of the Basuto nation? They had none; or, at any rate, none commensurate with such a task. They had only one regiment at their disposal, the Cape Mounted Rifles, a regiment newly developed out of the old Frontier Armed and Mounted Police; and, efficient as this new regiment undoubtedly was, they could hardly have imagined that it would suffice to quell a national revolt in such a country as Basutoland. Besides this they had the Burgher levies, which might be called out in case of necessity; but as the policy of the ministry was distasteful to a large minority of the Colonists, it was hardly likely that there would be any hearty response to the call. There were, in addition, two or three small, but effective and well equipped regiments of Volunteers, which might perhaps be available should the crisis become really grave, but that was all. They could not hope to obtain the loan of a single regiment from the Imperial Government, for that Government viewed their proceedings with ill-concealed dislike; and besides, it was evident that a reaction was fast setting in in the mother country against South Africa and all that belonged to it; indeed, there were not wanting those who even went so far as to counsel the abandonment by England of all her South African possessions, except a naval station or two at the Cape itself.

There had not been, there was not now, perhaps there never

L

could be, any consistent principle of action—any policy of continuity—brought to bear upon the native territories (least of all upon Basutoland) either by the Imperial Government or that of the Cape Colony. There was no guarantee that the policy which was in favour to-day might not be reversed in the near future; nay, within a very few months; a contingency which did actually take place, as we shall see. But, notwithstanding all this, the Disarmament Act was proclaimed in the Lesuto, and the Basutos were expected to submit to it and deliver up their arms forthwith.

The traders in the country were among the first to realize the danger of the Government policy, and as their goods and merchandise were uninsured they commenced at once, upon the proclamation of the Act, to remove them into the Orange Free State. In some cases they were forbidden to do so by the local officials; and all of them were warned that, as the removal of their stock-in-trade would tend to create a panic in the country, those who persisted in removing it would not have their licenses renewed, or be allowed to trade in Basutoland in the future. This had the effect of arresting the general trek which had set in. Most of the traders acted on the circulars put forth by the officials, and refrained from removing their goods. Wives and children were sent away into the neighbouring territories for safety, the men remaining at their trading stations as long as it was at all safe to do so. A few, secretly warned and assisted by friendly natives, succeeded at the very last moment in saving portions of their furniture or merchandise; others, not so fortunate, lost the whole of it. No compensation was ever made to them for their losses, notwithstanding that they were incurred through obedience to the instructions of the magistrates. I have had very little personal acquaintance with the traders in the southern districts, but of those in the north I can unhesitatingly affirm that they were, almost without exception, a quiet and well conducted body of men, who pursued their calling in legitimate ways, living in friendship with the natives, and for the most part setting them a good example as to sobriety and uprightness of dealing. The majority of them were members of my own European congregation, and were therefore well known to me; and some of them were not only valued personal friends, but also warm supporters of the Mission. During the rebellion several of them found their way, very naturally, into the army of defence, becoming officers of the loyal native contingent—a body of men which did splendid service in the cause of law and order, and protected our mission buildings more than once from entire destruction.

Unfortunately for the Basutos, Letsie, the Paramount Chief, has never displayed either the virtues or the force of character of his great father. A certain cunning, arising more from weakness and timidity than from sagacity or bravery, has always been his most marked characteristic; and accordingly he now attempted to " run with the hare and hunt with the hounds ": a double-faced policy, which was destined to bring about its own condemnation. Professing to obey the Act as soon as it was promulgated, he allowed his sons to seize and retain possession of the guns which he had sent to be delivered up to the authorities, while they were being conveyed to Maseru, and winked at the attitude of his brother Masupha, who was fast becoming the strength and backbone of the opposition. This chief, to do him justice, displayed throughout a more single and straightforward policy than is usually found among natives of his position and eminence.

In the Leribe district the people were still mourning the loss of Molapo, whose action and advice had been, as we know, distinctly in favour of submission. Through the chief's influence a large number of his people—perhaps at first the majority of them—were disposed to obey the Proclamation; and though Major Bell had simply read that document publicly, and then posted it up upon the door of his office (having no power at his back wherewith to enforce its obnoxious provisions), over 600 guns, good, bad, and indifferent, were voluntarily surrendered at once, and placed by their owners in the hands of the magistrate. Had the authorities in Capetown even then displayed any spirit of conciliation on the one hand, or any promptitude of action in supporting and protecting the loyalist party on the other, it is not too much to say that the north would have been spared the bloodshed which followed. But they did nothing. They seemed, indeed, for a time paralysed; taking no notice whatever of the repeated appeals made to them by their representative at Leribe. The result of this inaction was that the opposition faction, worked upon by the "patriotism" of Masupha, Lerothodi, and others, rapidly grew in numbers and organization; while the large body disposed to obey rapidly dwindled away into a tiny minority under the leadership of the young chief Jonathan Molapo.

The position of this man—destined as he was to become ere long the central figure of the north, round which the whole loyal force of the nation concentrated itself—requires a few words of explanation.

Josefa, Molapo's eldest son by his great wife Mamusa, had, on attaining to manhood, become hopelessly insane. He was, therefore, declared incapable of succeeding to the chieftainship, and his father nominated his *second* son *by the same wife* as his heir and successor. This second son was Jonathan.

But polygamy is sure to bring its curse with it in one form or other, and among the African tribes it comes usually in the shape of war—most frequently a war of succession. That was to be the case here. Jonathan had a powerful rival in the person of his half brother Joel, the eldest son of the second wife of Molapo. Already, during the father's lifetime, small feuds had occurred between the two brothers, and they were known to regard each other with ill-concealed dislike. Molapo endeavoured to smooth things over by removing them to a distance from each other—a common method of procedure by African chiefs under such circumstances. He placed Jonathan on the southern border of the district at the village of Fobane, close to the Putiatsana; giving him the charge of the entire south. with the right of succession to the chieftainship of Leribe. Joel he ordered northwards to Buta-Bute, giving him a small strip of country between Matela and Sinate, and bidding him dwell there in peace. Each of these chiefs had, of course, his own attached followers and "balekane," or comrades; the latter being specially bound to him by the common ties contracted together in the circumcision lodge in the days of their youth.

It was feared that upon the death of their father an open rupture would take place between the two sons, and there would be a desperate struggle for supremacy. The struggle was bound to come; but it would have come sooner, and would probably have been of short duration, but for the action of the Government. The people knew that Jonathan was the rightful heir, and the great majority of them were ready to support his claim by force of arms if need were. From the first the young chief had declared for the Government; partly from obedience to his father's dying wishes, and partly no doubt with the idea of strengthening his position all round. He wished to stand well with the authorities, who might on that account be the more inclined to support his claim to the chieftainship of the northern district; and he had perception enough to see that in the long run the Queen's power must triumph in the Lesuto, as it had done elsewhere in the other native territories of South Africa.

For a time Joel also professed obedience to the Government, and sent frequent messages to Major Bell, assuring him of his loyalty to the Queen, and his intention of obeying the new law. But after a few months, when it was apparent that the Government would do nothing to protect those who were running the gauntlet of loyalty by the surrender of their arms, Joel, feeling that his time was come, seized the opportunity of placing himself at the head of the increasing numbers of the malcontents, and was henceforth acknowledged as their leader in the northern division of the country.

It was in Masupha's district, however, that blood was first drawn. There was living in it, at a village not far from Advance Post, a small chieftain named Tukunya. He and his people were Fingoes; but living as they were in Masupha's country, they were of course under his jurisdiction. The Fingoes have always been renowned for their loyalty to England, and Tukunya and his people were no exception to the rule. They refused to join their " over-lord " in his resistance to the Proclamation of the Governor. However distasteful the present policy of the Government might be, they resolved to remain loyal and true to their protector across the sea, and to give up their arms when called upon to do so.

Then Masupha sent a commando against them, which on the 19th July attacked them, and after some hours' sharp fighting, in which the Fingoes defended themselves with great bravery, burnt their village and took nearly all their cattle. Eaten up by superior numbers, Tukunya and his surviving warriors fled, and together with their wives and children found refuge at Maseru, the headquarters of the Government. The Resident of the district and his police were compelled to abandon Advance Post at the same time, and do the same. Masupha was triumphant; officials and loyal natives had all been driven out of his territory, and from henceforth he reigned supreme. This was the signal for a general rebellion. Armed bands of the insurgents were to be seen patrolling the country in every direction, threatening to attack the magistracies, which were only defended by a few native police whose loyalty at such a crisis could hardly be depended upon. In the centre and the south the rebel party carried everything before them; only a tiny handful of the people having the courage to declare themselves for the Government. In the north, thanks to the firm attitude of Jonathan, the loyal party was still strong, though, owing to the unpreparedness and inactivity of the authorities at the Cape, it had begun to lose spirit, and was indeed in danger of melting away altogether.

At this juncture of affairs Col. Griffith, who was still the chief official in the Lesuto, did his utmost to place Maseru in a state of defence. In this he was materially aided by several Englishmen living along the border of the Orange Free State, who realized the danger of the situation, and saw that the few Europeans remaining in the country were liable at any moment to be massacred. The Colonel also authorized the formation of a small European volunteer corps, numbering between forty and fifty men, under the command of Mr. Stanton. This force, united with seventy of Tukunya's Fingoes, was despatched early in September to Thlotse at Major Bell's request, news having reached us that Jonathan and his people had had to fly from Fobane and take refuge near us at Tsikoane, a flat-topped mountain to the south over the Thlotse, only three miles distant. The rebel party in the north was meanwhile increasing in numbers daily, Joel attracting to his standard party after party of the waverers, now that Jonathan was practically a fugitive and unable to hold his own, much less to help them.

By the end of September Thlotse had a defensive force of forty-seven whites and 110 natives, these latter including Tukunya and his men, and the men of the mounted police. This was a very small body with which to defend a long, straggling township, in addition to the Residency and the buildings of the Mission. With as much haste as possible the place was put into something approaching to a state of defence. Walls, among them those of our Mission garden and cemetery, were thrown down and levelled to the earth, in order to prevent the enemy using them as cover. The gaol, with its enclosed courtyard, was turned into a fort, the sod walls round the police camp were loopholed, and two large loopholes were made in the east wall of the Mission Chapel. Anxious to preserve the chapel as far as possible from profanation or injury, I had urged the authorities to throw up an earthwork outside it where it was most exposed to attack, and to use it and the school as a hospital for the sick and wounded as soon as the campaign should really begin. This might easily have been done at the time, but my wishes were overruled, and the poor little chapel was soon afterwards pierced in every direction with loopholes and used as a barrack. When war actually broke out, and indeed all through the campaign, the sick and wounded had no better shelter than that of a tent in the courtyard of the fort—a sorry protection from the burning rays of an African sun with the thermometer sometimes as high as 105 degrees in the shade. There was no building in or near the fort large enough for the purposes of a hospital, and it was impossible to build one, neither money nor material, not to speak of time, being at hand for the purpose. Through the combined efforts of Major Bell and Dr. Taylor, a cottage hospital was in course of construction, the Government having given a small grant for the purpose, before any sign of rebellion had manifested itself; but the structure was unfinished, and too remote from the fort to be available for use at the present crisis.

And now there began a series of threatening messages on the part of Joel, Ramanella, Khethisa, and Tlasua, the principal leaders of the rebel party. Why they did not attack us in July, when Tukunya and his people were driven from their homes and Jonathan compelled to retire from Fobane, is past comprehension. One can only regard it as a signal manifestation of God's providence towards us; for during the two months that elapsed between these events and the arrival of the defensive force I have mentioned *we were absolutely at their mercy.* They could have come at any moment, by night or by day, and burnt our dwellings over our heads and killed us all. I do not see how one of us could have escaped. There was no force to defend us except about fifteen police, who could not possibly have saved either themselves or the place. But the good hand of our God was upon us during those weary weeks when we were waiting for succour; our enemies were held back and restrained, and not a hair of our heads was injured. All this time the rebels were everywhere on the alert all round us. The war bulls had been killed, the paths spread with charms, the warriors "doctored" and made invincible for the fray, and the assagais sharpened, and made bright and keen. Everywhere man, horse, and gun were in readiness, the ammunition served out, and the little skin pouch filled to bursting with a three days' supply of mealie or mabèlè meal. From July onwards very few of us slept at night, the alarms and threatening messages were so continuous and the danger so great. Yet the enemy did not come. He could have annihilated us then, but he allowed his chance to slip by and did nothing. Only seven white men were left in the place, and two of these, Mr. Champernowne and myself, were non-combatants. The few white women and children had been sent away over the border into the Free State at the first tidings of the outbreak at Tukunya's. One only remained, Miss Champernowne, who could not be persuaded to go, but bravely elected to remain for the present at least at the Mission. Mr. Reading had left us in June. He had gone to the Theological College at Bloemfontein for a year's reading preparatory to his ordination.

By this time the Cape ministers had begun to realize the gravity of their position, and were at last doing what little they could to meet the crisis. But that little was not much. All that they could do at present was to send up in September between two and three hundred men of the Cape Mounted Rifles to the southern districts; for the north they could do nothing. The weary days, weeks, months dragged on, and yet in spite of threatening messages, war dances, innumerable incantations, doctorings, castings of spells, and much swagger and brag, no one had yet come near to molest us.

Then Masupha, having been the first to draw blood, began to

taunt Joel and his allies with their inaction. "Why had they not wiped out the English at Thlotse, and their aiders and abettors, long ago?" "Because they were cowards!" "They feared Jonathan, who although he had turned Englishman was a far better man than they!"

Joel and his friends, stung by these reproaches, at last resolved to act. "They would eat up Thlotse at once," and to that end they began in good earnest to organize an attack upon us.

Masupha, who has a keen sense of humour, used to banter us every few days upon the possession of "his property." He sent messengers to Major Bell "with his compliments and greetings." "He desired to know how it fared with the stray goats that the Government had in their kraal," alluding to Tukunya and his Fingoes, who, as we have seen, were now with us. "These goats," he said, "are mine." "They were very lean and sick, and covered all over with scab"—alluding to their loyalty to the Government—"when they were last with me." "But I hear that they are fatter and more well-favoured now, and so I intend to send and fetch them."

Then, receiving no response save the greetings of the Major, he would send again a few days afterwards to let us know that "his *brand-ziek* (scabbed) goats were still in our kraal, and that he should come himself to fetch them. And woe be to us when he came, for he would eat us all up together!"

But he never did come. He had ousted the Government from his own domain, and was now sole monarch of all he surveyed; and he was shrewd enough not to leave his own stronghold at Thaba Bosigo and go on a doubtful expedition to Leribe. Still he undoubtedly succeeded in stirring up our adversaries against us, and his continued gibes and taunts compelled them to prove the truth of their boastings by their deeds.

At last, on November 8, the attack came.

It was sudden, swift, well planned, and delivered with great spirit. But thanks be to God it failed.

MASUPHA.

The day was Monday. We had held our usual services on the Sunday, though with diminished numbers; many of the men being posted round the heights on sentry duty. In the evening a heavy rain set in and poured down all night. Penetrated with the happy conviction that the rebels would not venture a twenty-five miles' ride from Buta-Bute in such a downpour, most of our men had for once gone to bed, and were soon fast asleep, though from the reports of our spies and scouts an attack seemed imminent. Their confidence was misplaced; for Joel, rightly judging that he would thus the more easily surprise us, resolved to eat us up at daybreak next morning.

Mr. Champernowne and his sister had retired to their huts, which were close to my own, and near the mission chapel. At my wish they had gone to bed, it not being necessary to leave more than one of our party on the watch.

The night passed wearily enough. Drip, drip, from the swollen thatch was all that was heard, save now and then when the rain pattered against the four small panes of glass in the one window of the hut. Without all was black: a thick, inky darkness, so intense that literally one could not see one's hand close before one's eyes. Worn out and lonely, a chill, creepy sensation came over me. All seemed gruesome. Everything around felt cold and clammy in the unutterable darkness. The moist air had penetrated everywhere: my very cassock was dank and damp. It was dangerous to light a candle, as its light might be seen through some chink or crevice, and serve as a guide to the foe. So I had to sit in the darkness, and meditate as best I could upon "the vanity of human wishes."

What an irrational creature man seemed to be! Here were thousands of people squabbling and fighting, biting and devouring one another, over the possession of a wretched iron tube which could not possibly be of any real use to them, for they had no use for it. Nevertheless, childlike, they would not give it up at the bidding of their superiors, though they were to be paid the full value of it, and to lose nothing by their act of obedience. It was theirs, and they would, on no consideration, relinquish the possession of it; nay, rather than do so, they were in all probability at that very moment on the war path, coming down to cut our throats. Perhaps there were even then fifty of them only a few yards away, at the bottom of the garden, waiting for the signal to advance, and burn down my poor little hut and disembowel me.

And then there was the Government. It seemed impossible that a number of " grave and reverend seigniors " could so provoke, and that so heedlessly, a multitude of savages—" children, with the passions of men "—as to goad them into butcheries and deeds of blood, from which, in their better moments, every one of them would shrink. Truly, the game was not worth the candle. Yes, thought I, " Sam Slick " is right. " Human nature is a very queer thing, and there is a great deal of it in man."

Then deeper thoughts would steal over one's soul: thoughts of those at rest in paradise, beyond the jarring scenes of earth. For " the souls of the righteous are in the hand of God, and there shall no torment touch them."* They had been taken away from the evil to come, and I thanked God that it was so.

After all, what did it matter? One was in the Father's hands, and to embrace His will was the only happiness. So doing, all would be well—come life, come death; come deliverance from danger, or the deadly thrust of the assagai.

Thus the long, weary hours passed away. A little before dawn the rain ceased, and at day-break—five o'clock—I heard the rapid clatter of a horse's hoofs. It could not be a sentry returning from night duty, for it was still early, and the horseman was evidently riding in hot haste. I listened, too tired and worn out to rouse myself and see. Then in a minute or two the well-known notes of the " alarm " burst forth from the bugle at the fort. That was a plain call to duty, so I went forth to see;

---

* Wisdom of Solomon iii. 1.

and there, before my eyes, not 1,000 yards off, was the enemy, forming into line on the rising ground opposite for the charge. At last, then, the rebels had really come, and the ball was about to open.

There was not a moment to be lost. Hastily I roused my two sleeping friends, and in a few seconds they were on the way to the fort, where I knew they would be under cover and safe as long as the place could hold out. Then I went into the chapel, which was rapidly filling with volunteers, both black and white, awaiting the onslaught of the foe.

The horseman I had heard was Captain Stanton, who, ever on the alert, had ridden out alone just before daybreak to see that all was well, and had hardly proceeded a mile when he observed, not far off, the whole of the northern detachment of the enemy rapidly advancing. Putting spurs to his horse, he rode back with all speed, just in time to rouse his sleeping men, and see them and the native contingent posted at their appointed places, before the enemy, with a great rush from the brow of the hill, swooped down upon us.

The Basutos are all light cavalry, well mounted on tough, wiry ponies, which will go anywhere, their riders never thinking of dismounting even in the steepest and most break-neck bridle paths and mountain passes. Five thousand of these warriors now attacked us, our straggling village being defended by the handful of men I have mentioned, who had the advantage of being all of them under some sort of cover. Mercifully for us and our dwelling place the rain had rendered the Thlotse impassable, thus preventing the eastern detachment under Ramanella from scaling the heights and attacking us in rear. Had the rebel forces been able to combine and carry out their well conceived plan, it is at best but doubtful whether a single hut would have escaped destruction, or a human being remained alive in the place. Eight thousand men, armed to the teeth with assagai, rifle, hatchet, and short stabbing spear, against one hundred and forty, who had to defend many buildings and many more huts, covering altogether a large expanse of ground! The odds would have been too great; and we saw, in the swollen river and the three thousand balked and inactive savages on the other side of it, God's protecting hand stretched out to help us.

So vigorously was the charge delivered that at one point the Snider carbines of the native police and the Martini-Henrys of Joel's picked troopers crossed each other through the same loopholes! The action lasted a little over an hour, and then our enemies, foiled and beaten at every point, began to draw sullenly off. They had succeeded in burning two houses and two or three huts, besides looting and partially destroying the Residency and the Doctor's cottage; but, being exposed at close quarters to a galling fire, they lost heavily. We counted twenty-eight corpses on the spot when the fight was over, and we knew that they had carried off many others. They acknowledged afterwards that in this first attack they had lost thirty-nine killed, and about double that number wounded; but as natives are never accurate in their numbers, and it is always difficult to find out the actual losses in these native wars—insignificant as the numbers are when compared with those of the battle-fields of Europe—it is probable that their losses were heavier than the number stated. Our loss was but trifling, the cover being so good. Two men were dangerously wounded, and one slightly, and both the former recovered. One of our men had a narrow escape. He was a young fellow named Pitso, a Mosuto, in the service of Major Bell. The Residency was too far from the native township to be defended, and the Major had, therefore, been sleeping of late in his office, a wretched little apartment in what was known as the "Court-house," or general Government Office, near the fort. But Pitso would not abandon the old abode in which he had spent so many happy years. He insisted on keeping guard over it and sleeping in it, though quite alone; alleging as his excuse for doing so his master's need of his "early coffee," which could be prepared there earlier and better than elsewhere. This cup of early coffee, which is usually ready at sunrise or immediately afterwards, is one of the most cherished institutions of South Africa, and English settlers speedily learn to adopt and appreciate it.

On the morning of the attack Pitso was suddenly awakened by the sound of windows being broken and doors crashed in. Springing to his feet he saw the outbuildings in flames, a great crowd of the insurgents all round the house, and all chance of escape cut off. There seemed to be no hope whatever left for him, for the enemy would be all through the house itself in a few moments, and a dozen assagais plunged into his body. In his despair *he crept into a cupboard in the passage*—the very last corner one would consider a safe place of refuge. Yet it proved to be so to him. The surging crowd of rebels pressed forward, beat down the doors, and took possession of the house. They hacked and chopped everything they could find into pieces, and only the iron roof of the building prevented it from sharing the fate of the cottages and huts around it. Yet, strange to say, they never thought of opening that cupboard! The other cupboards and recesses were all of them disfigured and ransacked of their contents, but that particular cupboard remained untouched. Groups of men, cursing and swaggering, passed and repassed it, hacking with their hatchets every bit of woodwork that came in their way, but *it* was left alone. This is the more remarkable when we consider that the native under such circumstances invariably gives way to the spirit of curiosity, which dominates him as easily as it does a child. But they passed and repassed, little thinking that within the small recess there lay coiled up in utter helplessness one whom they could have pinned to the wall in a moment with their spears.

Great was our joy when Pitso emerged unscathed, and with a whole skin, from his hiding-place, which he did not many minutes after the rebels had been beaten off. We had all given him up for lost, and Major Bell especially had felt greatly distressed at the faithful fellow's untimely fate. But he was saved after all, and certainly had a most remarkable escape.

As soon as the enemy began to retreat, our men rushed forth, mostly on foot, in pursuit, and in so doing captured thirty-six riderless horses, which were at once brought into the fort. I think that was almost the only spoil we took throughout the entire campaign.

What a piteous sight the poor little mission chapel presented when the fight was over! The windows were all chopped to pieces, the walls loopholed in every direction, and the unceiled iron roof riddled with shot. The walls of this peaceful sanctuary of God had hitherto resounded with songs of prayer and praise, but now they were given over to the clang of warlike weapons and the horrid din of the instruments of death. The deafening noise of the firing as volley after volley was discharged from within and without, the sickening smell of the powder, the suffocating volumes of smoke which filled the whole building, and the mangled corpses lying around, all combined to make one realize the havoc wrought by war, and the terrible hindrance the rebellion would be to the spread of the Gospel among the Basutos.

Henceforth, for a considerable time, our mission work came to an end. Thirty men (ten whites and twenty blacks) were quartered in the church and school, where they remained until the following August.

In the mission garden two of Joel's men had been shot down from the sanctuary window on the north side of the church: one was already dead, but the other was still breathing when I took the doctor to him after the enemy had begun to retire. Nothing could be done for the poor fellow: he was shot through the head, and died a few minutes after we reached him.

By eight o'clock our enemies had retreated to the hills of Sebotoane, and could we then have followed them up, thereby making our victory a decisive one, their power would have been so broken that the rebellion would almost certainly have come to an end in the north. But we had not strength enough to do so, and, moreover, very few of our men were mounted. Nearly all our loyal natives had lost their horses in the fight at Tukunya's, and the white volunteers were as yet only infantry. The northern insurgents were, therefore, still able to hold together, notwithstanding the check they had received; and in the evening when they effected a junction with Ramanella's men, they became more formidable than ever.

On going up to the training college compound a ghastly scene presented itself. We passed sixteen dead bodies of our enemies, some of them horribly disfigured; and when the garden was reached we found the main path slippery in several places with blood. A hand to hand fight had raged here for some minutes before the enemy was dislodged, and the cattle kraal at the bottom of the garden was a horrible sight. Several of Joel's men must have lost their lives there in trying to carry off our cattle. One horse only was left, and the poor thing was trembling all over from excitement and fright when we entered the kraal. All that was portable in the huts, including most of our food, had been carried off; but a ham we had succeeded in procuring from the Free State a few days before was left on the ground outside the kitchen, being probably dropped from the saddle in the hurry of retreat. This we thankfully reappropriated, and, after making a note of the few other things remaining from the general wreck, we returned to our huts near the chapel, which, thanks be to God, had escaped injury. I was much distressed that Miss Champernowne should have been called upon to witness such a dreadful scene of havoc and death as that which had just passed before her eyes. The sight of the mangled remains of the poor heathen men who had fallen in what they believed to be the path of duty moved her greatly, but she behaved bravely through it all.

M

We returned to the huts with the intention of taking counsel together as to the future, but there was in truth no need to do so. The matter was quickly decided for us. The rebellion having now actively invaded Thlotse itself, the seat of the magistracy of the north, martial law was proclaimed, Major Bell becoming Commandant of the Forces, such as they were, at the disposal of the Government for the protection of the place. Notice was accordingly given to us that no non-combatant Europeans but myself would be allowed to remain at the station, and Mr. Champernowne and his sister were escorted next morning to the Free State, where they remained until peace was proclaimed, Mr. Champernowne taking charge of the parish of Harrismith for a portion of the time.

Towards noon on the day of this first attack upon our station, the Thlotse became fordable some eight or ten miles up the stream, and Jonathan Molapo, who had been prevented from coming to our assistance before, now crossed over and came into Thlotse with 1,500 of his men. They congratulated us heartily upon our deliverance, and together with our own men united in a great war dance in celebration of our victory.

Jonathan, whose headquarters were now at Tsikoane, had fully intended marching to our relief, but had been prevented, as we have seen, from doing so; but the swollen river which hindered him from carrying out his intention enabled him nevertheless to keep Ramanella in check for several hours on the south side of the Thlotse until all danger to us had for the time passed away. This action of our loyal ally brought down upon him the vengeance of the entire northern band of rebels. Repulsed at Thlotse and unsuccessful in their attempt to destroy the place, they retired to the gorges of Sebotoane, where they knew themselves to be perfectly safe, calculating as they did upon our inability to follow them up.

The next day the entire party, Ramanella included, held a council of war, at which they resolved to eat up Jonathan for his temerity in having dared to go to the rescue of the white man. They proceeded on the morrow (the 11th) to carry out their resolution. Jonathan had in the meantime returned to Tsikoane and fortified his stronghold to the best of his ability. A furious fight took place, which lasted the whole day, and resulted at last in a great and decisive victory to the rebels. As for us at Thlotse we had to content ourselves with looking on. We were powerless to assist the man who had acted so generously towards us, and our feelings may be better imagined than described when we saw, in the afternoon, his village on fire, and learnt that though his men still held out in the rocks against desperate odds, all hope of recovering their position was at an end. The women and children had long before taken to flight, and were now safe in the Free State.

Outnumbered as Jonathan was by at least five to one, it is doubtful whether his enemies would have accomplished their purpose had it not been for the treachery of one of his counsellors, who in these pages shall be nameless. Suffice it to say that he was a man who had been greatly valued and trusted by Molapo, and who declared himself ready to follow Jonathan to the death, notwithstanding the unpopular side which the chief had taken. This man had been posted with a strong force to hold the main path leading up to the mountain camp, and at the critical moment of the battle he suddenly and basely betrayed his trust by going over to Joel. Most of his men followed his example, and thus the rebels at once gained an entrance into the centre of the stronghold. Not content with this, he acted with perfidious cruelty towards a younger brother of his chief, a little lad, who in the confusion of the fight had become separated from his protectors and was left alone in a corner of the battlefield. The traitor saw him, and lured him to his death by promises of friendship and protection. "Come to me, my child," he cried, "do not be afraid. You know I was your father's friend, and now I will be yours.

Trust yourself to me and I will see that no one shall harm you."

The boy, though hesitating at first, having heard of the man's treason, was in the end beguiled by his smooth speeches, and crossed over to him. But no sooner had he done so, than the old monster turned upon him, and butchered him in cold blood with the assagai. The whole scene was witnessed by several of Jonathan's men but a short distance off, and in a few minutes the perjured savage met, at their hands, the same death that he had meted out to the confiding, but unfortunate, child just before.

No one knows the numbers of the killed and wounded on that fateful day, but they must have been heavy; for both sides fought with great obstinacy, and very often at close quarters, the assagai doing on such occasions much more deadly execution than the rifle.

By sunset, Jonathan, weakened by the defection of so many of his men, and altogether overpowered by numbers, was completely beaten: his town was burnt to ashes, his cattle were swept off, and he himself was a fugitive flying for his life. Just before dark he, together with about 500 men who were still faithful to him, contrived to escape over the Thlotse and take refuge in "the Camp," as our station began now to be called. I remember so well the scene. The men cowed, beaten, and demoralized, looking like so many whipped curs, coming in by twos and threes, with their chief and his body guard bringing up the rear; all of them hungry and exhausted, and most of them stark naked, having thrown off their blankets when the hand to hand struggle began. By the time they all reached us it was quite dark, and Mr. Charles Bell and I went out with lanterns and distributed among them several bales of coloured blankets, which had fortunately been left at a local trader's. "What are we to do with them?" said Major Bell; and, indeed, it was a problem. They were, of course, utterly destitute, and had to be rationed every day from our not over abundant supply of mealies; there were no huts or tents for them, and until they could build for themselves they had to huddle together for several weeks outside the fort, sleeping in rows round its walls.

These men proved to be a great stand-by to us as time went on. Their loyalty to their chief had been thoroughly and severely tested, and was beyond dispute; and since he had chosen to stake his all—power, wealth, possessions, reputation, ease, and comfort—on behalf of the Government they were ready to follow his example, and be loyal too to the Queen of England, even to the loss of worldly goods, nay, to death itself. They had now gone too far to recede, and must take the consequences. Most of them were soon afterwards formed into a "Native Contingent," in company with Tukunya's men and others; and this force, numbering a little over 700 men, was placed under the command of Mr. C. Bell, an officer personally known to all of them, and one in whom they all had confidence.

The victorious rebels, having wiped out the chief obstacle to their progress, now carried everything before them throughout the entire district. There was still a small body of loyal natives left outside Thlotse. These were the people of Manamasoane, the French Protestant Mission, about six miles to the north of our own. Most of them were Christians, the fruits of the devoted labours of M. Coillard in years gone by. M. Coillard had, as I have said, left Basutoland some time before, and gone northwards to preach the Gospel to the Banyai. These loyal Christians were under the command of Nathanaele Makotoko, whose name is already familiar to the reader, and who proved himself to be in every way worthy of their confidence. Nathanaele and his people, both Christian and heathen, were devotedly attached to the house of Molapo, and they resolved, happen what would, to remain faithful to Jonathan as his son and heir. They were now speedily marked out for destruction, more especially as their village was quite undefended, for it was situated close to the church at the French Protestant station. The rebel party accordingly proceeded to eat them up with all speed, and with the utmost thoroughness. Their village was burnt, everything they possessed taken from them, and they themselves compelled to take refuge with us at "the Camp." Their pastor, who sympathized with the rebels, remained unmolested, and during the whole campaign was the only white man who could go at large wherever he pleased throughout the district. His people were eaten up under his very eyes, but he made no sign, though, doubtless, he would have been unable to save them had he tried to do so. No doubt he acted from conscientious motives, but there could, of course, be little affection or confidence between him and his flock; and it is, therefore, no wonder that soon after the termination of the rebellion he returned to France.

Under the Leribe mountain, not far from Manamasoane, there is a cave to which some twenty or thirty of Molapo's men retreated, determined to hold out to the last extremity. They were surrounded by the rebels, who in the end starved them out and compelled them to surrender. Poor fellows, in their distress they succeeded one night in sending a messenger to Major Bell to implore his intervention, but nothing could be done to help them. How the man managed to get through the enemy's lines is a mystery; but he did, under cover of the darkness; and we all deplored our inability to rescue his comrades. It was impossible for him to return to them, and a few days afterwards we heard of their surrender.

The whole loyalty of the Leribe district being now concentrated at Thlotse, the rebels, after holding a series of councils, determined to besiege the place and starve us out. They put out their whole strength, and formed a cordon which surrounded us on all sides, and which drew closer and closer every day. They worked hard night after night in constructing earth works, narrowing the circle, and drawing it nearer to us morning by morning. They poisoned the water in one of our springs, and cut off our supply from another, and that the principal one, so that there was very little water to drink, and none for any other purpose. From daylight to dark they kept up a desultory, dropping fire upon us, which was exceedingly irritating, though it did but little real harm. They burnt all the outlying huts; among them our own in the college compound, which had escaped the first attack. This was done on a Sunday afternoon (12th December) while Mr. Champernowne and other friends in the Orange Free State stood upon a tongue of land on the west side of the Caledon, watching the flames as one by one the huts became a heap of ashes.

Our case was fast becoming desperate. There were now over seven hundred half-starved natives to be fed daily, besides fifty Europeans; the water from the principal fountain was entirely cut off, and it was only with great difficulty that any was to be procured elsewhere. Wells had been sunk, but they had not been successful; food was rapidly failing, and there was no means of getting a fresh supply from the Free State, the rebels having not only surrounded us but carried off the one boat on the Caledon. Each morning saw their lines advancing nearer and nearer, and in less than a week we should be starved out and completely at their mercy.

In this strait Major Bell happily succeeded in sending off a dispatch to the commanding officer at Maseru, the headquarters of the Government, and now a fortified camp, informing him of our condition, and requesting aid at once if the place was to be saved. We could not learn whether the native who took the letter had succeeded in scrambling down the rocks, and making his way through the lines of our besiegers during the hours of darkness, and our anxiety was becoming very great, when, one morning while it was still dark, almost a week after the messenger had left, the welcome news reached us that the Kimberley Horse was on its way to our relief. The Commandant at Maseru, on learning our pitiful plight, had at once ordered the right wing of that regiment—a corps of cavalry lately raised at the Diamond Fields, and but recently arrived at Maseru—to proceed by forced marches to Thlotse. The regiment marched through the Free State, with the permission of the President, the country between Maseru and Leribe being entirely in the hands of the rebels. The relieving force so promptly sent to our relief numbered 275 men, well mounted and well equipped, under the command of Major Laurence, a brave and competent officer, who rode forward in advance alone, and at the risk of his life made his way up the heights before daylight, and brought by word of mouth the welcome tidings that relief was at hand. A few hours afterwards his men appeared on the west bank of the Caledon, forced a passage across the river (which was then running high) under a galling fire from the rebels, cleared the enemy before them up the rocks, and off-saddled at the fort amidst the ringing cheers of the whole garrison.

They had not come a moment too soon, for it would have been impossible for us to hold out more than a day or two longer. Fatigued as they were with their long march, they nevertheless only off-saddled for an hour, for absolutely necessary rest and refreshment for themselves and their horses; then mounting, they spurred forward to charge the allied rebel force under Ramanella, Khethise, and Tlasua; our own natives, now inspirited and full of hope for the future, making short work of Joel's men on the northern side of the town. The success of this fine body of men was astonishing. They charged an enemy at least ten times their own number with the lightheartedness and gaiety of school boys, drove the rebels from their magnificent position in the rocks round the heights, forced them to retreat over the Thlotse, and finally chased them across the broken country between us and the Malutis, almost up to the foot of their mountain villages. Thus for the second time Thlotse was saved. Indeed, and in truth, the Kimberley Horse did splendid service that day, for but for them we must have perished. God bless the Kimberley Horse.

Not long after the advent of our deliverers, another regiment of light cavalry arrived. This was the Transvaal Horse, a body of volunteers recruited at Pretoria, and under the command of Lt.-Col. Ferreira, C.M.G. This regiment occupied the rising ground directly opposite our mission garden to the north east, and protected us against the attacks of Joel and Matela. A fort was built, and a nine pounder mounted upon it close to the regimental lines, and from henceforth the rebels were unable to come to close quarters with us, except on rare occasions on the south side; on which occasions they would scale the rocks with the agility of cats, and give our native contingent a great deal of trouble in and around the cattle kraals.

Everything at Thlotse was now organized on a military basis. Redoubts and other earth works were pushed forward vigorously; food for man and beast was obtained through escorted and well guarded convoys from the nearest towns and villages in the Orange Free State; and our enemies, observing all this, were for the time cowed. Major Bell received from the Colonial Government the rank of Lt.-Colonel, and was confirmed in his post of Commandant of the Forces in the Leribe district.

Mission work, in the ordinary sense of the term, was at an end, but daily Matins was said in Sesuto in one of our huts, and there were always five or six of our native Christian volunteers present at it. On Sundays there was a celebration of the Holy Eucharist soon after sunrise in the same hut, and I am thankful to say that there were always a few of the more earnest of the men, both black and white, who attended it, and received together with myself the Bread of Life. A parade service in English in the open followed, the men of all three regiments forming three sides of a hollow square; and in the afternoon, if fighting was not going on, I held a mission service in Sesuto for the native contingent and the police. The government showed a commendable anxiety to provide for the spiritual needs of the men in the field, appointing four Chaplains to the Forces: two Anglican, a Roman, and a Wesleyan. Three of these were with the main column under Brigadier-General Clarke in the south; the fourth, myself, was appointed to Leribe.

I may mention here that a party of Joel's men attacked the Sekubu mission soon after their first defeat at Thlotse. Miss Woodman had removed to Harrismith, in the Orange Free State, some time before; and the night before the attack Mr. Woodman, who had been warned in time by a friendly native, escaped over the border with his Mosuto boy. He could save nothing except the communion vessels, which he slung over his shoulder; and it was a special mercy that he succeeded in crossing the Caledon in the dark, the river being very high at the time. But he and the lad got safely across, and found their way at midnight, drenched to the skin, to the house of a Dutch Boer in the "conquered territory," where they were received and cared for with the utmost kindness and sympathy. This attack upon the mission station does not reflect much credit upon Joel, since he had given repeated assurances to Mr. Woodman that, whatever happened, he and the mission should not be molested. But no doubt it was difficult for the chief to restrain his men from violence, smarting as they were under the severe repulse they had just experienced.

There was now for us at Thlotse a little breathing time, and meanwhile the rebels were holding daily pitsos, and maturing their future plan of action. During this period of inaction the absence of efficient discipline was conspicuous among the volunteers, and drunkenness became very rife. This latter evil attained at times to such proportions that the very sentinels were often unfit for duty; and on one occasion a commanding officer sallied forth *sjambok* in hand, and soundly flogged into soberness one of his sentries, who was endangering the lives of his comrades by repeatedly discharging his rifle in all directions at imaginary enemies. This was at night, too; and, of course, tended to increase the number of scares and false alarms which darkness generally brought with it. Rumours were rife of an impending attack by the combined rebel forces on Christmas Day, their spies and scouts having learnt the condition of the garrison. They were told that Christmas was the great "Drinking Feast of the Englishman," and imagined, naturally enough, that on that day the whole place would be at their mercy. What a heathen satire upon English Christianity! To the credit of the officers, and happily for Thlotse, this design was frustrated by an order put forth just before the festival, forbidding the sale or circulation of any spirituous liquors beyond a small regulation quantity once a day to the men on active duty. Thus we were at once preserved from danger, and saved from humiliation and disgrace.

Christmas Day was spent very quietly, and with entire sobriety, and it was very pleasant and refreshing to have my dear fellow workers, Mr. and Miss Champernowne, once more uniting together in worship with myself and our small band of Christian converts at the early Celebration in our little hut. They had managed to cross the river, and come over to Thlotse for a few hours, under an escort of volunteers, the rebels having, within the last few days, drawn off their commandos from the drift. It was the last time we were all three privileged to receive the Holy Communion together, and I am sure that the little company of communicants, both native and European, who united with us in that quiet and soul-refreshing service on the Birthday of the Lord, will ever remember it as one of the brightest and happiest moments of their lives. All the services of the day were well attended, and in their way joyful and hearty, and for once the anticipations of our enemies had in no wise been realized. There was no drunkenness and no disorder, and the holy day seemed to have brought with it, in the midst of danger, a special benediction from the Prince of Peace.

CHAPTER XI.

Dreary Days.

1881.

Position of Affairs—Third Attack upon Thlotse—Skirmishes—Commandant Saunders—Captain Hanson—Major Laurence—Ntoana—Ruined state of the Chapel—Defective Hospital Arrangements—Great Rain—Scarcity of Food—A Poet—An Escape—Work among the Troops—Scenes at Deaths and Funerals—Palm Sunday—Death of Lt.-Col. Bell.

The new year opened with very little that was hopeful. The rebels were again becoming aggressive and insolent, and they were, moreover, better organized, armed, and equipped, than ever before. They had taken so much loot, and carried off so much cattle, that they could well afford to part with some of the spoil to unprincipled gun-runners, both Dutch and English, on the border, who, "for a consideration," procured them improved arms and an abundant supply of ammunition. The whole of Basutoland was now in their hands, with the exception of the three fortified camps held by the Government at Maseru, Mafiteng, and Thlotse, together with the ground on which General Clarke's main column actually encamped from day to day between the two former places. The war dragged itself along slowly and unsuccessfully, and what little was done seemed for the most part to be done unwisely. It appeared to be nobody's fault, for nobody seemed to know anything of what was going on or to have any responsibility; in fact, it looked at times as if the whole of the defensive force, from the general in command down to the rawest volunteer, was suffering from paralysis. Individual acts of heroism and bravery were not wanting on the part of both officers and men, as any one can testify who went through that ill-starred campaign, but they availed little or nothing to counteract the baleful influence of the mental and moral confusion, which from first to last appeared to reign supreme in the councils of those most responsible for the situation of affairs. A skirmish now and then, in which a few huts were destroyed but no cattle taken, marked the most vigorous of our efforts, both at Thlotse and elsewhere. Occasionally the rebels, wearied by our inaction, or anxious to dispute the path with the main column when it sought to advance, would come forth from their hiding places, and boldly attack us; the result being that, though we contrived to hold our own, and beat back the enemy, it was usually with the loss of some of our best men.

Large numbers of Englishmen were in the ranks of the Cape Mounted Rifles or the different volunteer regiments in the field, many of whom, young and inexperienced, were cut off in the flower of their manhood in these skirmishes. Among them was young Bernard White, of the C. M. R., who was killed at Kalabane, in one of the first skirmishes, in September. He was the only son of a well known and revered parish priest in England, the Rev. G. C. White, of Newlands, who had been a generous supporter of the Church's work in the Lesuto from its commencement, and who, at the termination of the war, erected a mission chapel at Mafiteng, a station not far from the spot where the young man fell.

The Feast of the Epiphany saw us attacked once more for the third time. Some of our men had been out engaging a small body of the enemy at the Kimberley Kopje—a hillock renowned as the scene of many a stubborn hand to hand fight between the Kimberley Horse and the rebels—when just before sunset large commandos were seen advancing upon them from all quarters. They retreated at once into camp, and soon there poured forth, stream upon stream, the whole rebel host. Down they rushed from the slopes and gorges of Sebotoane, and over the "neck" from Khethisa's; upwards they clambered from Ramanella's and

Tlasua's; all in hot haste to make one more combined and successful attempt upon the hateful and still remaining loyal centre. In twenty minutes we were completely surrounded, and for six hours—from sunset until one in the morning when the moon went down—an incessant fusilade was kept up; but as our men were all well under cover only very few of them were hit. A desperate attack was, however, made upon the cattle kraal, which was built on the top of the crags to the south of the fort, and where the few head of cattle, remaining to our people from their once numerous flocks and herds, were jealously and unremittingly watched and guarded. The contest here was fierce and stubborn, and confined entirely to the two sections of the natives, who fought it out in native fashion. Twice did the rebels, through their superior numbers, succeed in scaling the walls of the kraal, but they were in the end driven off without having captured even a single calf. We never knew how many of our men lost their lives in this encounter, nor could we ascertain the losses of the enemy; but the losses of the latter must have been much greater than our own, for the rocks were slippery with blood next morning, and we could mark the trail of the dead and wounded for a considerable distance where they had been carried away down the heights.

With the setting of the moon the rebels drew off, taking their killed and wounded with them; the younger braves shouting to our men to look out for them next night, when they would come in still greater numbers, kill every loyal, and take every head of cattle in the place. "Come on then," shouted the cattle guards in reply. "Why don't you come on now that you have got the chance? You are ten times our number, and yet you cannot eat us up! You cowards! You are a multitude, and we are only few, and yet you are not enough! You must needs go home and get more help! Bring your wives with you to help you, they will fight better than you! Dog eaters,* we defy you!

---

* The name by which the rebels were first known in our district. They were afterwards called Mabèlète, and the loyals Matikete.

We will pin you to the earth with our spears the moment you leap into the kraal. You shall never take a head of cattle from us again."

They did not come the next night, nor did they ever attempt to get into the kraal again; they had learnt too lasting a lesson for that.

Fruitless skirmishes were now the order of the day on both sides. The rebels kept henceforth at a respectful distance, rarely coming within a mile of the camp; but every few days there would be a small encounter, generally at or near the Kimberley Kopje.

On one occasion a strong detachment of our men went out before daylight to ascend Sebotoane with the object of dispersing about 2,000 of Joel's bravest warriors, who were bent on forming an encampment on the mountain, from which they might sally down upon us, and give us a good deal of trouble whenever they pleased. They were driven off and dispersed, but not without serious loss to ourselves, and not before our ammunition had almost failed. Our men retired slowly down the mountain and came back to camp, bringing their dead and wounded with them. Had Joel's warriors only known that their ammunition was spent, it is certain that they would have allowed very few of them to return to Thlotse to tell the tale.

Among the killed on this occasion was a personal friend of my own, Mr. Ernest Saunders, a young Englishman who had been residing at a trading station close to Leribe before the outbreak of the rebellion. He was a bright, intelligent young fellow, a Roman Catholic by birth, and had been educated by the Jesuits at their school at Stonyhurst. When I first became acquainted with him, I found that, like many other educated and thoughtful men, he had revolted from the Roman Church in disgust at its superstitions, and had unhappily, as is often the case with such men, lost his faith in the Incarnation likewise; but he seemed grateful for any little kindness shown him, and soon began to ride over to S. Saviour's every Sunday to attend the English service, usually spending the remainder of the day with us at the Mission. I never heard a word against his moral character or conduct, and he was fast regaining his faith in the cardinal truths of Christianity when the war broke out. The establishment in which he was a clerk was looted and burnt, and he then offered himself to the Government for active service, having already gained some experience in military affairs in the Zululand campaign of the previous year. He was appointed to the command of the Native Mounted Police, and fell in this his first engagement. Two of his men were killed with him; one a heathen, the other—Sergeant Jeremia—a Christian, and by common consent the bravest non-commissioned officer in the little force. There were only twenty-three police in the action, and they were quickly marked out and surrounded. A rush with the assagai followed, and the three men perished, my poor friend receiving five assagai stabs, any one of which would have been fatal. One assagai had pierced right through him, and had stuck so fast that in order to extract it it was necessary to place the foot upon the young fellow's lifeless body.

Another promising officer cut off in early manhood in his very first encounter was Captain Hanson, of the Transvaal Horse, who was shot down with some of his men while charging the enemy, revolver in hand, on the slopes of the Kimberley Kopje. He was a favourite with the whole of his regiment, and his death was greatly lamented.

A few weeks afterwards Major Laurence, the officer in command of the Kimberley Horse, met his death exactly in the same manner, and almost at the same spot. Brave and accomplished, having the interests of his men more at heart than his own, and gifted in no small degree with military talents of the highest order, he was the idol of his regiment. It will be remembered that it was he who, at the risk of his life, rode forward alone in advance of his men to bring the commandant of the garrison the welcome news of their approach. He was mortally wounded while at the head of his men, waving his hand to cheer them to the charge, and died a few minutes afterwards while being brought into camp. The body was laid on my own mattress in my own hut, and reverently cared for and guarded with a guard of honour until it was buried next day in the Mission cemetery by the side of the others who had fallen in the field. He was beloved and mourned by all, and the whole garrison turned out at the funeral, and followed his remains to the grave.

Our old friend Ntoana, the native mentioned in a preceding chapter as the builder of our huts, also met his death during the campaign, though not near the same spot. A troop of the Transvaal Horse had been ordered out to Tsikoane on a foraging expedition for fuel, the Thlotse being then fordable; and Jonathan, thinking that their presence would be a protection to him, endeavoured to get two waggon loads of mealies into camp from the Free State by that route. His men were greatly in want of food, and he undertook this hazardous and unwise venture on their behalf; and that, too, without acquainting the military authorities of his intention. The Transvaal troopers were therefore in ignorance of his presence on the south side of the Thlotse, and imagined that he was still in the camp. All went well until the chief and his little party were rounding the foot of the Tsikoane mountain, when they were suddenly attacked by a commando of the rebels, which had been lying in wait for them for some hours. The struggle which ensued was short and decisive. The waggon drivers, guards, and most of Jonathan's own body guard were killed—the short stabbing assagai doing its deadly work in a few minutes. Seventeen men perished; among them our poor friend, who defended himself with great bravery until overpowered by numbers. Jonathan and the few men left then rode for their lives, and ultimately escaped into Free State territory. Probably the chief owed his deliverance more to his birth and position than to anything else; for so great is the reverence of natives for their chieftains, especially for those of the house of Moshesh, that a "*mothu fèèla*"—a common person—would hardly dare to lift a hand against one of them. It would be regarded as a species of sacrilege. Chiefs rarely fall except by the hand of other chiefs, but a stray bullet may find its way anywhere; it is no respecter of persons. After their victory, the rebels carried off the waggons and their contents in triumph, leaving Jonathan the poorer in purse, provisions, and prestige.

With so much continual warfare the chapel was in a ruinous condition: great gaping loopholes disfigured and injured its walls, and the roof was so pierced with bullet holes that the rain poured through in streams. It made one's heart ache to look at it. I tried in vain to get the authorities to remove the men who were quartered in it, and have the building repaired so that it might be used as a hospital.

The surgeon, as skilful as he was humane, was indefatigable in his duties, but the sick and wounded were still lying under canvas in the fort, though fever and dysentery were rife; and it was not until many months afterwards, when the volunteers were disbanded, and a solitary troop of the Cape Mounted Rifles was left in their place, that better arrangements were made.

To add to our miseries, that year's rainy season was unusually wet and prolonged. It rained almost incessantly during the months of February, March, and April. So persistent was the deluge that the rain would sometimes come down in torrents, as it only can in Africa, for a whole week together with hardly the least cessation. During these months we suffered much from want of food. Provisions were scanty, supplies could only be procured with extreme difficulty, and at famine prices, and there was often no fuel wherewith to cook the half ration of meal doled out morning by morning. Man and beast alike suffered the pangs of hunger. Often, when there was something in the way of food, there was nothing to cook it with; and often when there was fuel there was little or no food to cook. The sentries on night duty suffered most. Sometimes they would have to be on picket duty the whole night. They would stand hour after hour in the driving, pitiless rain, their ears ever on the alert, and their eyes strained to the utmost in the inky darkness which reigned around, for it was at such times that the enemy was most dangerous. And in the morning, when they returned to their quarters, it was often impossible, sodden with wet, and exhausted as they were, to procure even a cup of coffee. Poor fellows, one's heart ached to see them; and I did not wonder that the rank " Cape Smoke," of which, alas, there was always an abundant supply, was laid at such times under undue contribution.

Towards the middle of March the rebels, failing to drive us from our position, began to get weary and dispirited. The four months' almost continuous warfare had been a strain upon them as well as ourselves; indeed, the native is rarely able to hold out in the field for more than three or four months together. His commissariat arrangements are not adapted to lengthy campaigns; and what with poor feeding, constant action, and vigilant watching, he soon wears out, and requires to return home for a time, and rest. As the rebels had put almost the whole of their forces into the field from the very first, they had no reserves worthy of the name to fall back upon; and, under such circumstances, it was inevitable that by the middle of March they should be tired out, and incapable of doing more than holding the positions already assured to them.

Taking advantage of this lull in the tide of affairs, my colleague, Mr. Champernowne, came over from the Free State to stay at Thlotse for as many days as it might be possible to do so. I on my part was feeling jaded, and needed a change. So it was arranged that I should go to Ficksburg for a week, more or less. Mrs. Bell and other friends from Basutoland were in refuge there, and I should be able to see my little daughter. Moreover, I had been suffering of late from neuralgia, and it was hoped that a change of diet as well as of scene, not to speak of a good, long, continuous sleep, might be beneficial in every way. Accordingly, I rode over to this prettily situated Free State village, and spent a very pleasant three days there. On the fourth a letter came from my brother priest to say that " a queer old man, who gave himself out to be a poet, had arrived at the station, and greatly desired to see me. He was 'seeking a Government appointment,' requesting meanwhile food and shelter at the Mission." Mr. Champernowne added that "he did not think the poor man quite right in his head," and that " he did not know what to do with him."

Feeling now in better health and spirits, I thought it well to return at once, ere this erratic genius might take it into his head to burn down our remaining huts, or attempt some other thing equally unpleasant. So next morning after breakfast I saddled up and started homewards. The roads were in a sorry plight from the incessant rain, and one had to proceed carefully even on level ground; while on the hillsides the paths were so slippery and worn out that riding down them was no easy matter either to man or beast. I had ridden about an hour's journey from the village when, nearly opposite the Zout Kop Hill, I perceived on the road before me a small group of our volunteers, evidently on their way to Thlotse, and as evidently the worse for liquor. One of them had just tumbled off his horse, and his comrades were trying to seat him again as firmly as they could in the saddle. I rode up to them, and finding that they were on their way home, offered to accompany them. The party consisted of five: a captain and a trooper of one regiment, and a sergeant and two troopers of another. They were all dressed in the usual Bedford cord uniforms of our volunteers, and were unarmed; and they had evidently been on leave in Ficksburg, where, apparently, they had been drinking deeply. The officer, to his credit, was the least tipsy of the party, and he and one of the troopers were sober enough to recognise me, which they did seemingly with a pleasure not unmixed with some degree of shame. One of the others was madly intoxicated, a second good humouredly so, and the third helplessly. It was, of course, this latter who had fallen off his animal. Finding them in this plight, and knowing the condition of the roads, I thought it best to ride with them and see them safely into camp. Rain was again threatening, and I knew that if they missed their way, and were left in the veldt all night, the exposure would certainly do them harm, and might even cause their death. Such a thing had happened more than once before.

They gladly accepted my offer, and the hilarious brother forthwith proceeded to draw from his pocket the remains of a bottle of brandy, which he quickly despatched before my eyes. Happily they had no more liquor with them, so there was at least a hope that we might all reach home in safety. We had only an hour and a half's ride before us, but it took us *four hours* to accomplish it. The human log would insist on falling off his pony into the mud from time to time, his facetious comrade cracking jokes at his expense while placing him again in the saddle. The madman glared wildly about him for some time, and then, after having delivered a volley of oaths and imprecations, clasped his horse round the neck, and relapsed into silence. The others said and did but little.

In this way we proceeded slowly on our way along a fairly level road until we reached the "kloof" or gorge in the mountains on the Free State side of the Caledon, over against Thlotse. Going down this gorge was the reverse of easy. The track was full of holes and very slippery. Moreover, it was so narrow that two men could barely ride abreast on it. We descended at a snail's pace, cautiously, saying little or nothing to one another. Even the merry brother had become silent. It required all our care to steer our way in safety, especially with one of our number so helplessly incapable.

On we went, splish splash in the mud and slush, two abreast, when suddenly the man with whom I was riding—who happened to be the madly drunk one—to the amazement of the whole party, pulled out of his breast pocket a six-chambered revolver, and shouting "Kafirs!" "Rebels!" and I know not what, deliberately aimed at me, and had *fired three times* before the captain (who was immediately behind him), with the cry of "My God!" could spring forward and wrench the pistol from his hand. I was riding so close to the man that our horses constantly touched each other. He had fired three shots at my luckless head, which was barely a yard distant, and yet not one of them had touched me!

I have had several narrow escapes in my life, but I never had a narrower one than that. The whole thing happened in a moment, and I suppose the bullets missed me because we were moving forward at an irregular pace as the madman fired. Or there may perhaps be another explanation. I was riding at his right, on the off side of him, and, therefore, on lower ground; and as the path was a very sloping one, the shots probably went over my head. But, whatever the explanation may be, does not much matter; all I know is that the three shots whizzed past me as they were fired, and that I remained unhurt. "All's well that ends well." The man was now disarmed, and, thank God, I was safe.

Then there ensued a scene which would have been ludicrous had it not been somewhat dangerous. His four companions wanted to lynch him on the spot for attempting to murder me! They yelled, and the horses plunged, while I expostulated and tried to screen him; my facetious friend made frantic efforts to drag him down from his saddle; and even the helpless lout, who had hitherto taken notice of nothing, roused himself, and joined in his idiotic way in the general confusion and hubbub. Certainly the poor, patient, dumb beasts we were riding seemed to be much more sensible than their masters, for it was only by their surefootedness, and dogged determination to stick to the path, that we arrived safely at the bottom of the glen.

The Caledon was fairly high—quite high enough to wet us—and just as we got into the middle of it the rain began to come down in torrents, drenching us all through and through to the skin. In half an hour we arrived safely home, though in a half drowned condition; the whole party sober enough now, with the exception of my friend of the six-shooter, who still appeared bereft of his senses, and was speedily confined to the guard tent on a charge of attempting to murder the chaplain! Poor fellow, he was sober enough the next morning; and when, fortunately for him, I succeeded in begging him off, and getting the case quashed, he came to me in real distress of mind at what had occurred, declaring—what, I am sure, was perfectly true—that he knew nothing whatever about it, and protesting that I was the last person on earth he would have thought of injuring.

So much for the effects of drink.

What a curse it was at Thlotse, and along the Free State border, in those days, every volunteer or official who was engaged in the campaign will well remember.

The rained ceased as I reached the door of my hut. I was just about to enter it when I heard a strange voice accost me in the blandest of accents, and, on turning round, I beheld before me the "poet." Yes, there he was; evidently an eminently respectable member of society; important, benevolent, and voluble. He was a veritable Pecksniff. It is needless to say that he was scrupulously attired in black, and held in his hand a portly and ancient umbrella—an article quite unknown at the camp at that time. Such sort of people always do carry about with them a substantial-looking and capacious umbrella; though why, I never could quite make out.

Our new friend introduced himself at once with all the unctuous pomposity imaginable. "He was a poet by profession, and had recently come from Australia." Australia, the abode of the Muses, thought I. There is hope now even for South Africa !

But even poets are not always exempt from the reverses and troubles of ordinary mortals, and this was the case with our friend. In blunt, but pathetic prose, he declared that he was "hard up." Poets, he assured me, were "hard up at times," and such was his case then; and he had come to Thlotse "hoping to obtain the post of Private Secretary to the Commandant of the Garrison." "He had no doubt that he would be able to obtain it *with my kind recommendation.*" And so on, and so on, and so on.

Then he offered to recite one of his poems to me, "feeling sure that I should admire it." This was too much. "Sir," I said, "do you think that a man wet to the skin after a four hours' ride in the rain and the mud, his teeth chattering from cold, and his body shivering from clamminess, could be captivated by *any* verse whatsoever—however majestic or mellifluous ? Do you not think that even Shakespeare himself would pall under such circumstances ? "

With the blandest of smiles he allowed that it might be so. Good man, he was human after all.

" I will see you this evening," said I ; and, so saying, turned into my hut and at once took a bath—the best preventative of a cold, after having been thoroughly wet through, that I know of, at all events in South Africa. A cold bath, with plenty of friction while drying, and a hot cup of coffee afterwards : it sounds " Homœopathic," but, however that may be, it is true ; though perhaps it might not suit every constitution.

The old gentleman was never tired of reciting his compositions. He thoroughly believed in them, which was, no doubt, quite natural. As for ourselves, we were not gifted with such robust faith, and he used sometimes to try our powers of repression very cruelly by insisting on spouting what he called his " masterpiece "—a " poem " on Ferdinand and Isabella of Spain.

Choking with suppressed laughter we listened to him as he burst forth in his most magniloquent manner—

"O Queenly Isabella!"

The turgid bathos of this production was overpowering, and suggested various parodies, one of which

"O Gingham Umbrella!"

was frequently upon our lips, though, happily for himself, our poet guest knew it not.

It is needless to say that our friend was unsuccessful in obtaining the post he sought. But he accepted his disappointment with quite a Pecksniffian air of resignation; came down from his stilts, and informed me that in lieu of anything better he "would not disdain to accept the humble position of tutor to the younger members of a genteel family."

Poor dear, he often used to bore us when we were particularly busy, and came one morning with a profoundly solemn countenance to ask our advice as to his future. Two courses of duty presented themselves to him, he said; and he was in doubt which to follow. One was to go into the *Hooge Veldt*, one of the most monotonous flats in the Orange Free State, and unite himself in matrimony to a wealthy Boer widow with nine children residing on a sheep farm there; to which lady he "flattered himself that he was not altogether unacceptable;" the other was to proceed at once to Europe, and enter a monastery connected with the severest order in Christendom! It is needless to say that he did neither.

We kept him at the Mission for some weeks, and eventually succeeded in getting him a tutorship in a respectable Boer family, living at no great distance from us; but he did not remain there long. He left suddenly for Natal, after borrowing over five pounds from the confiding Boer, and was never heard of more.

We have had, from first to last, all kinds of curious people at our station, but I think our poet was the most original of them all. At this time especially the place was full of some of the most remarkable specimens of the human race. It was, of course, the war which had brought all these together. The volunteers of the three regiments forming our camp were not only men of every grade of society, but of all races and nationalities. Englishmen, Irishmen, Scotchmen, Canadians, Australians, Africanders, Americans, Germans, Swedes, Norwegians, Danes, Hollanders, Frenchmen, Italians, Russians, Poles, and even a Corsican, were to be found in their ranks. Nay, one of them told me pathetically one day that he had no country at all. "I was born in a haystack," said he, "and the cow ate up my country."

Their religious beliefs were hardly less varied. Not only was every form of Christianity represented, from the most extreme Romanism to the wildest and newest sect of yesterday, but there were also Agnostics, Deists, Theosophists, Fatalists, and believers in the Anglo-Israel theory. "Many men, many minds;" and so we found it.

As to social position, reckoned on the score of birth, they ranged from scions of noble houses down to the village barber and the navvy. Promotion from the ranks was the general rule, and many of the troopers and non-commissioned officers were quite the equals of the officers who commanded them. In such a body of men, hastily recruited and thrust together cheek by jowl, there was of necessity a considerable sprinkling of roughs, nay, even blackguards; but I am bound to say that I never received a rude word from any of them. The language of a military camp is by no means choice; but I do not remember that bad language was ever indulged in in my presence; and often at night when going my rounds between the lines, as the shadow of my cassock was caught sight of against the tents, I have heard exclamations like the following: "Dry up there,

Bill; don't you see who is passing?" Or, "Look out, old man; draw it mild; the chaplain is just outside."

At times, when fuel was not to be had, and they were half starved with hunger, they would often, under cover of the night, steal out and appropriate any piece of wood or other fire-kindling material they could lay their hands upon, even taking doors off their hinges, and carrying them off to cook their food with; but they never confiscated a single door of any of our Mission huts, though I do not think I could have blamed them much had they done so. Perhaps it was because they knew that these huts had been so often the last resting places of their friends and comrades who had fallen in the field, before they were finally committed to the earth; for the soldier has, in his way, very keen instincts of reverence and respect. Many of these men would come at times to a voluntary service in the ruined chapel, or in my study, and some few of them were communicants.

It was touching to see the care and reverence with which they treated the dead. When some poor fellow was brought in to be laid on the couch of death, with a bullet through his brain, or half-a-dozen assagai stabs in his body, his comrades would gather round and perform the last offices of love with the greatest delicacy and gentleness; and at the prayers which followed, when the corpse had been carefully washed and laid in its blanket shroud, I have seen the strongest and most hardened weep and sob like little children, as they knelt around in the doorway of the hut, or on the ground outside. And before they were disbanded, at the end of the rebellion, each regiment gave a day's pay (it was their own suggestion) towards the enclosure of the hallowed spot where their dead lay buried.

Poor fellows, they had a bad character throughout South Africa; and no wonder. But they were not all bad, and had they been properly handled by such a man as Gordon, they might have been moulded into an "Ever Victorious Army," as his volunteers were.

Palm Sunday, the 17th April, was the last fighting day at Thlotse during the rebellion proper, or " gun war," as it came afterwards to be called.

We had but barely finished our celebration of the Holy Eucharist (which, I am thankful to say, was kept up almost every Sunday in one of our huts all through the troubles), when shots were heard in the neighbourhood of the camp of the Transvaal Horse on the hill opposite. The rebels had planned a surprise. Half an hour before they were nowhere to be seen; now they poured down upon us from all quarters. In a few minutes every man was at his post, and from 9 o'clock till noon the firing was almost continuous. Happily there was little or no work for the assagai that day, neither party having come to close quarters; and by half-past twelve the enemy was beaten off, and retired sulkily to the heights of Sebotoane.

In the afternoon a flag of truce came in with the information that Lerothodi, the insurgent general, whose head-quarters were two days' journey from us to the south, had sued for peace. An armistice followed, which ended finally in a treaty of peace being agreed upon between the majority of the rebel leaders and the Government.

In June an event took place which cast a deep gloom over the whole place. Our kind friend Colonel Bell died, worn out prematurely with the worries and the follies of both the contending parties in this miserable and abortive strife. That he was deeply respected for his integrity and personal rectitude goes without saying, and his loss was for a long time felt, at times severely, throughout the district. Even the rebel leaders mourned his untimely decease, and followed his remains with lamentations to the grave.

Soon after this sad event Mrs. Bell removed to the Transkei, several hundred miles to the south of us, where her eldest son had been appointed to a magistracy in the Idutywa native reserve. She took with her my little daughter, of whom I now lost sight for several years. It was a new grief to be thus severed not only from friends of long standing, but also from my only child; but I felt that it was safest to leave all in God's hands. Indeed, I was powerless to act otherwise. I did not feel justified in leaving the work to which God had called me in Basutoland, and that was the only alternative. I had " put my hand to the plough," and it would not do now to " look back."

CHAPTER XII.

Patching up a Peace.

1881.

Cessation of Hostilities—Reversal of Government Policy—Peace at any Price—Efforts of the New Governor—Departure of Col. Griffith—The Forces Disbanded—Results of the War—Scourges, Moral and Physical.

The winter of 1881 was indeed a dreary time: everything seemed hopeless. The Government had been foiled in their endeavour to enforce disarmament, and now a new Cabinet came into office whose one object it was to bring the war to an end and make peace—peace on any terms and at any price, with the practically victorious rebels. Sir Bartle Frere had been recalled, and Sir Hercules Robinson had succeeded him. Lerothodi, the ablest of the Basuto chiefs, took in the political situation at a glance.

He saw that the attempt of the ministry had proved abortive and had been discredited, thanks mainly to the efforts of himself and his friends. He knew also that in England there had been a change of Ministry, and that the new Cabinet took no pains to conceal their disapproval of what had been done in Basutoland. A change of Governors meant a change of policy, and Lerothodi saw his chance. He knew that his allies were all but exhausted, and that if the forces of the Government could but hold their positions for another month or two, they would in all probability succeed in dispersing the insurgent bands now roaming about the country. Natives cannot endure the hardships and privations of a winter campaign in a country like Basutoland; while, on the contrary, the white man prefers the bright dry days and cold frosty nights of June and July for military operations. And Lerothodi knew well that, were he once thoroughly beaten, it would be almost impossible for him to rally his scattered forces. Great numbers of the waverers, who had hitherto cast in their lot with him, would go over to the loyal side the moment the Government became victorious.

There was, too, a still greater danger looming in the distance. How were he and his friends to procure food when their present supplies came to an end? Native tribes live only from hand to mouth, and it would be impossible to plough and sow with the country convulsed by war. The loyal natives would, of course, be fed by the Government. They had lost their lands, and, therefore, had none to cultivate. But to Lerothodi and his following these lands would be useless, as well as their own. The Basuto General saw hunger staring him in the face. He was fully alive to the danger of his position, and resolved, therefore, to seize the opportunity to make peace.

Thus both parties were anxious to bring the campaign to an end; the Government appearing to be even more eager for peace than the rebels. Masupha, indeed, still held out, declining partly from jealousy, and partly from his innate obstinacy of disposition, to submit to the dictation of an inferior. But Lerothodi had his father, the Paramount Chief, on his side, and he was so convinced of the necessity of coming to terms with the Government that he resolved to act without his uncle, and accordingly made, as we have seen, overtures of peace. These overtures were gladly, nay greedily, clutched at and accepted. "Peace; peace at any price" was now the cry both at the Cape and in Downing Street; and, in their desire to bring the war to an end, the Cape Ministers were ready to go any lengths in the direction of concession or accommodation.

As I have said, Lerothodi made his first overtures on the 17th April, and on that day a conference was held between him and Col. Griffith, the Governor's Agent, near the village of Molipa. The old ministers had not yet gone out of office, though it was clear to everyone that the Cabinet was moribund. It could not survive the advent of a new Governor and of the new policy he brought with him, backed up as that was by all the moral influence of the English Colonial Office; and, accordingly, when his Excellency offered to mediate between his Ministers and the Basuto chiefs the offer was at once accepted.

The Governor, on hearing that Lerothodi had sued for peace, proclaimed an armistice, and a few days afterwards, on the 29th April, put forth his "Award," which certainly could not be said to err on the side of severity towards those who had been in arms against the Government. The Award was accepted by both the belligerents; and had it been adhered to, the loyal Basutos would have secured a fair indemnity for their losses, together with the prospect of being able to return to their ruined homes and cultivate their lands. But the rebels, while professing to accept it, took good care to evade its most important provisions—those, namely, which bound them to restore to their rightful owners the cattle which they had taken from the loyals; and the new ministry, which had meanwhile come into office, and endeavoured to reverse, as far as possible, the policy of their predecessors, prevailed upon the Governor to have it cancelled altogether, while pledging themselves to secure to the loyals a just compensation for their losses. But this pledge, though solemnly and publicly reiterated on several occasions, was only partially and inadequately carried out. The rebellion had cost the Cape Colony almost four millions, and the Cape Parliament was in no mood to add to its burdens. The final result of the promise was that Jonathan and his people did, after long intervals, receive two instalments of the amount due to them; but the third has never yet been paid, and nobody, I suppose, now thinks that it ever will be.

Col. Griffith, the Governor's Agent, a most capable and experienced official, did not see his way to accept the new policy; and he was, therefore, granted a year's leave of absence, upon the expiration of which he was placed upon the pension list, to the regret of everyone in the country. He knew only too well, from a dearly-bought experience, what everyone comes to know who has to deal with natives, that the worst of all policies is to threaten and not to punish, and to promise and not perform. He did not consider the new policy a righteous one, and he had the courage of his convictions. He was therefore sacrificed to the political expediency of the moment.

The black man has a keen sense of justice, and a thorough appreciation of strength of purpose. You may govern him with a tight rein if you will; and though, in that case, he can hardly be expected to like you, he will, nevertheless, respect you as long as he sees and knows that your rule is just and righteous. Moral rectitude in the white man is everything with him, but scoldings and threats are only signs of weakness; and a promise unfulfilled or evaded destroys in his breast all respect for the maker of it.

This sudden reversal of policy on the part of the Government; this determination to meet the rebels more than half way—nay, to regard them as oppressed and injured patriots, suffering for their fatherland and their rights—did not commend itself to either party among the Basutos. The rebels regarded it as a sign of weakness, and treated it with ill-disguised contempt; the loyals knew that it meant to them social ostracism and loss, perhaps even absolute destruction. "Ba etsa jualeka bana"— "they act like children," said an influential chief to me one day when the news of this sudden reversal of policy came to us. He could not understand the action of the Cape ministers. It was a complete puzzle to him; and he only reflected the general opinion of the people.

The new Secretary for Native Affairs and other officials from Capetown now appeared upon the scene, travelling in hot haste through the country, and disbanding the forces everywhere with the utmost speed. Within a month there was not a man left, with the exception of the small regiment of Cape Mounted Rifles; a troop of which, numbering about sixty men, was now stationed at Thlotse. These sixty men were placed there for show rather than for anything else, it being understood that they were to adopt an attitude of non-intervention between the *Matikete* and the *Mabelete* should these again attempt to fight. But we felt that, for the present at any rate, Thlotse was safe. It was the depth of winter, and both parties were exhausted by the struggle. Hostilities were, therefore, not likely to break out again until ploughing-time, which would, at least, secure to us two or three months of peace. As to the future, we feared, and as the event proved rightly, that the time was not yet come when the two contending parties would consent to "beat their swords into plough shares, and their spears into pruning hooks."

On the 10th May I had written to the Bishop describing the condition of affairs, and summing up my report in these words:

"Mr. Champernowne's place has entirely disappeared. Your lordship would not know it in the least. Even a part of the main *foundation* of the training college has been dug up. We have had a large tent made, which, with our remaining huts, must serve us until we can build. The armistice has come to an end, but it will probably be renewed, as the Government seem bent upon making 'peace upon almost any terms. It is the general conviction here that a patched-up peace, such as the one proposed, can never last. The rebel party will break out again in the spring, as soon as they have got their harvest in. Meanwhile the loyal natives, so cruelly abandoned, are wringing their hands, as well they may. It certainly *does not pay to be loyal.*"

O

And later, on the 18th August, I wrote as follows as to the political situation :—

"I regret to say that affairs in Basutoland are still in a very unsettled state. Four months have been spent in endeavouring to patch up a peace with the leading rebel chiefs, but up to this time very little substantial progress has been made. Lerothodi in the south, and Joel in this district, are said to be anxious for peace, and have expressed their willingness to accept the terms offered them by the Governor; but Masupha and Ramanella still hold back, and are said to be threatening a fresh attack upon Maseru. A large number of loyal refugees, chiefly women and children, have lately settled here, 3,000 of whom—all heathen—are at our very doors."

The results of the war may be summed up in a few words: loss of British prestige, a Colonial debt of four millions, and the alienation of a great tribe. The Colony had gained nothing and lost much by its futile attempt to disarm the Basutos. Nay more, the sudden change of front, issuing in the virtual surrender to the rebels of all that they asked for—for, of course, they were allowed to keep their guns—struck a direct blow at the confidence of the law abiding section of the people in the British Government, whether Imperial or Colonial. These latter had incurred, as we have seen, all kinds of obloquy, had shed their blood, had lost their lands and cattle, in fact everything that they possessed, on behalf of a power which had suddenly deserted them in the hour of their greatest need. Bitter and deep was the feeling of injury—the feeling of injustice and wrong—which rankled in the breasts of these faithful allies of England, when they saw themselves thus abandoned to the mercy of their enemies. There was no guarantee worthy of a moment's thought that they would be able to return to their ruined homes, and sow their fields for the coming harvest. A few, indeed, did attempt to do so, but they were so effectually harassed and boycotted that life became a burden, and they gave up the attempt in despair, returning to their intrenchments at the camp.

Throughout the whole northern district the loyals only regained the possession of their lands, and a portion of their flocks and herds, through their own strong arm, in the inter-tribal war which followed that of the rebellion. This struggle was protracted for four years, during which time the loyals under Jonathan and his captains recovered inch by inch, by their persistent patience and splendid courage, the ground they had lost, the Government looking cynically on while the two parties "fought it out." For the few Europeans who remained in the country this was not only, as we shall see, a time of personal danger and discomfort, but a time which made men blush for the tarnished honour of the English name.

There were other results of the gun war which ought not to be passed over, leaving as they did a baleful trail behind them. These were both moral and physical, the former being especially harmful in their influence and their outcome; indeed, it may be said with perfect truth that this miserable campaign did much to permanently lower the morals of the Basuto people.

Given a mob of natives huddled together for well nigh a year in a hot climate, and a small space, with an utter absence of the simplest sanitary regulations, and we know what the result will be. This was the case with us. The very atmosphere became tainted, and typhoid fever raged throughout the place. Festering corpses of man and beast polluted the air all around. The "slums" in the centre of the camp, where the fugitives were cooped up closest, were in a shocking condition, and grew worse and worse as time went on. Crowds of men, women, and children came flocking into Thlotse, which had now become the one great camp of all the loyals of the country, and the stronghold of all who followed the banner of Jonathan. To their honour be it said, the little band of Christians in the place did what they could, both by influence and example, to mitigate the misery and diminish the filth, keeping their own huts neat and tidy, and the approaches to them as clean as circumstances would permit.

Moreover, small parties of them, headed by the veteran Nathanaele, went forth outside the camp, as soon as peace was proclaimed, and it was safe to do so, and buried the skeletons of their foes still lying on the battlefields around, the vultures and wild dogs having, in most cases, picked the bones quite clean. But fever had got too firm a hold upon the place to be easily dislodged. It raged on violently, and with it dysentery. Dr. Taylor was in attendance night and day, completely overworked; nurses, at least for the natives, there were none. Men and women were dying daily, and the survivors, cowed and dazed at the turn which events had taken, looked on in sullen apathy and despair.

Those who escaped the fever were attacked from time to time by violent fits of nausea and vomiting, which would come on quite suddenly and unexpectedly, especially at meal times. These were sometimes as distressing as they were inconvenient, but they usually passed off in a few hours, and I do not remember that any evil results followed them.

A more serious trial was that of opthalmia, which became so common that hardly anyone in the place, either black or white, escaped it.

To add to these miseries there was at the same time quite a plague of flies. I have seen these little creatures very numerous in the summer at the sheep farms in the Karoo, but I never witnessed anything to equal the swarms of them that settled down upon us at this time. They were so numerous, so persistent, and so irritating, that they became what I have termed them—a veritable plague. They were loathsome and poison-laden too, and it was the general impression that they were the chief cause of the ophthalmia from which we suffered. I have no doubt that this was so in my case, for I had escaped the malady for a considerable time, and had begun to hope that I might do so altogether, when one day a fly settled for a moment on my right eyelid. I felt a sudden burning sensation when the insect settled down—something like the sting of a scorpion, but by no means so acute—and then in a few minutes the eyelid began to swell, and the mischief was accomplished. The one eye quickly affected the other; and the result was that for eight days I was laid upon my back in a darkened hut, with eyes swollen, sore, and smarting from pain. Mr. Champernowne had been attacked in the same way a short time before, and suffered, I think, even more acutely than I did. Our good doctor was indefatigable as usual, doing his utmost to mitigate the pain of his many patients, and supply eye lotions to all who were suffering, until one day he succumbed likewise, and was laid up with a severe attack which completely prostrated him. For ten days not a ray of light was allowed to enter his chamber, and it was not until many weeks had elapsed that he quite recovered.

These were miseries enough, the reader will think; but there was one evil more, greater than all these, from which the natives now began to suffer: an evil which cannot be referred to here further than to say that it was the direct outcome of licentiousness and vice. This loathsome and terrible disease was but rarely met with anywhere in the country before the war, but it now became rampant, and, sad to say, has remained ever since. Two years ago it had so infected every district, and its ravages had become so dangerous to the community generally, that the Government officials were roused to make a united and determined attempt to stamp out the dreadful scourge. That this attempt has largely proved successful is matter of great thankfulness to all who have the welfare of the Basutos at heart.

Yet another evil must, I fear, be regarded as the heritage of this untoward time—that of dishonesty. Before the rebellion no one thought of locking a door, or scrupled to leave all kinds of property outside his house should necessity so require. But now the natives rapidly became adepts in the art of "picking and stealing." They had never scrupled to do a little in the way of cattle lifting whenever the opportunity presented itself, but other forms of depredation were rare among them. But now pilfering became a settled habit with many, and I greatly fear that they learnt it from the more dishonest among the white volunteers, many of whom, if the truth were told, had been by no means unacquainted with the inside of a gaol. But during the last three or four years there has been, I am glad to say, an improvement in this respect, and there is now, one would fain hope, a prospect of a gradual reversion to the former condition of things, when doors needed neither lock nor bolt, and everyone's goods and chattels were secure.

But it is time to leave these unsavoury subjects, and turn our thoughts to the Mission and its prospects.

CHAPTER XIII.

Reorganization.

1881-2.

Reorganization of the Mission—The Compensation Question—Abandonment of the Native Training College Scheme—Death of Mrs. Woodman—Visit of General Gordon.

Though the spring of 1881 brought with it little or no prospect of a substantial and permanent settlement of the affairs of the country, yet hostilities were for a time at an end. We therefore thought it our duty to endeavour, as far as was possible, to reorganize the Mission. And here let me remind the reader that, when I speak of "Spring," I am referring not to the earlier months of the year, but to the later—to the months of September and October.

The Mission chapel was restored to us at the end of July,

when the garrison vacated it, and we turned our first thoughts towards its cleansing and repair. It was indeed in a sorry condition. Its walls were full of holes, its windows without a single pane of glass in them, and its roof still riddled with shot-holes. Every time it rained the water streamed down from these holes as from a shower bath; and besides this the earthen floor was furrowed all over, the walls besmeared and defiled with grease and filth, and the whole place alive with vermin. By the aid of friends in England, who had heard of our evil plight and who prayed daily for our deliverance, we were enabled to restore the building to some degree of decency and order. The walls were scraped and replastered both inside and out, new corrugated iron roofing was put up, the floor was relaid and resmeared, new windows replaced the old, the furniture that remained was repaired, thoroughly washed and cleaned, and in a few weeks we had the privilege and the joy of again being able to worship the Lord in His own House, and before His own Altar. The restoration of the schoolroom was, of course, accomplished at the same time, and, from a mission point of view, was only second to that of the chapel. Mr. Champernowne returned to us from the Orange Free State as soon as there was a prospect of peace, and at the end of September Mr. Reading came to us from Bloemfontein. My junior colleague was now in deacon's orders, and the school was reopened, and placed once more under his charge. Fifty children, the majority of whom were heathen in the utterly "raw" stage, entered it at once, and their numbers steadily increased. A native catechist, Alfred Motolo, soon afterwards entered the service of the Mission, taking the charge of the junior classes when not engaged in evangelistic work among the heathen in the surrounding villages. We greatly missed the services of Miss Champernowne, who had been married at Easter to the Rev. T. Woodman, then in temporary charge of the town of Harrismith during the abeyance of the work at Sekubu; and the cares of housekeeping—no light burden as anyone knows who has undertaken it under such circumstances as ours—again devolved upon myself.

We repatched and rethatched our rondavels and re-enclosed the garden, planting many young fruit trees, chiefly peaches and apples, to replace those which had been trodden down and destroyed during the year that the garden had remained unwalled and open to every passer by.

There were now more than three thousand heathen at our doors, and among these we began to labour. Such a time of political and social ferment and upheaval was hardly favourable to the spread of the Gospel, yet, thanks be to God, several converts were then made who have continued faithful to their baptismal vows, and are still among the most regular communicants of the Mission.

When the chapel was first taken possession of, and loopholed, and the garden walls thrown down, we were assured by the authorities that full compensation would be given to us by the Government for the damage done, or for any losses that the Mission, or we ourselves, might incur through the war. Forms of claim for damages were sent to us from Capetown, and these were carefully filled up, and the amounts of the claims attested and approved by the Basutoland executive. Nay, we were required to *sign in duplicate a receipt* for the amounts of our claims, with the promise of immediate payment. We signed these receipts, *but received nothing*. After waiting in vain for several months we applied to the Colonial Secretary at Capetown for our money, when we were courteously, but decisively, informed that no such documents as those signed by us were known at headquarters, and that no record of them existed. And our case was not singular: the traders and Europeans generally suffered in the same way. But in the September of the following year, 1882, a commission appointed by the Colonial Government to examine all claims for compensation arrived at Thlotse, and we were awarded—though not until the month of November,

1883—a portion* of the amount due. I hope we were grateful. We had given up all hope, and had not expected to receive a farthing ; so we took the money with a hearty " thank you," on the principle that half a loaf is better than no bread.

A considerable part of the amount claimed was in compensation for the loss of the Training College building. This had been levelled to the ground by the troops, and even its site could hardly now be recognised. Its garden had of course gone also. Nor was this all. Some of the native refugees, who were still coming in in small parties, had taken possession of the ground, and built their huts upon it. It was therefore impossible for us to think of rebuilding the institution on its old site ; and, indeed, in view of the still unsettled state of the country, we considered it highly impolitic to attempt the establishment of a training school at all, until the advent of more propitious times, We therefore gave up the idea, and, with the consent of the donors of the original building fund, erected, as soon as the condition of the country warranted our doing so, a large and well-built schoolroom of burnt brick for our day schools, thereby supplying one great and increasing need of the Mission.

On the Ash Wednesday of 1882 it pleased God to call to her eternal rest a third member of our little band of workers. This was Mrs. Woodman, who died, after a few days' illness, at a farm on the Free State side of the Caledon almost opposite our station. The Woodmans had made that place their headquarters after leaving Harrismith, Mr. Woodman having seized the first opportunity of returning to Sekubu, and it was while he was engaged in rebuilding the huts and reorganizing the work of his old Mission that this bereavement fell upon him.

Mrs. Woodman was endeared to us all by her unaffected piety and gentleness, as well as by her untiring devotion to the work of Christ among the heathen. She was buried in the

---

* This was for damage done to the buildings *by the Colonial forces* ; no compensation being granted for that done by *the rebels.*

Mission cemetery, now greatly enlarged through the war; and her remains were followed to the grave by a large number of natives, who had learnt to love and esteem her for her labours among them. Their hearts, I am sure, went out in unison with our own to her stricken and desolate husband. Among the mourners was her brother Philip, a bright young fellow fresh from Oxford, who had come out to us on a visit to her and his elder brother, little dreaming that, in a few short weeks, he and his brother would be called upon to follow their sister to the grave.

The month of September, 1882, was a memorable one in the history of S. Saviour's, for in that month we received a visit from a very distinguished man—General Gordon, the hero of Khartoum.

I shall ever account it one of the greatest privileges of my life to have been permitted to make the acquaintance of so remarkable a man. Certainly one would never have expected to do so at a place so utterly remote, and out of the world, as Thlotse. In common with other Englishmen, I had heard of "Chinese Gordon," but seeing him face to face, and enjoying long conversations with him for hours together, was a possibility never even dreamt of. Yet it did actually happen, and in this wise.

In the April of 1881 the General, distressed by what he had heard of the state of affairs in Basutoland, telegraphed to the Premier of the Cape Ministry, offering to go out to South Africa, and assist in terminating the war, and reorganizing the administration of the country.

"The Cape Government," says Sir W. F. Butler,* "did not even think it necessary to reply to Gordon's offer of service." But "early in 1882 the new Cape Government suddenly bethought them of the man whose telegram their predecessors had not troubled themselves to reply to. Basutoland had proved

---

* Butler's Gordon, p. 180.

too hard a nut for the Colonial forces to crack." "Manifestly the sooner this very disreputable business was brought to an end the better for all parties. Would Gordon renew the offer he had made a year earlier? Yes, he would." *

The Ministry offered him the post of Commandant General of the Colonial Forces, and he was speedily on his way to the Cape. The appointment thus conferred on him necessitated his remaining in the Cape Colony for some months after his arrival; but in September he was free to proceed to Basutoland. He started at once, arriving in the country towards the end of the month in company with the Hon. J. W. Sauer, the new Secretary for Native Affairs. The Secretary's presence was urgently needed at Thlotse, and Gordon went northwards with him. Thus it was that I was privileged to meet him.

He could only stay in the place three days, and was, of course, during the greater part of the time, busily employed in investigating the details of the quarrel between the Basutos and the Government, as well as the position and prospects of the loyal natives at the present crisis. Once in the heart of the country, he soon grasped the situation of affairs.

With his enthusiastic love for Mission work he naturally felt drawn to our Mission, and when he learnt from actual observation how much our work had suffered, he deeply sympathized with us in our misfortunes. The whole of his spare time at Thlotse was spent in my hut. I remember so well his first visit to us. We were at breakfast, and he came in and joined us, sitting down on a bag of meal in lieu of a chair. The hut was mean and dilapidated. It had suffered grievously from the ravages of the war, and had not yet been properly repaired. It happened that that morning we had been unable to procure any meat, and there was therefore little upon the table except mealie meal porridge, and coffee.

* Ibid, p. 181.

I apologized for the scanty repast we had to offer, and our uest answered, in his quick, bright way, that the simpler the food the better he liked it, and that he admired asceticism. I confess I felt very guilty, for the " asceticism," if there was any, was by no means voluntary on my part.

Then we adjourned to my own rondavel, and had a good long talk about the affairs of Basutoland, and the best method of righting them. The next day he came and stayed with me four hours—four of the most delightful hours I have ever spent in my life. The General smoked his cigarettes, and I my pipe of Transvaal, while we discussed Mission work and its methods, gradually sliding off into Theology, and ending with the symbolism of the Old Testament ritual.

I have never yet met a man who knew the Bible—more especially the Old Testament—as he did. He was simply *saturated* with Scriptural knowledge, and knew by heart every provision of the Mosaic code. He had worked out in his own mind the symbolism of the Ceremonial Law down to its minutest details. I felt humbled and ashamed in the presence of this man " mighty in the Scriptures ": a layman, great in his own profession of arms, who had nevertheless found time, amid manifold duties and distractions, to study the Word of God so thoroughly that he put me, a commissioned ambassador of Christ, entirely to the blush.

Now and then in these conversations his own well known peculiar views came out; but they were at the worst quite harmless—at least, so it seemed to me—and on the essentials of the " faith once delivered to the saints" he was sound, orthodox, and Catholic to the core. He struck me as really humble minded, and penetrated with the mind and spirit of Christ. He had been drawn, he told me, " to realize more and more the blessedness of sacramental union with Jesus," and had an intense longing for frequent Communion. " One of my greatest trials," he said, " is that I am so often placed in circumstances where I cannot get THE BREAD—I mean the Sacramental food I value so much."

Yet we know he never shrank from duty, or from going to places where no sacramental means of grace, or even of corporate religious worship, was to be had, when the call came to do so. He spent the best years of his life in places, and among scenes, where the great Sacrament of Love was unknown, or where it was impossible to have it celebrated. Even in his last hours, and heroic death, there was no last Communion, no *Viaticum*, for one whose longing for it was so intense. Perhaps after all he hardly needed it as much as we do : he was so spiritually minded, and lived so habitually in the invisible. In any case, we may be sure that this privation was abundantly made up to him in spiritual communion with his Lord and Master, for General Gordon was *above all things a man of prayer*. In the midst of great and manifold distractions he was constantly alone with God, and mental prayer was a settled habit of his life.

There was about him, as we might have imagined, a dash of fatalism. He had spent long years in the wildnesses of Northern Africa, where this tone of mind is most marked ; and it was, perhaps, augmented by his natural tendency to mysticism. He often told me that he regarded himself " simply as an instrument, a tool—a very poor sort of tool, no doubt—but still a tool, an instrument in the Great Father's hands for carrying out His Divine purposes and will." Hence arose his fearlessness and absolute honesty of purpose. He feared no man ; and nothing would move him when he was once convinced of a certain truth, or a certain line of duty.

Speaking on one occasion of the future, he said that " he did not know where his lot would be cast, and he did not care so long as it would find him doing the will of God."

He had already come to the conclusion that there was but little hope of his being able to agree with the plans proposed by the Government for Basutoland. He trusted neither the measures nor the men. Rightly or wrongly, he had come to regard them as crooked. "I feel," he said, not long before he left us, "as if I should go up yonder," pointing to where the chief officials were, "and explode."

I besought him to remain, were it in any way possible, telling him that, at such a crisis the future of the country was in his hands, and that if Masupha could be induced to listen to anyone, I felt sure it would be to him. Alas! his foreboding was verified only too soon, as we all learnt to our cost.

But penetrated as he was with the conviction that God had a certain work for him to do, or rather that he was the instrument for working out the Divine will under certain circumstances and conditions, there was with this conviction another—I am sure not less deep—the conviction of his own unworthiness. This he bewailed to me more than once; and it was this humility of soul, this realization of his own frailty, which impelled him to cast himself daily and hourly at the feet of Christ in self-abasement. He longed to be like Christ, and have the mind of Christ, that he might be able in the spirit of Christ, and of Christ alone, to do the Father's will. And it was this aim that kept him *straight* as well as courageous. Without it I can imagine him becoming a fanatic: with it he was a devout soldier of God: an enthusiast if you will, but no fanatic.

It goes without saying that such a man could not remain unmoved when he came to know, by personal investigation, the wrongs which the loyals had suffered, not only at the hands of the rebel party, but also through the vacillation of the Government, and more especially through the sudden reversion of their policy. He no sooner knew the whole truth than, with the facts before him, he sought an interview with the loyal leader.

"Jonathan," he said, "I know all about you. I have heard everything, and I feel for you as much as one man can

JONATHAN MOLAPO.

feel for another who has been wronged. But I cannot help you. I have no power or position to enable me to do so. I am only on a visit here, and have come up into the country to try to make peace. But because I feel for you, and know what you have suffered for your loyalty to the Queen of England, I will do the little I can for you. That little is in the way of advice. I have no power or authority to do more. But I have seen many men of many nations, and some of them were in positions like yours. So I will give you my advice as a brother who feels for you in your trouble, if you care to take it."

The chief replied that " he was most grateful to the General for his kindly greeting, and his words of sympathy. It was the first time he had heard such words from an officer of the Queen of England, or of her Government, for a very long time."

" Well," said the General, " this is my advice. Let nothing tempt you to desert the Queen of England, or her Government, whether it be her Government in England, or at the Cape. Do not join your enemies and rivals here merely for the sake of getting back the men who have deserted you. You will gain nothing by doing so, either from the Government or from the rebels. They will both of them despise you, and no one will believe in you. And do not expect the Government to help you now. They cannot. It is beyond their power at present, even if they wished to do so. Remain faithful and obedient, and then at some future time, when the wheel turns round once more, they will be able to help you and support your rightful claims.

" And then as to your people. Rule them justly and uprightly. Do not oppress them. Do not eat them up when you have the chance of doing so, as so many chiefs do. Be gentle with them, and show all the mercy you can. But, above all, be just, and straight, and upright in your dealings with them. Then you will gain their respect and their affection too.

Then, you may depend upon it, before very long, all those men who have deserted you will gradually come back to you. They know that you are their lawful chief, and they will contrast your mild and just rule with the harsh methods of the other chiefs.

"You will thus have two ways of winning them back to you: your birthright, and your personal character. These will, I am sure, tell upon them now that the question of the guns is settled, and you will see that they will come back to you by twos and threes. Then, by and bye, when your position becomes strong, and your influence stronger, *you will be able to use your faithful followers as a whip with which to flog your enemies and reduce them to subjection.* In that way you will recover, not only your rightful position in the tribe, but also a great part of the cattle which has been taken from you."

Jonathan Molapo was wise enough to take the advice thus tendered to him, and General Gordon's words were abundantly and literally fulfilled. The chief ruled his people firmly, but gently, doing all in his power to conciliate and attract waverers, until gradually his seven hundred men became more than a thousand. These he used, as we shall see in the course of this narrative, and used most effectively, " as a whip with which to flog his enemies," until the tables were completely turned, and he became, as he continues to-day, the most powerful, as well as the most loyal chief in Northern Basutoland.

Just before leaving Thlotse, Gordon came into my rondavel, and had a last talk about the Mission and its prospects. These were far from bright at the time, as the reader knows; and I felt much cheered by our conversation, and by the General's hopeful and kindly words of sympathy and encouragement. Then he suddenly turned to me and said, " How are you off for money?" I told him that we had very little, but could not say that we were in *immediate* need of any, as we did not think it safe or prudent to venture upon erecting permanent buildings during the present unsettled state of the country.

" You will need some before long," he replied. " You will need it when you begin to build, and I hope that will be soon. I wish I could give you more, but I shall be very glad if you will take the little mite I have to offer."

So saying, he took out his purse, and put five sovereigns into my hand.

I felt much touched by this spontaneous act of generosity towards a mission which had no sort of special claim upon him; but, indeed, it was only in keeping with his lavish charities and manifold deeds of love at Woolwich and elsewhere.

Then we went together into the House of God and prayed for each other, for the work of the Mission, and for poor torn, distracted Basutoland, still bleeding from its wounds; after which I said some collects from the Prayer Book, ending with the Apostolic Benediction.

Half-an-hour afterwards the General was on his way southwards to Masupha, and three days had barely elapsed when we heard, to our dismay, though hardly to our astonishment, that he had resigned his post, and was already on his way to England.

How this happened is well known to many in South Africa, and has been already told to the world by an authority which few will question. In Sir W. F. Butler's words, " it was necessary to get rid of this just steward. . . . At last the opposition " (to Gordon) " reached a culminating point. Three out of the four Basuto chiefs had agreed to terms; the fourth, Masupha, still refused to accept magistrates and levy a hut tax. Gordon felt certain that if he could personally interview the chief, he, too, would accept the terms now offered. For this purpose he starts for Masupha's stronghold. It has been agreed between him and the head magistrate that no overt act of hostility was to be made against Masupha until Gordon had first tried his hand at personal negotiation. After that had failed, pressure might be applied. But no sooner had Gordon reached the Basuto chief's

P

stronghold, and while he was yet negotiating with him, than news arrived that a hostile expedition was approaching. If Masupha Moshesh did not make the envoy pay with his life for this breach of all the rules of fair fighting, it was assuredly not because the men, who were at the bottom of this movement, had taken steps to prevent such a calamity. After this it was not possible to continue in the service of the Cape Government. Gordon resigned his post as Commandant General, and, embarking for England, arrived home early in the month of November, 1882." *

I will only add to this that from what I have heard, and from what I know of Masupha personally, there was every chance of the negotiation succeeding, and of the obstinate old chief being induced to listen to reason, when the conference between the two men was thus broken in upon and brought to an end. Gordon had been too outspoken and too straight. He had told the Ministry and their supporters many unpalatable truths, and he must go.

They certainly took the most effective means to make him throw up his commission. To stand before a heathen chief as a base deceiver was a position which General Gordon, of all men, would never consent to occupy, and his opponents knew it. Their stratagem succeeded; to the injury and loss, it must be added, of the Basuto nation.

After Gordon's departure a report was circulated that he was mad. That, no doubt, was the shortest and easiest way of getting over the difficulty of his resignation. A then highly placed official in the Lesuto repeated the report to me, and declared that he believed it to be true. "He is mad, I tell you ; perfectly mad," said he. And when I, with some pardonable indignation (as I venture to think), demanded his evidence or authority for such a statement, this was his reply : " Gordon had said and done things which only a madman would say and do."

---

* Butler's Gordon, p. 183.

"What things?" I asked. "Well, I know of two things," was the answer.

"The first is that on one occasion, in my hearing, he declared that his greatest wish was to retire to Mount Carmel, and get the monks there to let him have two or three rooms in the monastery, in which he would be able to board, lodge, and instruct some of the Syrian boys of the lower classes. Now I am sure you will grant," continued my friend, "that a man in General Gordon's position would never talk of throwing up his appointment, and sacrificing his prospects, in order to devote himself to the education of a lot of little Arab cads, if he were not out of his mind. He must be mad; perfectly mad, I repeat."

"And what other mad thing did he do or say?" said I.

"Oh, I will tell you! He did a most extraordinary thing! I did not see it myself, but a friend of mine, upon whose word I can rely, did. He actually went out into the veldt alone one day, knelt upon the ground, stretched out his arms at full length in the form of a cross, and prayed! It is absolutely true, I assure you; for my friend happened accidentally to come upon him when so engaged. The thing is beyond doubt; and no sane man would dream of doing such a thing. No; you do not know Gordon. He is mad; perfectly mad, I assure you."

The reader may smile, but this was the only evidence I could ever get for the truthfulness of the report that had been so industriously spread abroad.

Gordon was mad because he desired to do a deed of love to the little ones for whom his Master laid down His life: he was mad because, like his Master, "he went out into a solitary place alone and prayed."* Happy madness! "If they have called the Master of the house Beelzebub, much more shall they call them of His household."†

These two assertions were quite true. I can myself bear independent testimony to the truth of the first, for I well remem-

---

* S. Mark i. 35. † S. Matthew x. 25.

ber how, in one of our talks together, the General told me that he could conceive no more delightful work than the training of the young. We were speaking of our Mission school at the time, and presently our conversation glided off, as it often had a tendency to do, to the East and to Palestine. It was then that he told me "he had a great wish in his heart which he feared could never be carried out." "It is," said he, "to retire, when I am no more wanted in the world, to the monastery on Mount Carmel, and to establish there, with the consent of the good monks, a little refuge or school for poor Syrian boys, where they could be instructed in the Christian faith, and at the same time trained to be useful in the world." He added, "This is only a wish, you know. And I don't know whether the monks would let me do such a work, or spare me a few rooms for the purpose. And besides, I doubt whether I shall ever be able to undertake it. But I think it would be a really good work to undertake, and I have no doubt I should be happy in it."

He never was able to undertake it, as we know. He was called by duty to a sterner and more heroic task.

I have said that the other "charge" against him was also true. From what I have been able to gather, I believe the facts to be these. While on his way up to us he stayed one night, together with some of the officials, at one of the southern magistracies. The condition of Basutoland was causing him great anxiety, and he was trying to find the best plan for meeting and settling the difficulties of the country. At such times he had a habit of retiring into his room, sometimes for hours, in order the better to think out the problem before him, often seeking guidance concerning it in prayer. Everyone who has travelled in South Africa knows that such privacy is not always to be found, especially during a hurried journey up country. The General, wishing to find a little time for himself before starting for the north, and anxious not to cause inconvenience to anyone, rose early and walked out alone into the veldt. One of his fellow travellers went in search of him when breakfast time drew near, and, to his astonishment, came unexpectedly upon him kneeling behind a rock with his arms stretched heavenwards in prayer.

It may have been that some of the officials with whom Gordon was at this time associated were not men of prayer. I do not say it was so: I have no right to say such a thing, and I hope that the supposition is altogether incorrect; but it *may* have been that such was the case. And if so, I suppose it would be quite natural for such persons to regard the General as eccentric, when they heard that he had actually been seen praying in the veldt. But it was not he who was mad. Certainly it may be affirmed with perfect truth that, among the swarm of new and continually changing officials with which Basutoland was at that time beset, there were some who could not in the least understand him. He was altogether too far above them. Their thoughts were not his thoughts, nor their ways his ways. But whatever may have been their opinion of Gordon, one great fact stands out very clearly in the subsequent course of events: that they themselves were not conspicuous examples of success in the administration of the affairs of the country.

"The horses of the pacha went down to the water to be shod, and the *beetle* put out his leg too," says an Eastern proverb.

General Gordon will long be remembered at Thlotse, and by no one with more gratitude and veneration than by Jonathan Molapo. When the news of his tragic death at Khartoum reached us—but little more than two years after we had parted from him—all hearts were moved, and the chief bewailed his fate with lamentations of sorrow and with tears.

Mad or not mad, so long as England can produce men like Gordon, she will continue to be great.

CHAPTER XIV.

Inter-tribal Warfare.

1883.

Matikete and Mabelete—Jonathan and Joel—The Opening of the Ball—One More Attack upon Thlotse—The Fight over the River—Defeat of the Eastern Confederates—Burning of the Crops by Lepoko—Burning of Molapo's House—Thlotse Saved—Joel and his Allies driven Home—Massacres—Weakness of the Government—Rumours of Abandonment—Increase of Drunkenness—Revival of Heathenism—An Important Pitso.

We have now to deal with the inter-tribal warfare which convulsed the northern part of the country for a period of three years—from November, 1882, to November, 1885.

Such a struggle was inevitable. Abandoned to their fate by the Government on whose behalf they had taken up arms; despoiled of their possessions by the party which was now in high favour at head-quarters, both in England and at the Cape; with a promise of compensation for their losses not yet even partially performed; cooped up in a narrow space at Thlotse camp, and unable to return to their ruined homes or cultivate their former fields; Jonathan and his men felt that the hour had come when they must do or die. There was virtually no government in the country, or at any rate none with sufficient power to restrain them from striking a blow at their enemies whenever they might feel strong enough to do so.

Jonathan was biding his time, and acting on the advice which Gordon had given him. The old officials, who knew the sacrifices that he and his people had made on behalf of law and order, had been carefully got rid of. They had been either removed or pensioned; and their successors were instructed, no doubt with the best intentions, to reserve their sympathies and favours for the disaffected party.

The struggle which now broke out afresh in the north between the two parties was a struggle for supremacy, a question of *borèna* (chieftainship), though it had its roots in the old question of loyalty *versus* rebellion. Neither party fought against the Queen's Government as such, but the old names of Matikete and Mabelete were retained, and only ceased when, three years afterwards, the struggle came definitely to an end. It is by these names, rather than by those of "loyals" and "rebels," that the two parties will be henceforth known in these pages; the two latter appellations being no longer literally applicable to them.

At first the Mabelete were altogether the stronger. They outnumbered the Matikete almost ten to one, were better armed, richer, and in possession of almost all the northern districts. But there was, as Gordon had foretold there would be, a continuous leakage from them to Jonathan; for the principle of loyalty to the chief is deeply enshrined within the native breast. "By twos and threes" the more moderate party among the "rebels," who had probably never wished to break either with the British Government or with their chief, began to return to their lawful leader, encouraged to do so by the reports they daily heard of his gentleness and uprightness in dealing with his people.

When Molapo died, he had by his wives and concubines over one hundred and twenty children who survived him. The exact number is doubtful, but as far as I have been able to gather it is 128. His eldest son by Mamosa, his great wife, was Josefa, who, as has already been mentioned, early developed a tendency to mania, and became, soon after he attained to manhood, completely imbecile. His claim to the succession was therefore set aside; and the *second* son by Mamosa was nominated by Molapo as his heir and successor in the chieftainship.

This son was Jonathan, and his right to the succession was universally acknowledged throughout the tribe during Molapo's lifetime.

But he had a formidable rival and competitor to his claims in the person of Joel, his half-brother, Molapo's eldest son by his second wife. It is well to remind the reader of these facts once more, since they are so very important. The other sons of the old chief were divided in their sympathies. All, however, sided, ostensibly at any rate, with Jonathan until the "gun" question arose; when, finding that he had resolved to obey the law, the great majority of them threw in their lot with Joel. The most celebrated among these half-brothers were Khethise and Tlasua; the former proving himself an able and intrepid leader in many of the fights which took place in and around Thlotse; the latter becoming celebrated for his tenacity of purpose and ferocity of disposition—a ferocity which gained for him among the Matikete the name of *Nkue*, (Tiger).

Tlasua's territory was the nearest to Thlotse, and he was a most troublesome neighbour. He was the most vigilant and ruthless of our enemies, distinguishing himself in many an independent skirmish on his own account until he was finally subdued in 1885. True to the last in his hatred to his half-brother and elder, he elected to occupy a remote strip of country in the Malutis as the nominal vassal of Joel, rather than remain on his own ground and acknowledge the supremacy of Jonathan. The hatred between the two parties was inconceivably great. Family feuds are proverbially the most bitter, and in the case of these half-brothers, and indeed of the whole house of Molapo, the spirit of "hatred, malice, and all uncharitableness" reigned supreme. They seemed to forget, utterly and entirely, their common bond of brotherhood as the sons of one father, so implacable was the hate they bore to one another. Polygamy had, indeed, brought with it its curse in the case of the sons of Molapo. Like Solomon, the old chief had gone after many strange women, who turned away his heart from God and from the faith he professed in his youth; and now his sons were biting and devouring one another, and filling the land with violence and bloodshed.

The first really serious engagement took place on S. Andrew's Day, 30th November, 1882, at Sebotoane. The Mabelete had provoked it by their continued ill treatment of those of Jonathan's people who had gone out from time to time to plough and sow their fields. They made life unendurable to the luckless Matikete, and, notwithstanding the disparity in numbers, Jonathan resolved to strike a blow at them, or perish in the attempt. The officials looked on and did nothing: there was, in truth, nothing that they could do. They prophesied Jonathan's utter and speedy destruction; while the other Europeans in the place sympathized with him, and felt that, great as were the odds against him, it was by no means certain that he would not succeed. It is true he had only 700 men with him, but they were veterans; and his general, Makotoko, was a host in himself. Moreover, the Matikete were becoming desperate. They said, and with truth: "We cannot live on any longer as we do. We have no homes, no lands, no hope of a future before us, and we are in daily and hourly danger of destruction. The Government has cast us off, and we must do what we can for ourselves. We do not *live* now: we only *exist*. We must all die sooner or later, and it is better for us to perish at once on the field of battle than live the lives of dogs, as we do now. Let us win back our hearths and homes, or die in the attempt to do so." And so they prepared in this desperate mood for the decisive day. In this spirit they marched up the heights of Sebotoane to confront the 5,000 Mabelete who awaited them.

Joel and his allies had taken up a strong position on the table-land above, from whence they could command the country for miles round, and effectually harry, by their marauding bands, any of the Matikete who attempted to cultivate their old fields;

and it was necessary to dislodge them, and compel them to retreat to their own districts, if the Matikete were to escape starvation during the coming year.

The battle which ensued was fierce and long contested, but in the end the Matikete were successful at all points, driving their enemies right across the mountain slopes, and pursuing them for a distance of twenty miles—almost, indeed, to the very doors of their huts. A large number of the Mabelete, with Joel at their head, fled over the Caledon into Free State territory, much to the annoyance of the border farmers, who protested against this invasion of their homesteads by an armed multitude of demoralized and fugitive savages. The Government officials, amazed at the turn which events were taking, and alarmed at the incursion of a host of their own barbarians into the territory of a foreign country, besought Jonathan to return home without delay; *congratulating him upon his victory*, but at the same time threatening him that, if he did not at once desist from further hostilities, *he and his people would forfeit the compensation money due to them*. This threat proved effectual, and the Matikete returned to Thlotse in triumph, celebrating their victory with the usual war dance.

The action at Sebotoane proved to be the turning of the scale. From henceforth Jonathan's star was in the ascendant, and he and his followers were no longer treated with contumely by the officials, or hindered from cultivating their fields by their enemies. Sebotoane brought us peace for a time—the first real peace we had known for three years. The country for many miles round Thlotse was open to us, and, although the season for ploughing and sowing mabèlè was ended, there was still time to put in maize. To work, therefore, everyone now went with all his might. The plough and the pick took the places of the rifle and the assagai, and during the next three weeks the ground was everywhere broken up, and large quantities of maize were sowed, most of which was above ground, and looking strong and vigorous by Christmas. It was very late, but there was just a chance of its ripening before the winter frosts set in. Everyone was once more in good heart, and hopeful for the future.

But we were not yet out of the wood, for, in the following March, we were aware that a general combination of the Mabelete was again being formed against us, with the redoubtable Masupha at its back. The combination was well-planned and exceedingly formidable. Thlotse was to be invaded, plundered, burnt, and levelled to the ground, and the ripening crops were to be trodden under foot and destroyed. Jonathan and his friends, both white and black, were to be eaten up entirely and absolutely, once and for all.

The danger was no light one, for Masupha was very powerful, and was at this time the sole ruler of his own territory. He altogether ignored the authority of the Government; would have no magistrate or official of any kind, European or native, in his country; and issued his own passes, which were stamped with his own seal, and recognized as valid in the Orange Free State. The Volksraad of that state regarded British authority as practically defunct in Basutoland—a conclusion which was certainly not altogether unwarranted by the actual condition of the country, in which, as we see, chaos reigned supreme.

But the astute and masterful old chief was not without his difficulties. He was, in truth, divided between political policy and personal affection. On the one hand, he hated and despised the Government and all its doings; and small wonder that he should do so after all that had happened—more especially after what had taken place while Gordon was with him treating for peace in the Queen's name. But, on the other hand, he loved Jonathan, the avowed leader of the loyals. Nay, he not only loved him; he admired and respected him. The old man had been, as we know, a great and renowned warrior in his younger days, and he could not help admiring the bravery and consistency of his nephew. Jonathan was his own favourite brother's son, and was, moreover, his son-in-law, married to one of his best loved daughters; and " blood is thicker than water" everywhere. It is very seldom that a Basuto chief will turn against his own brother, the son of his own father and mother; and, I for one, judging from my own observation and experience of the natives, did not believe that Masupha would do any actual bodily harm to one who stood to him in the twofold relationship of son-in-law and nephew. Still, as the Mabelete of the north had appealed to him for aid, and as he was regarded as their virtual leader and chief, he felt himself bound to support them.

The Paramount Chief, Letsie, was at this time, through his persistent double dealing, in favour with neither party. He had indeed enough to do to hold his own, and control his multitudinous and turbulent sons in his own special district. He was therefore, for the present, put out of consideration; though both parties at times, when it suited their purpose, made a show of appealing to his judgment and authority.

The summer passed away peacefully, the rainy season was over, the crops were fast ripening, and the early frosts were just about to set in, when the storm burst upon us in all its fury. This was on the 3rd of May. For a week previously each day had brought rumours of an attack on the morrow, and very few of us were able to trust ourselves to sleep at night, not knowing when the enemy might appear. Our scouts brought us news from day to day of the movements of the confederates, and on the 2nd we received a boastful message from Tlasua, the Tiger, that he intended to sleep at Thlotse on the following night. The town was to be razed to the ground, and everyone and everything in it to be made an end of; "but," said he, " I shall save one house—only one—that I may be able to sleep comfortably in the place." Threatened men live long, thought I. Thlotse has gone through so much, and has escaped so often, that it will not do to despair yet. Still, the situation was undoubtedly grave—grave in the extreme. We knew that the confederates had at last agreed upon a common plan of action, thought out with commendable skill; and our position seemed desperate, if not absolutely hopeless.

Their plan was this: the northern detachment, about 5,000 strong, under Joel and Matela, was to advance through the Leribe Pass, leave a guard at the village of Leribe (six miles distant), cross the undulating country that intervened, and attack us at our most vulnerable point, the north. This was, as the reader knows, exactly where our Mission was situated, and it would, therefore, be the first object of attack. The eastern detachment, numbering nearly 6,000, under Ramanella, Khethise, Tlasua, and Makoa, was to cross the Thlotse, and charge us up the slope in the direction of the Residency; while the southern, Masupha's, under his eldest son Lepoko, and about 2,000 in number, was to surround us on the south, and cut off our retreat in that direction. The west was, of course, open, but it would be difficult, if not impossible, for us to escape over the Caledon, the heights being everywhere precipitous, and lined with gigantic rocks and slippery boulders. Moreover, our village no longer possessed any fortifications or earthworks worthy of the name, all these having been suffered to fall into decay; and the space covered by the 1,500 houses and huts in the place was so considerable, that it was impossible with our numbers to defend even the half of it. We were thus exposed to the enemy on all sides except the west.

Jonathan's men now numbered 1,700, one thousand of whom were seasoned soldiers, devoted to him heart and soul. The remainder consisted of seceders from the Mabilete, who had come to recognise him as their rightful chief.

On the morning of the 3rd, looking across the undulating country over the Thlotse, we could see the different regiments of the eastern contingent advancing in good order from their several starting points. They came on leisurely enough at a walking pace, until by nine o'clock they were within half-a-mile of the river. Here they halted, united, and rested for a few minutes before crossing. Masupha's men were reported to be massed behind Tsikoane on the south, and were, therefore, not yet visible. The northern contingent was said to be in the Leribe Pass, attempting to force an entrance through the village.

Jonathan had posted his nephew, a young chief named Motsuène, at the foot of the pass, with orders to hold it at all risks. This young chief was the son of the insane eldest son of Molapo already mentioned, and, in accordance with the declaration of Moshesh, was regarded as heir to the Paramount Chieftainship of the whole tribe. During the rebellion he had been residing at Matsieng, under the care of his grandfather, Letsie, and he had only recently come into the northern district. He was an untried man, and proved himself on this occasion to be quite incompetent in the field. It must, however, be said in justice to him, that probably he was not altogether accountable for his actions, since, shortly afterwards, he developed symptoms of the same distressing malady as that to which his father has been the prey. He had with him some 800 of his own men, sufficient, that is, to hold the pass and the village against all comers, had they resolutely determined to do so.

Jonathan's plan was a bold one. Perhaps it would be truer to call it audacious. Relying on Motsuène to hold the northern confederates in check, and thinking it impossible to defend so large a place as Thlotse with only 1,700 men, he "took the bull by the horns," and galloped across the Thlotse at the head of his whole force to give battle to Ramanella and his allies on the rising ground above the eastern bank of the river, ere they could cross and surround us. It was an exciting moment. I stood on the stoep of the Residency, only about a mile distant from the scene of action, and saw through a powerful glass all that happened. Our men went down the slopes almost at a hand gallop, as only natives can do, crossed the Thlotse, which was then low, and rode up its eastern bank in excellent order. It must be remembered that they were all mounted, as were the enemy. They then extended with the chief at their head, the veteran Makotoko riding by his side. The allied forces were drawn up, apparently awaiting them. Evidently it was to be a hand to hand encounter.

For a moment the two contending parties stood irresolute, contemplating each other. Then Jonathan, seeing that the enemy made no sign, gave the word to advance; and he and his men galloped up to within 300 yards' distance of the allied forces. Both parties then opened fire, at first without much effect, for natives are in general but poor marksmen, and waste a great deal of powder and shot to no purpose. But soon several men were observed to reel in their saddles, and some fell to the ground, notably on the side of the Mabelete. These were at once picked up, and carried off on horseback, by men evidently told off for the purpose. Then Jonathan, seeing, I suppose, that the decisive moment had come, ordered a general charge. With a great "Hurrah!" which they had learnt from the English in the preceding war, he and his men dashed forward into the very ranks of the enemy. They were outnumbered by nearly four to one; but, fighting as they were for hearth and home, wives and children, and everything else that was dear, and smarting under manifold and accumulated outrages and wrongs, their onward sweep was irresistible. Then ensued a fierce fight at close quarters, in which the assagai did its deadly work all too well. The Mabelete, disorganized and dislodged from their ground by the first onslaught, nevertheless managed to rally, and their superior numbers made us tremble for the fate of the intrepid band that had attacked them—nay, if the truth must be told, made us tremble for our own, for we well knew what awaited us in the event of Jonathan being driven back.

I looked on in breathless suspense, sending up a heartfelt prayer to the God of battles that He would defend the right, and give victory to the oppressed. For about ten minutes the issue seemed doubtful, when suddenly our brave fellows charged again with redoubled vigour into the very midst of the confederates, stabbing right and left, and using the battle-axe in all directions, until the foe began to waver once more, and then, in another moment, to fly.

Then there ensued a great chase—the most exciting chase that I ever witnessed; and I have, alas! seen many during these African experiences. The Mabelete ran for dear life; galloping furiously across country through ravines, dongas, and sloots, over hill and dale, rock and stream, right onward, helter skelter, to their mountain villages, eight, ten, twenty miles distant. But the Matikete pursued them everywhere, cutting down every straggler in the retreat. Each regiment of the confederates made for its own villages, and our men divided themselves into companies and followed them separately, chasing them up to—nay, beyond—their kraals, and setting fire to village after village. From eleven o'clock until dark we could see volumes of smoke arising from every townlet and village along the slopes and spurs of the Malutis. Khethise's and Tlasua's were the first in flames; then followed Makua's and others of lesser size and importance. Ramanella's alone escaped, being very distant, and built on a spur of the Malutis, most difficult of access — a fitting stronghold for such a nest of robbers as Ramanella and his men have always proved themselves to be.

But what of Masupha's contingent? At this all-critical moment they did nothing. They might easily have marched into Thlotse from the south, when they saw that our men were absent from the town, pursuing their own flying allied forces; but they did nothing. I suspect that Lepoko had received secret orders from his father not to attack his brother-in-law, or suffer the blood of his men to be shed in defence of Joel and his supporters, who were by no means personal favourites with the old warrior. At all events, whatever was the reason, Masupha's two thousand did nothing in the way of fighting that day, but contented themselves for a time with looking on at the defeat and utter rout of their friends. But when the smoke of the burning villages in the mountains began to fill the air, Lepoko, thinking, I suppose, that some sort of action was expected of him, instead of retaliating by burning our roofs over our heads and piercing us to the ground with the assagai, as he might easily have done, revenged himself and his friends in another and characteristically savage way. Ordering his men southwards, he proceeded to ravage and lay waste the whole of the country along his line of march, right down to the Putiatsana, the stream which divides Jonathan's territory from Masupha's. It is true that he burnt no villages, for there were hardly any to burn; the Matikete, as we know, not having yet dared to return to their former dwelling-places and rebuild them. But he seized and carried off whatever grain had been harvested (it was not much), and cut down or trampled upon, and destroyed, all the standing corn, both Kafir corn and mealies, in every field that his men came to. When it is remembered that nearly every valley, as well as the greater number of the uplands, for a distance of twenty miles—the route he had to traverse—was nothing less than a continuous series of cornfields, some idea may be formed of the havoc caused by this ruthless proceeding.

But he did not even stop at that. Though it was winter, and frosts were beginning to set in at night with all their rigour, this unfeeling ruffian ordered his men to strip every Matikete woman they could find in the mealie fields, or hidden away behind the rocks, take from her her one poor garment, her blanket or petticoat of skin, and leave her naked and helpless in the bitter cold of a Basutoland winter's night. And these indignities were accompanied, in many cases, by the grossest outrages, which the hapless victims were powerless to avert. Some of the poor creatures died from ill-usage and exposure; others fled to "caves and dens of the earth," where they remained for days until they were rescued by their husbands or brothers; while the remainder escaped into the Free State, where the border Boers, to their honour be it said, received them with kindness, providing them with food, shelter, and clothing, until they could return to their relatives at Thlotse or elsewhere. It may be as well to say here that the young chief who thus distinguished himself did not live many years after these occurrences. Lepoko literally drank himself to death a few years ago while yet in the flower of manhood, leaving a little son to succeed him, who, let us hope, may prove a better man than his father when the time comes for him to occupy the chieftainship of the Berea district.

But though the eastern column had been routed and put to flight, and Masupha's men had retired, we were not yet safe. Nay, the greatest danger of all was yet to come.

About eleven o'clock we were startled at seeing a dense pillar of smoke arising from the north in the direction of Leribe. We at once guessed that the worst had happened: Joel had forced his way through the pass, and was burning the town. A mounted man was despatched in hot haste to ascertain if such was really the case, and in less than an hour he returned with the news that our surmise was only too true. Leribe was in flames, and Joel, flushed with success, was rapidly advancing upon Thlotse. Motsuene had proved to be no Leonidas, and Leribe no Thermopylæ. He and his men had either been bought over by the enemy, or they were arrant cowards. In any case, they allowed themselves to be dislodged from their position without so much as striking a blow, and retired ignominiously southwards, leaving the Mabelete masters of the field. The path being thus open to him, Joel at once advanced and burnt the town. This township, lying under the Leribe mountain, was founded by his father Molapo; and the reader will remember that it was there that Mr. Lacy and I had our first interview with that chief before settling in the country.

Not content with burning every hut in the place, the Mabelete chief did a deed which struck awe into the hearts of the whole people. He burnt down his father's house with his own hands! This act, so unparalleled in native warfare, displayed the depth of his jealousy and hatred of his half-brother; for the house, a large and, in its way, not unhandsome structure of stone, went with the chieftainship, and was, of course, claimed by Jonathan, though he had been as yet unable, from the force of circumstances, to occupy it. There is, as we know, among the Basutos a great reverence for their ancestors, and a father, whether living or departed, is always held in honour by his sons; and thus the burning not only of his father's village, but even of his very house, the house which was Molapo's special pride and boast, was an act which drew down upon Joel the execrations of the whole tribe. There can be no doubt that old Letsie marked it and remembered it; for from that time forth the Paramount Chief showed Jonathan more favour, though he was not yet prepared to side with him openly.

Leribe destroyed and Motsuene disposed of, there was now no obstacle to an easy march upon Thlotse, and by 12 o'clock the northern column was on its way to the town. It seemed now that nothing could save us from destruction. Jonathan and his men were miles and miles away in the east and south-east, still pursuing the eastern Mabelete, and were, of course, unconscious of our danger, relying as they did upon Motsuene. But even had they known of our peril, they could have done nothing to save us, for by the time they returned Thlotse would have become a heap of smoking ruins. Added to this, we were as yet ignorant of the movements of Lepoko, and expected every moment to hear that he was advancing upon us from the south.

So great and so imminent was the danger, that I began to

think that our last hour was indeed come. There was only a tiny handful of men left in the place. With the exception of the Fingo Chief, Tukunya, and thirty of his warriors, every fighting man was out with Jonathan. There were also some fifteen or sixteen native police and six white men, the latter being the Resident (Mr. Bailie), his clerk, a young trader, Dr. Taylor, Mr. Champernowne, and myself. The few European women and children had been sent away in the morning over the border to Ficksburg; and Mr. Reading, at my earnest desire, had also gone over the Caledon, taking with him our native boarders and domestics. He was a high spirited young fellow, and it went much against the grain to go off and leave Thlotse and its people to their fate; but he was very good about it; obeyed my wishes to the letter, and sat with our little mission family upon the banks of the river all through the weary hours, expecting every moment to see the smoke of the town rising in the distance.

The danger being now so pressing, I desired Mr. Champernowne to ride over the border likewise, and join our party there, telling him that I hoped, please God, to be able to find my way down the rocks, and effect my escape by the bridle path, when the worst came to the worst. Both my colleagues were very good in thus sacrificing their own wishes to mine, for I am sure it cost them a good deal to do so; but they could do nothing to avert the threatened destruction, and it was an unspeakable relief to know that they, together with the other inmates of our Mission huts, were safe on Free State soil.

And now was seen a sight which moved me strangely—a spectacle which I hope never to behold again, and which stirred every pulse of one's being. In the doorway of each hut in the town stood a woman, with blanched cheeks and clenched teeth (natives when greatly scared often present a ghastly drab-green appearance), holding her assagai in her hand, ready to defend herself and her little ones within to the last. Though the men were all away, the women and children had remained: there was no place for them to escape to. And now each woman brought out the spare assagai and stood awaiting her fate, resolved to sell her life as dearly as she could. I went round to several of the huts. The whole place seemed absolutely deserted, save for the little knot of loyal Fingoes who were gathered together in one corner, each man standing at his horse's head, straining his eyes for a sight of the enemy. Not a woman or child was visible: they had all retired in terror to their huts. The very dogs, as if scenting danger, had retreated likewise to their hiding-places; not one was to be seen anywhere. My own horse was standing outside the garden gate, saddled and bridled, tethered to a willow tree.

Our doom seemed certain; our fate sealed. Human aid there was none. I thought that nothing but a miracle could save us. I stood outside the study, looking intently towards the Leribe road, expecting every moment to see the dreaded forms of our foes emerge from the hollow, and appear upon the brow of the hill in front of us, from which they would with the greatest ease descend upon us, and cut our throats, or stab us to death, and burn our village to the ground.

I had stayed behind simply from a sense of duty, feeling that I ought to be one of the last to leave the place, should I, by the mercy of God, be spared to do so. I felt at that moment anything but heroic, and I do not think I can honestly say that I *liked* the situation in which I found myself; but, as an American hero (in fiction) observed on a celebrated occasion, " Vocation is vocation, and dooty is dooty—some." So I stayed to see the end. Furthermore, it must be remembered that nearly all our Christian women and children were in the place, and I could not help hoping that, were I permitted to escape, I might be able, in my flight, to afford some little help to these helpless members of my flock, or, at least, succeed in rescuing one of the children from the jaws of death and carry it off triumphantly on my saddle.

So as I strained my eyes in the direction of the enemy, I lifted up my heart in prayer, commending myself and the poor souls around me to Him Who is able to save even unto the uttermost, and beseeching Him to extend to us the arms of His mercy, and deliver us even at the eleventh hour, when all earthly succour had failed us.

While thus engaged, I felt someone touch me on the shoulder, and, looking round, I saw at my side a Hottentot—a convert whom I had baptized two years before—by name Hermanus Norkie. He had been living for the last year in the Orange Free State, and I was therefore doubly astonished to see him standing close to me at such a moment.

"Hermanus," said I, "what brings you here at such a time as this? Why have you ventured into such danger?"

"Mynheer," he replied, "I was riding along the frontier to pay a visit to a friend, when I heard the firing, and saw the smoke in the distance yonder. They told me in Ficksburg that Leribe was already burnt, and that Thlotse was being attacked, and could not possibly this time escape destruction. So I thought of Mynheer, and made all speed to get here, taking the short cuts which are still open on the Free State side, and thinking that I might be of some use in helping Mynheer or some of the brethren to escape before it was too late. I am well mounted, and my horse is ready outside the gate at Mynheer's service." "The rebels," he added, "are advancing sure enough, but they are not riding hard. They are coming on at their ease, feeling, no doubt, sure of their prey."

"Well," I said, "it is indeed kind of you to come, and to risk your life for mine. But I do not need your horse; my own is saddled up waiting for me. As to the brethren, they are safe on the other side of the river. But since you are here, I will tell you what you can do for me. You can make haste and light the fire, and make a cup of coffee for each of us."

I was feeling, truth to say, hungry as well as weary, having tasted but little that day, and it was now past noon.

The Hottentot's face brightened up and broke into a broad smile at the suggestion. Under what conceivable circumstances would a Hottentot not welcome the idea of a fire and a bowl of coffee?

But there was more to follow.

"Mynheer," he replied in his very best Dutch—it must be remembered that Cape Dutch is now the language of most natives of Hottentot extraction—"Mynheer, that is a good thought, and if Mynheer likes I will prepare a little meat in the frying-pan likewise.

"But," said I, "that is impossible. There is no meat in the house, and, besides, we should have to fly before it could possibly be ready."

"Mynheer," he rejoined, "I have two or three *ribbetjes*" (ribs of salted mutton) "with me in the saddle-bag, and a couple of onions too. I thought I might find Mynheer in this strait, and so I bought some in Ficksburg, and brought them with me. Let me fry them. The rebels will hardly be here for half-an-hour, and before that time the *ribbetjes*, as well as the coffee, will be ready. Then, if the worst comes to the worst, and we cannot escape, we will eat our last meal together and die together. But the rebels have not got us yet into their clutches, and *the Lord is great*. So, do you keep a sharp look out from the gate, and let me go inside and do my duty."

"Ruling passion strong in death," thought I. So I bowed to my Hottentot brother's decision, grateful to him for his kindness, and appreciating, I trust, the spirit of love and self-sacrifice which had prompted him to come at such a time of danger. In a moment he had disappeared inside the rondavel used as a kitchen, and in a few moments more the fire had begun to blaze.

At this juncture I noticed Tukunya's men and the Resident,

accompanied by about half a dozen of his police, crossing the road which runs along in front of our station. They were evidently going out to the Leribe road to see how far off the Mabelete still were. I mounted and followed them, joined by the doctor, who, true to his profession, had remained at his post to the last. He shook his head gravely over our prospects of escape, agreeing with me that, as far as we could see, the town must fall. We rode on and attached ourselves to Tukunya's party, making straight for the Leribe road. We had no sooner reached the brow of the hill, about six hundred yards distant from our lower garden wall, than we saw the enemy in full force almost within a mile of us. To the right, under Sebotoane, were Motsuene and his men, who had off-saddled, and remained there out of danger to see the end.

Joel's host came on leisurely and confidently enough, advancing to within five hundred yards' distance of us, when they suddenly halted. Both parties waited, native fashion, to see what would happen, or who would strike the first blow. Then Tukunya's men formed themselves into two little groups of about fifteen each, at something like three hundred yards' distance from each other, in front of the long extended line of Joel's five thousand.

During this movement the doctor and I rode quietly back to our respective duties. Mine was to warn my faithful old Hottentot friend, and to make such hurried arrangements as were possible for the safety of our Christian women and children. A deathlike silence reigned around. Nothing living was visible in the place: everything was still. But just as I arrived at our gate I heard the report of a gun. It was from Tukunya's men, and was followed a few seconds afterwards by two or three shots in quick succession.

What could be the meaning of it? Surely Tukunya would not be mad enough to challenge such a multitude to the fight? But in very deed and truth he had done so! And, what is more: looked at simply from a human point of view, his very audacity proved to be our salvation. For the Mabelete, seeing these two little groups of men drawn up in front of them, and doubtless recognising them as Tukunya's Fingoes, must have imagined that heavy reserves were hidden somewhere close at hand, and that this was simply a trap to lure them into the town to their destruction. They could easily see that the place appeared deserted, and that there was no movement or sign of life in it, and this made them, no doubt, only the more suspicious. Yet they must have known from their spies and scouts that the whole of Jonathan's men had followed him into the field, and they knew equally well that, engaged as he was with their allies in the mountains, he could not possibly return to Thlotse before they had had time to work their entire will upon it. Yet they made no movement. They seemed paralyzed with indecision, and allowed the thirty Fingoes to take " pot shots " at them for at least ten minutes !

All this I saw while standing at my pony's head with his bridle in my hand, sipping the *Kommetje* of coffee which my Hottentot friend's kindness and self-sacrifice had procured for me. The minutes seemed very long as one by one they passed away, I straining my eyes to observe what was going on and when the next movement would be made, expecting every moment to see our enemies rush in upon us and overwhelm us. But they made no sign, until suddenly, to my amazement, I saw them turn their horses' heads in the direction of Sebotoane, wheel round, and quietly retire towards the bridle paths which led up to the top of the mountain !

It seemed a dream, an optical illusion, an impossibility; but it was simple, downright fact. They had actually abandoned the prey when it was absolutely within their grasp. It was inexplicable, but it was true. The words of the prophet concerning God's city of old came unbidden to my mind: "He shall not come into this city, nor shoot an arrow there, nor come before it with shields, nor cast a bank against it. For I will defend this city to save it."*

God had, indeed, wrought a great deliverance in thus turning aside our enemies and giving them over to the strong delusion which took possession of their minds, so that they might not harm us. When I look back upon that wonderful deliverance at this distance of time, I cannot help feeling more and more that the hand of our God was upon us for good on that memorable day.

I hastened into the chapel, there to pour forth my thanksgivings to our Father in heaven, Who had so signally saved us when all hope of deliverance was lost.

"Ah," said the Hottentot, as we shared together in peace and with hearts full of gladness the repast which his bounty had provided, "I told Mynheer that *the Lord is great*. See, I did not bring the *ribbetjes* in vain. I have had time to cook them after all. Eat them, Mynheer. You are tired and hungry, and they are done to a nicety."

I can honestly say that I required no persuasion to act upon his advice. I took my full share of them, and savoury indeed they proved to be.

Joel, after ascending Sebotoane, off-saddled on the top of the mountain, he and his men looking down upon us, but doing nothing. Our great hope now was that our own men might return home ere the enemy changed his mind, or removed from his present position. It was now half-past one o'clock, but not until nearly three hours afterwards did Jonathan appear. He and his men rode into the town exulting in their victory, only then for the first time to learn the extent of the danger we had gone through during their absence. They had fully relied upon Motsuene, and when they heard what had happened, their indignation was loud and deep, both against him and his men. They saw that even now the danger had not

* Isaiah xxxvii. 33, 35.

entirely passed away, for they beheld the Mabelete looking down upon them from the heights of Sebotoane. In less than two hours it would be dark, and they felt that Joel must not be allowed to remain where he was until the morning. Fatigued as they were, for they had been in the saddle since eight o'clock, they nevertheless resolved to follow up the enemy at once and dislodge him from his position. But their horses were so jaded and so unfit for further effort that an off-saddle, however short, was absolutely necessary if the field was again to be taken that day. So an hour's rest was ordered; and then, just as the sun was dipping under the horizon, the command was given to mount, and the whole force marched out towards the northern road.

My colleagues and our mission boys had in the meantime returned home, the tidings of our remarkable escape having become speedily known along the Free State border; and we all stood together and looked at our men as they marched down the path which skirts the wall of the Mission, in excellent order and with pealing hurrahs, on their way to Sebotoane. By the time they reached the bridle paths leading up the mountain, darkness had set in, and we lost sight of them. But an hour afterwards we could hear the battle raging in all its fury on the flat mountain top. The volley firing was incessant; the sharp, short crack of the rifles reverberating grandly through the mountain gorges. It was undoubtedly a critical moment, but we had every confidence in the bravery of our men, and could not bring ourselves to believe that they would suffer themselves to be defeated, since to be so would mean absolute destruction to them, and cruel wrong and suffering to their wives and children. Nor were we disappointed in our confidence. After a time the firing became more and more distant, and we trusted that it signified the retreat of the Mabelete. Such, indeed, was the case. There was a struggle—not very prolonged—and then our men, bearing down upon them with all their might, succeeded in driving them from their position. They fled over the mountain (Sebotoane is the extreme end of a long straggling spur of the Malutis), and were chased for more than ten miles through the night by Jonathan, who, with his victorious warriors, returned in the small hours of the morning, and bivouacked on the spot that the enemy had occupied.

Then the savage came out in the Mabelete. In revenge for their defeat and the failure of their enterprise, they put to death in cold blood, on the following morning, six helpless old men and three children, whom they found in one of the outlying villages belonging to the Matikete, after having burnt the half-dozen huts of the place.

Jonathan and his commando, after remaining three days upon the heights of Sebotoane, and assuring themselves that all was now safe and the enemy thoroughly beaten and dispersed, returned home, and celebrated their double victory by such a war dance as I have never witnessed either before or since, making the air resound for miles with their repeated shouts of joy.

Thus ended this signal deliverance from death and destruction—one of the most noteworthy, surely, if not indeed the greatest, in the history of Thlotse.

I could not ascertain the number of the killed and wounded on either side, partly, as the reader knows, because natives have but little idea of numbers, and partly also, because they like to hide their losses as carefully as possible. But it was certain that the Mabelete lost far more heavily than our own men, and, indeed, they themselves allowed such to be the case. Asking one of Jonathan's men, a few days afterwards, how many of the enemy had fallen, he replied that he could not tell. " They were many," said he, " but not so many as men thought." I was glad to hear it. And then he added complainingly, and with a rueful expression of countenance : " Moruti, we could not kill as many as we wished. They ran away so fast that we could not get at them ; *they would not stop to let us kill them.*"

The combination against the lawful chief was now, for the present at least, broken up, and for the first time since the middle of 1880 we began to breathe really freely, and to look forward to *a settled and permanent peace*. So great and decisive was the victory, that the name of Jonathan was henceforth spread abroad in song and chant throughout the country, while the very sight of a Letikete inspired feelings of fear and respect where hitherto he had been despised and contemned. Thus had Gordon's forecast been entirely realized and brought to pass: the chief had used his men "as a whip with which to chastise his enemies." Certainly it was a great deliverance; for from that time forward, though outbreaks occurred at intervals in the extreme north, Thlotse itself was never again in the danger that it had been. The tables were completely turned, once and for all; and every man could now "sit under his own vine and fig-tree" in peace.

But it may be asked what the Government had been doing during this time of anarchy and bloodshed. The reply is, nothing. The Government officials, having no power at their back, and little or no influence over the chiefs, were powerless to do anything effectual to check the outbreak. They had, in truth, an impossible task to perform. They were commissioned to govern the country by "moral force"; but such moral force as the Government had ever possessed was completely played out. A new Chief Magistrate, or "Governor's Agent," Captain Blyth, C.M.G., had recently been appointed and sent up to Maseru, and he hastened at once to Thlotse to investigate the state of affairs, and to endeavour to effect a permanent settlement between the rival factions. He was a high-principled, humane man, and was inexpressibly shocked and grieved at what he heard and saw. In particular, the massacre of the old men and the children, the indignities offered to the women, and the destruction of the crops, moved him greatly. Highly indignant as he was at these atrocities, he was powerless to bring the perpetrators of them to book, and could only return to Maseru and report to the Governor what had taken place.

There can, I suppose, be no doubt that the Government and the Parliament of the Cape were both of them getting sick of Basutoland, and desired to get rid of the country altogether. The President of the Orange Free State, too, was continually complaining of the condition of affairs in the nominally British territory, and pointed out with unanswerable force how injuriously it affected the peace and well-being of the Free State subjects in the eastern towns, and, in fact, everywhere along the border. It was rumoured that we were to be abandoned altogether. The Cape Government would have no more to do with us, and the Imperial Government were unwilling to step in and take us under their control. But, at any rate, now that the confederation of the Mabelete was broken up, we in the north had a real breathing time, and thankful enough we were for such a boon after the strain of the last three or four years.

What added to the misery of the situation all round was that drunkenness was rife throughout the land. For several years past the great majority of both chiefs and people had given themselves up to it, until it bid fair to be the destruction of the tribe. The strongest and vilest " Cape smoke " (we used to call it " Kill at forty yards ") was daily smuggled into the country by unprincipled white men, both Dutch and English, and a whole string of illicit grog shops and canteens existed along the border. Some of the chiefs, and many of the people, drank themselves to death. It was no uncommon thing to see a native take a whole bottle of brandy, and drink it off, raw as it was, in less than a quarter of an hour. Some of the people took to mixing the spirit with their joala, drinking large draughts of the villainous compound, which maddened and poisoned them at the same time. Ten years of such excesses would, I think, have gone far to destroy the nation, and a people of less splendid physique would have suffered from them much more than the

Basutos did. Of course, there were not wanting cynical white men with no faith, no principle, and no bowels of compassion, who looked on with indifference, or even gloated over this condition of things. "Let the niggers drink themselves to death," was their cry. "It is the best thing that could happen to the country and to ourselves." But the vast majority of the Colonists and the Free State burghers regarded the sight with very different feelings. They were profoundly distressed at the spectacle of such a promising people as the Basutos going headlong to destruction.

With this drunkenness there took place also, as was inevitable, a revival of heathenism. It looked as if the good that had been gradually accomplished in some parts of the country by fifty years of continuous and arduous labour on the part of the various Christian missionaries would be undone and swept away in five. I am thankful to be able to bear witness that during these days of "blasphemy and rebuke" our little band of converts at Thlotse stood firm to their faith in Christ. Not one relapsed into heathenism, and but few gave themselves up to strong drink. By God's grace and mercy nearly all of them came out of the ordeal unscathed, and, I would fain hope, with their faith increased and strengthened.

"When things are at their worst, they begin to mend," says the proverb; and it was so in our case. Early in November we heard that the Imperial Government had consented to relieve the Cape of the responsibility of governing Basutoland, and intended taking us under its own control. This proved to be the case, to our intense relief and joy; for, as I have said, we were in great fear lest we should be abandoned altogether.

A Pitso of the whole tribe was summoned by the Governor's Agent at Makolo-kolo, near Maseru, on the 29th November, 1883, at which a letter was read from Lord Derby, the Secretary of State for the Colonies, requesting the people to say whether they were willing to be taken over by the Imperial Government or not. All the chiefs and headmen, with the exception of Masupha and his subordinates, at once gladly consented to receive Imperial officers into the country, and pledged themselves to obey the laws and regulations laid down for them by Her Majesty the Queen. In particular, the Paramount Chief was urgent that he and his people should come under the direct control of England, feeling, doubtless, that this was the only means left of preserving the Basutos as a nation. It was hoped that the perverse obstinacy of Masupha might in time be conquered, and that he too might consent to be " taken up by his mother."

To this request of the majority of the tribe the Imperial Government acceded, and early in the ensuing year Lt.-Col. Clarke, R.A., was appointed Resident Commissioner in Basutoland, under the direction and control of the Governor of the Cape Colony in his capacity of High Commissioner for South Africa. There was thus a revived hope of a prosperous and peaceful future before us, and everyone rejoiced that the Basutos were once more in the "cave" that Moshesh had provided for them.

CHAPTER XV.

Gleams of Hope.

1884.

Outlook at the Commencement of 1884—Sir Marshall Clarke—More Fighting—Impaired Health of Mr. Champernowne—The Outbreak at Thaba 'Nchu—Tsipinare and Samuel—The Barolong Scattered—Opening of the New School Room—Tukunya and his People.

From what has been said in the preceding chapter, the reader will have gathered that very little in the way of solid progress in the work of evangelization could be hoped for while Basutoland continued in the state of ferment I have described. The outlook at the commencement of 1884 was undoubtedly much brighter than it had been since the rebellion; but we felt, nevertheless, that there were still " lions in the path." As long as Masupha continued in his present position of opposition to, and independence of, all government except his own, so long would the Mabelete of the north be encouraged in their lawlessness and contempt for all and every kind of authority. Yet, as we have seen, there was little or no fear of their being able to threaten our peace at Thlotse itself, and the daily routine of the Mission could therefore now go on without let or hindrance. Accordingly we resumed our work with renewed energy. The services were once more held without interruption or distraction; the congregations increased, and the school was full to overflowing. We felt that the present was a time of fresh ploughing and sowing rather than reaping, and we were content to go on, possessing our souls in patience, until, please God, the time might come when the harvest of present efforts might be gathered in. When, in the providence of God, the country should be restored to law and order, and the people no longer agitated by internal conflicts, we felt assured that Divine grace would triumph in the hearts of many who had been in a greater or lesser degree attracted to the Mission, but who had not yet been moved to give themselves to Christ. The Lord Jesus would yet, we believed, " see of the travail of His Soul and be satisfied " among the heathen of the Lesuto.

The arrival of the Imperial Commissioner in March shed a fresh gleam of hope across our path, and we all felt that his presence was a guarantee that England did not intend to desert us. It was also, as we would fain believe, an earnest of good government, which must, ere long, when the nation had had time to reflect and passions to calm down, result in a settled and abiding peace. Lt.-Col. (now Sir Marshall) Clarke was an officer of much experience, and his subsequent administration of public affairs proves that he came into the country with the best

R

interests of the Basutos at heart. Known personally by his friends as a man of high principle, unspotted reputation, and calm judgment, he assumed the reins of government at a time when the great majority of the people were growing weary of internal discord and internecine strife. It was, of course, in Masupha's district, and among the malcontents of the north, that disaffection and opposition would be experienced, and the Commissioner had a difficult, as well as a delicate, task to perform in reducing these districts to obedience and order; for it must be remembered that he brought with him no military force, and possessed no authority save that of the name of the Queen of England. That he has to a large extent succeeded in accomplishing his purpose is proof of his uprightness and sagacity, as well as his firmness and patience. The Imperial Government had granted to the Basutos practical autonomy—perhaps it may be better called local self-government, guided by the moral suasion of the Commissioner. A code of laws, simple in its aim and scope, and founded on that in force before the rebellion, was adopted and promulged by the High Commissioner, and these laws were to be enforced by the joint authority of the Commissioner and the Paramount Chief. It is but fair to say that Sir Marshall Clarke has from the first been effectively aided and supported by an efficient and able body of officers in his efforts to promote the well-being of the people.

One of the very first things he had to do, soon after his arrival in the country, was to endeavour to settle the long-standing dispute between Jonathan and Joel. In this he was ably assisted by Lerothodi, who, at the wish of his father, exerted his whole influence on behalf of peace; doing his utmost, though not with entire success, to overcome the perverseness, and curb the insolence of Joel, and so bring this upstart potentate to reason. Hostilities had broken out again on the 14th March between the Mabelete and the Matikete, the former, as usual, being the aggressors. True to their old methods, they had oppressed and maltreated those of the latter who endeavoured to occupy their old homes, and cultivate their old lands, near the borders of Joel's district, carrying off their cattle whenever they found a chance of doing so, and otherwise making their position intolerable. Thanks to this last defeat, Joel was no longer powerful enough to threaten Thlotse, or the villages and corn lands near it, but what mischief he could do north of Leribe he did. Jonathan was bound to protect and defend the rights and interests of his people, and he accordingly marched north, and punished the Mabelete severely, gaining a signal advantage over them at a spot not far from our mission station of Sekubu. But he was hastily summoned back to Thlotse before he could strike a final blow at these implacable foes, and disperse them once for all; for during his absence two of Masupha's sons had hastily organized a commando, and were again threatening to attack us from the south. Once more the European women and children were sent away in haste over the Caledon, and Jonathan marched southwards to meet the advancing commando. He encountered it at a spot about ten miles distant, and inflicted upon it a severe defeat, but only after a determined struggle, which lasted nearly a whole day. Masupha's men then drew off, and retreated to the Malutis, where they remained for some days, taking counse together. The upshot of this was that they formed a plan for seizing Jonathan's cattle, but were unsuccessful in carrying it out; and, failing in this, they fell back into their old methods of procedure, and revenged themselves by trampling down and destroying the greater portion of the crops still remaining between Tsikoane and the Putiatsana, a distance of more than fifteen miles.

Col. Clarke, who had arrived at Maseru during these disturbances, prevailed upon Letsie to command Masupha to withdraw his marauders to their own districts; and in the meantime Joel and large numbers of his men had, as usual, fled to the Free State, and taken refuge there after their defeat, leaving forty-six of the killed behind them on the battle-field. This was the condition of affairs which the new Commissioner found upon his entrance into the country, and he lost no time in trying to set things straight, and put an end to such destructive inter-tribal warfare.

At this time the state of Mr. Champernowne's health was causing me considerable anxiety. Never strong, he seemed now to be on the point of collapsing altogether, and I felt that the only thing which could permanently benefit him was a voyage to England. Six months before this he had felt very jaded and "worked out," and had, at my solicitation, taken a two months' holiday in Kaffraria and Natal; but though he returned to us in better health, the improvement was only transient, and at Easter he broke down once more. Evidently the only thing to be done was to pack him off to England as soon as possible, so that he might arrive there in time for the summer. He did not like the idea of going, but I was resolute about it, and after a good deal of persuasion, prevailed upon him to apply for a year's leave and start at once. He left us at the end of April, going home by way of Natal. An amusing incident occurred while he was at Pietermaritzburg, on his way to Durban. He was staying at one of the hotels in the city, and, as the weather was wet and wintry, was muffled up in a shabby-looking great coat and woollen scarf, which did not help to impart a clerical character to his appearance. Sitting down one day at luncheon, the individual next to him at table, a gentleman-like looking man, began a conversation with him after the free and easy manner of people in young countries, little imagining that he was a clergyman. After the state of the weather had been duly and sufficiently discussed in the usual introductory fashion, the stranger turned to my colleague and asked "where he hailed from, and where he was going to?"

"From Basutoland," answered Mr. Champernowne, "and I am on my way home to England."

"From Basutoland, eh?" said his acquaintance. "And you are bound for the old country?"

"Yes!"

"Oh, well, I am in luck's way to-day, for I have long wanted to find out all about Basutoland; and now you will be able to tell me. You have had a lot of fighting up there, have you not?"

"Yes, we have had nothing but 'wars and rumours of wars' ever since the rebellion of 1880. At least, that has been the case in the part of the country in which I have been living."

"What part is that, may I ask?"

"Leribe; the northern district of the country."

"Oh, yes, Leribe. I have heard of it. Rather a fine district for mealies, is it not?"

"Yes, and for Kafir corn too."

"Ah, to be sure. And what have you been doing up there? Trading, I suppose?"

"No, I am a missionary."

"A missionary!"

Then there was a slight pause; and then, with a sneer, "Oh, yes, to be sure. I see! *You have made your pile, and are about to retire from business!*"

The idea of such a man as my brother priest "making his pile," and "retiring from business" was delicious, and we laughed over it again and again.

Now this hotel stranger must not be taken to represent the feeling of Colonists generally on the subject of missions and missionaries. In my experience the Africander, whether of English or of Dutch extraction, though not usually as keen as could be wished on the subject of missions, never opposes them. and invariably treats missionaries with respect, no matter to what body of Christians they may belong. The greatest enemies of missions are a certain class of *Englishmen* who go out to South Africa, perhaps with the object of settling, more often only with the idea of "seeing the country" and writing a book about it; but who, wherever they go, take with them much flippancy and little faith. For the honour of our nation they are not very numerous, and South Africa is such a "slow" country that such people are not likely to settle down in it permanently. We need not, therefore, say any more about them.

In the July of this year we were startled by the news of a sudden and sanguinary revolution at Thaba 'Nchu, the capital of the Barolong territory. The reader may perhaps remember that about fifty years before a certain quantity of ground round the Thaba 'Nchu mountains had been granted by Moshesh to the Barolong fugitives, who had fled southwards when their country was overrun by the armies of Moselekatse. Upon the death of their chief, Moroka, in 1880, there was the almost inevitable dispute as to the right of succession. Two men, Samuel Lefulere and Tsipinare, claimed the chieftainship. The first was regarded as the actual son of Moroka, the second as a reputed son; and each considered himself to be the rightful heir and successor of the departed chief. Into the merits of the quarrel I have no wish to enter, and, indeed, to do so would be foreign to the purpose of this book. Suffice it to say that the great majority of the Barolong, as well as the tribes round about them, favoured the claims of Samuel, and regarded him as their lawful chief. But Tsipinare, who had been for some years, with Moroka's consent, the virtual ruler of the town of Thaba 'Nchu, had a considerable party there who sided with him. He was a man of much greater force of character than his rival, had displayed much more ability in public affairs, and had contrived to gain the favour of the European traders and other foreign residents. Samuel's party was strongest in the rural districts, especially in the northern division, where his own village was situated.

As there seemed to be no chance of a settlement between the two parties without an appeal to arms, the President of the Orange Free State, Sir John Brand, volunteered to act as mediator, and, if they desired it, arbitrator between the claimants. They both acceded to his proposal, each pledging himself to abide by his decision, and regard it as final. The President, after a patient examination of the evidence tendered to him, gave his judgment in favour of Tsipinare. Samuel was to retain his present rights at his own village and in his own district, but Tsipinare was to be Paramount Chief of the whole Barolong territory.

The President's decision was at once repudiated by Samuel and his supporters, who, as has been said, formed by far the majority of the people; and even among the Boers of the neighbouring farms there were not wanting those who roundly declared that the President had not been impartial in his judgment. That Sir John Brand would have decided otherwise than according to the evidence laid before him is a supposition that no one who knew that eminent statesman could entertain for a single moment. He was universally recognised throughout South Africa as the most fair-minded and upright of men, and if his decision ran counter to the convictions of so many who professed to know the rights of the case, it could only be because the whole of the evidence in favour of Samuel was not forthcoming, or because he was in possession of facts and testimonies with regard to Tsipinare of which people in general were ignorant.

The unsuccessful claimant contented himself for the time with protesting against the judgment, and allowed his rival to assume the chieftainship of the tribe; but it gradually became known that a fermentation of feeling was going on beneath the surface of things, and there had been from time to time ominous whisperings and rumours of an intended rising, which caused much uneasiness to the Europeans of the town of Thaba 'Nchu, as well as to the supporters of Tsipinare.

But latterly these rumours had ceased, and most people had begun to think that Samuel and his party had tacitly acquiesced in the new order of things, and that the power of Tsipinare was now firmly established. They were destined to be wofully deceived. In the July of this year, four years after the judgment of Sir John Brand had been given, Samuel and a large body of his followers, led on by several Boers, suddenly and unexpectedly fell upon the town of Thaba 'Nchu, burnt a large portion of it, overpowered Tsipinare's guards, most of whom made but little effort to defend their master, and killed the chief himself. Tsipinare fell, together with " Long John," one of his most devoted followers, overpowered by numbers; and for a few short hours Samuel gained his object, and occupied the seat of power of the Barolong.

I recollect very well the evening when the news of the rising first came to us. There was staying with us at the time one of the mission workers at Thaba 'Nchu, an enthusiastic, energetic young man of Irish extraction—a young fellow who was good nature personified, and who never tired of singing the praises of the green glades of the Emerald Isle in the raciest of " brogues." He had come up to S. Saviour's to spend a well-earned holiday, and, on the night when the weekly post came in, was sitting with me in the study, discussing over a friendly pipe the bright and promising prospects of the Thaba 'Nchu Mission. I opened the *Friend of the Free State*, the Bloemfontein paper, and, to my astonishment, the first words that caught my eye were "Terrible doings at Thaba 'Nchu." "The Stad burnt." " Tsipinare killed." " Samuel in Possession "; and other sentences of like import.

"Why," said I to my young friend, "what is all this dreadful news about Thaba 'Nchu ? "

"What news ? " said he, in his short, sharp, eager way.

I read the paragraph.

"What, what, *Fhwat* do you say?" he shouted. " Tsipinare killed! No, no, it can't be! Tell me again. Tell me that it isn't true ! "

I read him the detailed account of the attack upon the chief, and of the brave way in which he met his fate. Then my poor friend, who had formed a real attachment to Tsipinare, burst out in his grief and excitement:

"Tsipinare dead! Killed! Murdered! Murdered, did you say? Och, och! Poor Tsipinare! Dead! Assassinated! Murdered! *Murdered in his night-shirt; and I wasn't there to help him!* Let me go! Let me saddle up my pony at once and *go to his rescue!*"

"Go to his rescue!" I exclaimed. "Why, don't you hear that he is dead?"

The idea of a native chief meeting his death in such a garment, and that, too, at high noon, was too much. It was so inexpressibly droll that, in spite of the dreadful news, I could not refrain from laughing. I ought not, of course, to have done so, and it agitated my friend more than ever. He sprang up, made a huge stride, and, forgetting where he was, and that the hut was so small, came suddenly in contact with the wall, fairly butting his head against it in his forgetfulness and excitement. Finding no outlet in that direction for his wounded feelings, he began to stamp upon the floor (it was only an earthen one) with all his fury, shouting "Och, och, and I wasn't there! Murdered! Murdered, did ye say? Murdered, and I wasn't there! Poor Tsipinare!"

Then in his distress he proceeded to *tear his hair* (fortunately he had a good share of that article), beating his big broad forehead with his huge fist, as if it had not already been bumped enough by its contact with the wall.

I could not calm him. He plucked out his hair by the roots, "as if," to use the words of Montaign, "baldness were a cure for grief;" until at last the paroxysm was over, and I got him to bed.

I took care to keep him with us for at least a week afterwards, knowing only too well that, were he to return to Thaba

'Nchu, he would soon be in the middle of a mob of Tsipinare's partisans, and might be tempted to say and do things which would be good neither for the Mission, nor himself.

Samuel's triumph was short lived. The President ordered out at once a strong commando, and, after a few days' parley, the chief, together with his principal captains and the Boers who were with him, surrendered themselves to the Orange Free State authorities. They were conveyed to Bloemfontein, where they were tried soon afterwards upon the charge of murdering a chief in alliance with the Orange Free State. The trial caused great excitement all over the country, and ended in their acquittal, on the ground that the crime had been committed in independent territory beyond the jurisdiction of the court. Samuel, and Bogatcho his chief warrior, a brave, and in his way honourable man, and several other leaders of the Barolong, were conveyed to the borders of the State, proclaimed as outlaws, and forbidden to put their foot again upon Free State soil. The Barolong country was then annexed to the Republic of the Orange Free State, due regard having been had to vested rights and interests. The Volksraad granted certain portions of the territory to chiefs and others not implicated in the recent outbreak, and set apart a considerable quantity of land on the northern border as a reserve for the natives who wished to remain in the country. The remainder was divided into farms and sold, a magistrate being placed at the town of Thaba 'Nchu. Thus the Barolong ceased to exist any longer as an independent people.

How far these proceedings on the part of the Government of the Orange Free State were righteous and justifiable, is a question which it would not become me to answer. It is beyond my province to do so. No doubt a great deal could be said on both sides. I will only remark here that, surrounded as the Barolong country everywhere was by Free State territory, it is hardly to be supposed that the Government of the Republic would consent to allow a chief, whose claims had been officially rejected, to set up an independent authority at Thaba 'Nchu under such circumstances. When the choice lay between annexation and anarchy, there could scarcely be a doubt which would be preferred. As to the confiscation of much of the native land, one can only deplore it. But it is only fair to remember that, though such a proceeding is not the one usually adopted by the British power in South Africa, there have not been wanting many exceptions to the rule, and that on a larger scale than in the example before us. The Barolong country was a small one—only thirty-three miles by about thirty-six—and contained a population of something less than 20,000, ten thousand of which resided at the central town of Thaba 'Nchu.

Thus broken up, and their tribal unity and independence destroyed, the Barolong people were soon after scattered. About half of them acquiesced in the new order of things, and remained in their old homes; a considerable fragment found its way north to Bechuanaland, the land of their forefathers; some were spread over the Free State; and the remainder, with Samuel, Bogatcho, and other leaders at their head, found a refuge in Basutoland, where they were kindly received by Letsie. A considerable portion of these latter were Christians, most of whom were converts to our own Church; and these now form a portion of the congregation of S. Barnabas', Masite, under the charge of the Rev. T. Woodman.

The August of this year saw an important addition to our mission buildings in the shape of a new school-room. My readers will recollect that the buildings hitherto erected were merely temporary structures of raw brick, or sod, plastered with mud; but we felt that the time had at last come for the realization of our plans as to structures of a more permanent and substantial character. We greatly needed a mission house, our huts being, after so many years' wear and tear, almost beyond repair; but a still greater need was a suitable school-room for the rapidly increasing numbers of our children. Tukunya, the faithful old Fingo chief, and his people, had left us the year before, migrating far to the south, at the wish of the Colonial Government. There was no prospect of their return being permitted to their former homes in Masupha's district, and the Government therefore came to the rescue, and provided for them a place of refuge in the Matatiele division, where they would henceforth be allowed to dwell in peace, without molestation from their old enemies. They left Thlotse with real regret, and we on our part were sorry to lose them. Heathens as they were, they possessed that "honest and good heart" so necessary to the reception of the truths of the Gospel; and the seed already sowed seemed about to germinate, and spring up, when they were thus called away to a distant part of South Africa, remote from any direct Christian influence. Over thirty of their boys had attended the Mission school, and were among the most promising of our pupils, and they were such bright, manly little lads, that their departure was a special source of regret to us. I believe they were equally sorry to leave the school, but there was no help for it; and we could only hope and pray that the good impression already made upon them might not be allowed to dwindle away and die. Sooner or later some Christian influence would reach them, and we trusted that our early efforts for their conversion might not be altogether without fruit.

Notwithstanding the loss of these thirty promising lads, the school was now larger than ever, and we all heartily rejoiced when, on the 7th August, the new building was completed and ready for use.

It was opened by an impressive Benedictory Service, at which nearly all our native Christians, a large number of heathen, and all the school children were present; and this service was succeeded by a big feast—the greatest feast we had ever given. More than 1,000 natives came, with Jonathan at their head, to rejoice with us; and mainly through the kindness of our old and steadfast friend, Mr. Richards, of Leribe, we were able to give a hearty meal of bread, beef, and coffee, not only to the children, but to over three hundred of their elders. It was a happy day— the first real mission feast that we had been able to have since the commencement of our troubles in 1880.

The school-room was a substantial, well-built structure of burnt brick, fifty-two feet by twenty-eight, under a galvanized iron roof, and the possession of it enabled us to pull down the partition wall between the old school-room and the chapel, thereby giving us in the latter an additional space of twenty feet. This also was a great boon—indeed, an absolute necessity— in view of the increasing numbers attending the Sunday services. Even then we began to feel the need of a much larger place of worship, but, at any rate, this additional room would help to suffice for present necessities: and we hoped that, please God, some day in the not distant future, we might be able to realize the dream of years by the erection of a comely house of prayer and praise, suited to the needs and requirements of the Mission.

CHAPTER XVI.

Quiet Progress.

1885—1886.

Death of Canon Beckett—Return of Mr. Champernowne—Additional Compound—The New Mission House—The Liquor Trouble Settled—A New Mission at Masite—Election of a New Bishop—Last Struggles of the Mabelete—Submission of Masupha—Signs of Progress—Enclosure of the Cemetery and Compounds—Revival of the Choir—Visit of the Bishop—A Cannibal Story.

EARLY in 1885 the Mission, and with it the whole diocese, sustained a great loss in the death of Canon Beckett, a venerable priest and servant of God, who had been the founder, and for many years the Superior of the Community of S. Augustine,

and had always taken the deepest interest in the progress of the work at Thlotse. He had helped us, as the reader knows, by his wise advice as well as by his alms, to start the Mission, and only a few months before his death he had provided desks and other furniture for the new school. He entered into rest on the 23rd of February, after years of patient suffering, and more years still of tenacious, uphill work; and his name will be long held in veneration over all the eastern part of the diocese of Bloemfontein.*
" He rests from his labours, and his works do follow him." †

At Easter we were gladdened by the return of my colleague, in renewed health and strength His visit to England had proved of benefit to the Mission as well as to himself, since our friends at home had been able to hear from the lips of one of the Mission clergy a plain, unvarnished account of our actual position, of the trials which had beset us, and of the future prospects of the work. He had stirred up and stimulated the interest of many members of the Bloemfontein Association, and it was a great comfort to us to know that many whom we had never seen in the flesh, and perhaps never should see, were daily interceding for us at the Throne of Grace. It brought home to us in a very real way the invigorating and consoling verity of the Communion of Saints.

Some time before this the Resident, Mr. Alexander Bailie, had generously assigned to the Mission a new compound, in lieu of the former one, which, it will be remembered, had been occupied by the refugees who crowded into the place soon after the destruction of the training college buildings. In this compound I proceeded to build our long needed and long delayed Mission house; and on the 1st May, the Feast of SS. Philip and James, it was dedicated to God for the use of the Mission workers by a

---

* He was succeeded by the Rev. Canon Douglas, a devoted and widely loved man, under whose wise rule and guidance the Society of S. Augustine has been fruitful in many good works.

† Rev. xiv. 13.

Benedictory Service, according to the custom of the diocese. Thus, after a nine years' sojourn in rondavels, we at last had, thanks be to God, a good substantial roof over our heads, and rooms large enough to move about in, without our heads bobbing against a strip of biltong or a coil of riems hanging from the rafters, or our shins coming in contact with the edge of a box, bath, or bedstead. The house was substantially built of burnt brick, ceiled, and contained nine rooms. It possessed also a good broad *stoep*, to which a verandah has since been added, and last, but not least, it stood in its own grounds. These latter have since been laid out, and planted with trees and shrubs; a portion being reserved as an orchard, with a kitchen garden attached to it. This house was provided and paid for entirely by the Mission workers, and their relations, and personal friends, supplemented by the offerings of the European congregation, the diocese being at the time too poor to make a grant from its general fund for such a purpose.

The July of this year saw the end of the iniquitous, and soul and body destroying liquor traffic in Basutoland. Col. Clarke and his officers had been doing their best for some time past to suppress it; and now the chiefs, stirred up by an instinct of self-preservation, and by the earnest exhortations of Mopedi, began to second their endeavours, and co-operate with them in the good work. Mopedi was the chief of Witze's Hoek, a Basuto reserve in the north-eastern corner of the Orange Free State; and, seeing the havoc wrought by strong drink among his kinsmen, he made a tour through the Lesuto during the months of May and June, and succeeded in effectually rousing Letsie, and the people generally, to a sense of their danger.

Brandy runners had now "a bad quarter of an hour." They were tracked out, their waggons and oxen confiscated, the fire water spilled upon the ground (its stench was sometimes almost overpowering), and they themselves, when caught, heavily fined. The Government of the Republic did their share of the good work also, and did it so effectually that the border canteens and illicit grog depôts were put down, and extinguished once for all. The plague was stopped, and from that day to this there have been no brandy runners, either in Basutoland, or the Orange Free State. Let us trust that this nefarious traffic may never again be permitted to enter either country.

This year also witnessed a forward movement on the part of the Church. A new Mission was established at Masite, the village of the chief Bereng, in the centre of the country. In the general ferment caused by the rebellion, and by the anarchy that followed it, many native Christians in communion with the Church had settled in and around the central districts, and their numbers were augmented by the influx of Barolong Christians who had followed their Chief, Samuel Lefulere, into the Lesuto. Tentative efforts had been made from time to time to minister to these, and now Letsie, Bereng, and other chiefs and headmen united together in praying the Church to come permanently into the country. Recognising the need, Mr. Woodman, who had hitherto been located at Sekubu, volunteered to step in and supply it. Leaving his colleague, Mr. Ball, at that station, he removed to the south, and commenced the work now known as the Mission of S. Barnabas, which has become one of the most flourishing Missions in the whole diocese.

Before the year ended, the welcome news reached us that a priest had been found in England willing to become our Bishop. This was good news indeed, for the diocese had been without a chief pastor since the early part of 1883. The clergyman thus chosen was the Rev. G. W. H. Knight-Bruce, Incumbent of S. Andrew's, Bethnal Green, an important home mission centre in the East-end of London, and we hoped much from his appointment. He was consecrated Bishop of Bloemfontein on the festival of the Annunciation, 1886, in the Church of S. Mary, Whitechapel, in the presence of a great crowd of his own parishioners, and of the members of the Bloemfontein Diocesan

Association; and after several months of earnest effort on behalf of the diocese in various parts of England, his lordship set sail for his distant sphere of labour, and arrived at Bloemfontein in August, amid the ringing of bells and the jubilations of the people.

In November, 1885, the Mabelete made their last expiring effort for supremacy. Broken and disorganized as they now were, they nevertheless contrived to put upwards of 4,000 men into the field, and these were encountered by nearly the same number of Matikete. For two days the struggle continued. It took the form of a series of small fights, which took place at points from fifteen to twenty miles distant from Thlotse, and resulted in the complete defeat and dispersion of Joel's party, which fled in confusion to the Free State or to the Malutis. As usual, they had provoked this final conflict by their lawlessness and violence. They had deliberately violated the boundaries laid down some time before, in the interests of peace, by the Paramount Chief and the British Commissioner, and were constantly carrying off the cattle of the Matikete whenever they had the least chance of doing so. But they were now at last effectually subdued, and from henceforth troubled us no more.

The final defeat of our northern foes was not without its influence upon Masupha. The old man had long regarded his *quondam* allies with ill-concealed contempt, and he now began to show signs of a change of front. Confidential messages passed and repassed between him and Jonathan, and we knew that we had now nothing more to fear from our earliest and most dreaded foe. Jonathan paid a friendly visit to the redoubtable old warrior soon afterwards, and was received very graciously, and in a few days the feud of years was forgotten! The logic of facts proved to be too strong, even for Masupha; and now that the Mabelete of the north had lost their supremacy, and he was once more at peace with his victorious son-in-law, he saw nothing to be gained, either for himself or his people, by

s

continuing to hold aloof from the Government. His attempt at independence and self-government had not been supported by any of the other chiefs, and had not been a conspicuous success, and he therefore judged that the time had come for him to make his peace with the Queen's Commissioner. The personal respect which he must have felt for Col. Clarke contributed, no doubt, in some degree, to this change of action. In any case, he resolved to abandon his position of isolation and opposition, and in the following March made his submission to the Commissioner, and received with all due respect the officials appointed to reside in his territory.

Very pleasant was it once more to live in peace and quietness, with no foes to molest us on the right hand or the left, after so many years of bloodshed, chaos, and insecurity. We thanked God, and took courage. This settled state of quietness and confidence had also, as may be supposed, a happy effect upon the people. No longer harassed and agitated by fightings, fears, and scares, they began to settle down to more peaceful and profitable avocations—to build new huts, and to improve their old ones, and to cultivate the soil much more largely than before. Peace, too, disposed the hearts of many of them to higher thoughts, with the result that the number of our hearers at the Mission services was greatly increased, and that several among them were moved to give themselves to Christ.

During the year we succeeded, by the help of friends at home and abroad, in enclosing both our compounds with a strong stone wall, a protection greatly needed now that the sod ones were old and altogether beyond renewal. The cemetery was also enclosed in the same manner, and carefully laid out and planted with shrubs and flowers. Several costly memorials had been lately put up to the memory of officers who had lost their lives in the rebellion. These had been sent out from England by relatives, and as they were Christian and tasteful in design, they formed a handsome addition to the memorials already erected in the sacred spot.

The middle of the Trinity season marked the restoration of the Mission choir. The old one had come to an end at the outbreak of the rebellion, and we thought it best not to attempt to restore it until the advent of better days. Most of the old members had left the country or were dead, but the two or three who remained once more put on their cassocks and surplices, and, together with a dozen new lads whom Mr. Reading had carefully trained for the purpose, led the services effectively and reverently. This was another step gained, small, it might be, but not without its influence in mission work, especially in such a land and among such a people as ours.

Towards the end of October we received a visit from our new Bishop, who seized the earliest opportunity of making himself thoroughly acquainted with the work of the Church in Basutoland. Some extracts from an account of his visit, which I wrote at the time, and which appeared soon afterwards in the pages of a missionary magazine,* may perhaps not be inadmissible here.

"On Tuesday, the 26th October, I rode up to Riverland, a farm and trading station on the banks of the Caledon, and the residence of our friend Mr. A. E. Richards; and the next day I went on to Brindisi, where I was to meet the Bishop. His lordship arrived there from Bethlehem just before sunset, looking a little sunburnt after his long journey, but in good health and spirits, and much pleased at the thought of being so close to Basutoland. Mr. and Mrs. Allum had come with him from Bethlehem, and on the following day a considerable number of other old friends arrived from various places in the neighbourhood to be present at the Confirmation, which was to be held in the afternoon. Mr. Middleton, with his accustomed kindness

---

* Bloemfontein Quarterly Paper, January, 1887.

and urbanity, placed his house at the disposal of the Bishop and his party, and lent his lordship a horse next morning for the ride to Sekubu—the most northern mission station in Basutoland, and the first to be visited.

"The Bishop and myself, accompanied by Samuel Munnesammy, an intelligent young coolie convert, and Seauthlo, a newly admitted catechumen, arrived at Sekubu about noon on the Friday (the 29th), having called on our way at the Government sub-station at Buta-Bute to exchange a few words of greeting with the officials stationed there. A very pleasant day was spent at the Mission, the Bishop being satisfied that a good and earnest work was being done, which would, in due time, bear its fruit.

"On the evening of All Saints' Day, our indefatigable churchwarden arrived at the station, and the next morning drove the Bishop down to Thlotse in his spider. After a three hours' trek, we outspanned near Leribe, at a trading station belonging to Mr. Richards, where we found a substantial luncheon awaiting us, Mrs. Richards having most kindly come over from Riverland on purpose to prepare it for us. While we were engaged in doing justice to the good things thus bountifully provided, old Mikaele Ramokemane, our volunteer evangelist at Lekhalong (one of the Thlotse out-stations), arrived with two or three other native converts, being anxious to get an early glimpse of the 'Mobishopo,' of whose approaching visit they had heard so much. After an hour's rest in the heat of the day under the hospitable roof of our kind friend, we inspanned, and proceeded on our way to Thlotse. When we had driven a little more than half way, and were nearing Sebotoane, we suddenly found, on emerging from the valley at the foot of the mountain, that the Europeans of the town, with Mr. Wroughton, the acting Assistant Commissioner of the district, at their head, had come out to meet us. All our white people were there, some driving, some on horseback, and all of them ready with a hearty welcome for their chief pastor. After the interchange of cordial greetings, we all proceeded together on our way, the little band of horsemen acting as an escort to the Bishop, until we reached the brow of the hill overlooking the Mission station, at which spot we found my brother clergy and the native catechist and choir in their surplices, together with the school children, most of our native converts, and a considerable number of the heathen of the place, all drawn up ready to receive us. As the Bishop's vehicle approached, the choir commenced the Sesuto version of 'The Church's one Foundation,' which was taken up very heartily by all around; and his lordship, who seemed very much touched and impressed by the scene before him, alighted from the spider, and stood bareheaded in front of the little company of native Christians until the hymn was finished. He was then introduced to my colleagues, Messrs. Champernowne and Reading, to the sidesman, Mr. E. Pfaff, to Alfred Motolo, our principal catechist, and to the leading members of the Mission congregation, as well as to several of their heathen friends and relations who had come out with them to meet him. Fervid 'Dmelas' were heard on all sides, and everyone seemed glad to see the 'Moruti e Mogolo'—the Great Teacher.

"These salutations ended, the choir re-formed and preceded the Bishop into the town, singing hymns and songs of rejoicing in their own language as they proceeded on their way. The spectacle was a very unwonted one in heathen Basutoland; indeed, I suppose it is certain that such a scene had never been witnessed before in the country. The surpliced procession, with the sign of redemption at its head, standing out in the sunlight against the clear blue sky, the harmonious music wafted softly onwards by the passing breeze, the joy depicted on the faces of the converts, and the wonder expressed on those of the heathen who followed them, made the scene a striking one—one which will, I am sure, long linger in the memories of those who took part in it. While speaking of this, I may remark that the processional cross used on the occasion (a large and effective one of wood, beautifully carved) was made and presented to the Mission by Mr. Pfaff, a member of the choir, ever ready to help forward the interests of the Church in any way that lies in his power.

"And so we all proceeded, singing through the town, until we neared S. Saviour's, when another halt was made, and the choir having commenced the Alleluiatic Sequence in Sesuto, we moved onwards until we halted finally at the door of the church. The Bishop then addressed a few happily chosen words to all around him, and with evident emotion thanked them for the truly Christian reception they had given him; remarking that when he had started in the morning from Sekubu he felt tired, but that now all his fatigue had passed away at so kind and cordial a welcome, and that he was indeed glad to be at Thlotse.

"His lordship stayed ten days in our Mission district, not only making himself master of the details of the work at the main station, but visiting the out-stations, as well as the more important heathen villages in our part of the country. Forty-two converts were confirmed, the little temporary church being crowded to excess on the occasion, and a large number of heathen standing outside round the door.

"Friday afternoon was intended to be devoted to visiting the remaining half of the town, but soon after the confirmation service was over a dust storm arose, which interfered for the time with our programme. It was quite *à la Kimberley* in its violence, and reminded one somewhat too forcibly of Lord Beaconsfield's definition of dirt. The dust was everywhere. In the streets it was well nigh blinding and suffocating; in the houses it was "laid on thick." It penetrated one's eyes, mouth, and nostrils; it made one cough, and wheeze, and sneeze; it peppered one's food, it stuck to one's clothes, it sanded one's beard. We do not often get such a dust storm in the Lesuto, but, when we do get it, it serves to draw closer than ever the bonds of union between ourselves and our brethren in the far West at the Diamond Fields.

For undoubtedly from that far West it comes; and at times one could almost fancy that all the dust of the Kalahari, of Griqualand West, and the Free State, were accumulated together in one vast volume, and poured into every nook, and cranny, and chink, and crevice of Basutoland. There was nothing for it but to stay at home. So stay at home we did, practising as best we could the great African virtue of patience. The next day was calm, clear, and cool—indeed, almost cold for the time of year; but as the Bloemfontein mail had come in, the Bishop was kept in the study all day, busily writing letters. Sunday followed, and the services were all bright and hearty, and, of course, well attended. There were five of these, in Sesuto or English, beginning with an early semi-choral celebration of the Holy Eucharist, besides a Sesuto instruction and singing class in the afternoon.

"On the Tuesday the Bishop, Mr. Champernowne, and myself paid a visit to Jonathan at his new and rapidly increasing town, built on the plateau at the base of Tsikoane. We were received with genuine cordiality, the chief pleading with the Bishop for a 'Moruti' for his people in their new home. We had a long talk together over this important matter, which ended by the Bishop promising to remember the chief's application, and to do all he could to meet his wishes. After this we were regaled with leting such as chiefs alone can produce.

"His lordship left Thlotse on the following Tuesday, riding with Mr. Champernowne to Lekhalong, a place about eighteen miles to the south. All the Lekhalong people, both Christian and heathen, with old Sethleiko, their chief, at their head, came out to meet them, singing hymns under the direction of Mikaele, the good old Mosuto who is labouring among them as an evangelist out of pure love, and with no hope of any earthly reward. In the afternoon there was a Confirmation Service in the open air, the Mission possessing as yet no buildings there from want of funds. This was the first Confirmation ever held in the open in Basutoland, and some two hundred natives were present at it, the great majority of whom were, of course, heathen. Such a solemn and impressive service, together with the Bishop's earnest addresses to the confirmees, must, one would hope, have made a lasting impression upon those present. The chief was in every way most friendly, and placed his best hut at the disposal of his visitors, providing them with bread, tea, leting, and milk, the two former having, no doubt, been specially procured for them.

"The Bishop and Mr. Champernowne left Lekhalong early next morning, after Sesuto Mattins, for Tyatyaneng, visiting one of the cannibal caves near Lepoko's village on their way. In olden days this cave was a stronghold of the man-eaters, and not many years ago a great quantity of human remains was still to be seen in and around it. Most of these bones are now, however, embedded in dung, the cave being used as a kraal for goats and sheep. His lordship picked up a fragment of a bone which the shepherds on the spot pronounced to be human; but having no morbid fancy for the possession of such a melancholy *souvenir*, replaced it in the earth, remarking that if it was the bone of an animal he did not care to have it, if of a human being it had better remain where it was until the resurrection of the great day.

"A visit to Lepoko's followed, and as the party were riding along they came suddenly upon a number of young girls belonging to one of the circumcision lodges in the neighbourhood. The Bishop was staggered at the sight, as well he might be; for the poor creatures were almost entirely naked, and were daubed from head to foot with white clay, presenting altogether one of the most ghastly spectacles that can be imagined. They wore a small reed veil with which they partially hid their faces, and walked in solemn procession, keeping up a dismal sing-song, which ended every now and then in a series of unearthly howls. These and other ceremonies which they undergo are regarded, as I have stated at the commencement of this narrative, as an introduction to the rights and duties of womanhood; and during this time of discipline no one is allowed to approach them, or converse with them, except the directress of the lodge (generally a thoroughly heathen and hideous old hag), and they are regarded as unclean.

"At Tyatyaneng the Bishop spent a pleasant evening with our friends the Sloleys, and went on next morning to Maseru."

Speaking of the cannibal caves, I remember a story which was told me in 1878 by Col. Bowker, an officer of much experience in native affairs, who was at that time acting as the Governor's Agent in Basutoland. It illustrates the native character so well that it may be worth while to relate it here; and I will do so from notes of our conversation made at the time.

Col. Bowker told me that some time before—I do not recollect how long—he was at a French Mission station in the neighbourhood of one of the caves, and the missionary and he talked together over the changes that had taken place during the last half century, and the progress the Basutos had made during that time, especially of late years. His friend agreed that they had made great progress in several ways since the extinction of cannibalism. And then he went on to tell him the way in which the cannibals disposed of their victims. "I will tell you," said he, "how the cannibals disposed of their victims after they had captured them. Usually they tied a thick cord of twisted grass (thapo) round their necks and strangled them, but sometimes they cut off one of their fingers and also a large piece out of their lip, and then left them in the cave to bleed almost to death; after which they put them into a great earthen pot filled with cold water, and then (as the cookery books have it) *boiled them till they were ready.*

"Well, one day the inhuman wretches went out on a hunting expedition, and managed to entrap two handsome, well-favoured young damsels. These were bled in the usual manner, and left in the cave to die. The cannibals, having got ready the pot of water, went out on a fresh expedition, intending to return in an hour or two. But before leaving they placed the bodies in the pots, thinking their victims to be all but dead, and then duly made up the fires. But one of the girls was by no means dead: she had only fainted from loss of blood. Presently, when she came to herself, the horrible truth flashed across her mind, and with a yell she leapt out of the pot and bounded forth from the cave—her captors not having yet returned—and ran for dear life to a mission station which had been recently established, and which was not many miles distant.

"There she related her story, and was taken care of, and soon after was converted to the faith of Christ.

"A great many years afterwards, when this young girl had become a middle-aged woman, I noticed one day smoke issuing from her hut at an hour when it was unusual for natives to prepare their food; and, thinking there must be something out of the common going forward, I went to the hut, and enquired whether she was keeping festival that day. 'Yes,' said she, 'I am making a feast.' 'For whom?' said I. 'Who and where are your friends?' 'They are here,' she answered, 'inside.' I looked in, and saw three old men sitting round the fire, chatting together, and contemplating with evident interest the pot on the fire before them, the contents of which were simmering pleasantly.

"'Who are they?' I asked. 'Oh,' said she, '*they are the men who captured me when I was a young girl, and put me into their big pot to cook me.* I have not seen them since. But to-day they have come to see me *and congratulate me on my escape, and of course I can do nothing less than prepare a meal for them.*'

"And," added the missionary to the Colonel, "I will show you, if you like, the very woman of whom we are speaking." The Colonel said that he would very much like to see her. Whereupon his friend took him to her hut and introduced him to her. "And," remarked the Colonel to me, "I looked at her, and at once saw the mark in her lip where the piece had been cut out, and noticed also that she had lost the tip of one of her fingers."

CHAPTER XVII.

SUNSHINE AND SHADOW.

1887.

Departure of Mr. Reading—Temporary Help—Masupha Fined—The Jubilee Memorial Church—Laying the Foundation Stone—Visit of the Bishop and Mrs. Knight-Bruce—Tsikoane—Death of the Rev. R. K. Champernowne—His Life and Labours—His Last Day on Earth—His Funeral—His Example.

THE Bishop's visit had cheered us all, and had given the work a fresh start. While he was with us it was arranged that Mr. Reading should leave us the Easter following, and go to Modder Poort, in order to prepare himself there for the priesthood. As the reader will have gathered, he had been with us many years, and we were sorry on many grounds to lose him from the Mission; but it was felt that he had, by his steady and persevering labours, proved himself worthy of the higher degree of the sacred ministry, and we hoped that his experience at S. Saviour's would be valuable to him in any new sphere of labour to which he might hereafter be appointed. He is now doing good service for the Church in the Mohales Hoek and Quiteng districts, where important Missions have been committed to his care.

When Mr. Reading left there was staying with us a layman who had come on a little visit, intending to remain with us for a month or so. Seeing that we were now short-handed, he offered to take our brother's place, as far as he could, for a few months, and I gladly accepted his offer. He stayed with us until the end of June, working vigorously in the school, and taking the entire charge of the garden, besides helping us in other ways. But circumstances over which he had no control prevented him from remaining permanently in Basutoland, and he soon afterwards left for England. But he did not remain in the mother country many years. He returned to South Africa, and has for some time past been living at Robben Island, devoting himself to the care of the lepers (of whom there are a large number) at the leper hospital established by the Cape Government on the island—a work of heroic self-sacrifice, to which, I believe, he desires to give the remainder of his life. May He Who, when on earth, did not shrink from these outcasts of our race, but healed them with His touch of pity and of power, give His servant grace and strength to continue, and to carry out for many years to come, the generous ministration of mercy thus begun.

In the June of this year there was fighting once more : this time between Masupha and one of his former allies, Pete, the son of Ramanella. But it was outside our district, and affected us little or nothing. In this case Masupha's sons were proved to be the aggressors : and the old man paid the fine of cattle levied upon him by Letsie and Sir Marshall Clarke for not keeping his belligerent offspring in better order.

Our congregations had now increased so much that the need of a larger and more suitable church became a pressing necessity. Even though the partition wall had been removed, the present chapel would barely hold one hundred people seated close together on ordinary school forms, and these included the choir, who were cramped up in a small space close to the very step of the altar. Yet we often contrived to pack a hundred and thirty or more inside the building, while outside there were always a number of listeners at the door. Open air services were very exhausting to the preacher, as I had proved by experience, especially during the " Gun War " ; and besides, they could only be held with success in fine weather. On wet or windy days they were anything but effective, not to speak of the discomfort involved in attending them. It was manifest that an effort must be made, and made soon, to erect a larger and more permanent church.

Yet how to compass such an undertaking we did not know. The diocese was passing through a financial crisis, and was too poor to make anything like a substantial grant for building purposes to the Mission. Our own people consisted of a tiny handful of Europeans, none of them rich, and a congregation of native converts, nearly all of whom were very poor. But both whites and blacks were ready to do their utmost to help forward such a good work, and they did their duty nobly when the time came. Meanwhile, the need of greater accommodation was growing so pressing that it seemed useless, if not indeed a mockery, to go round to the heathen huts and kraals, and invite their inhabitants to come to hear the message of salvation, when there was no room for them in their Father's house. Often, in answer to our exhortations to come and listen to the teaching of the gospel, there would be the reply, " Moruti, I have been, but there is no room for me there. The church is too small. We cannot sit in it ; we cannot stand in it. As soon as you make the house big enough I will come, and I will bring my friends with me to hear your *thuto* (teaching), for I want to hear about God."

At this juncture an old friend of the Mission came to our rescue. Knowing how greatly this want was pressing upon us, Canon Balfour—who was now for a time in charge of Harrismith, one of the most important towns in the Free State—generously offered to raise £300 towards a permanent church for S. Saviour's, provided I would arrange that the foundation stone should be ready to be laid *on the day of the Queen's Jubilee*.

A friend in need is a friend indeed, and I eagerly caught at the offer. We had been saving for several years past every penny we could lay by for the purpose, and these small sums amounted now to nearly £100. A subscription list put out among the congregation and their friends produced, in the course of a few weeks, £100 more, so eagerly did everyone enter into the proposal. A design, with plans and specifications, had been carefully prepared some time before, and I immediately set about getting a competent man to put in at least the foundation stone of the building.

Canon Balfour's promise was speedily performed, his own purse, I am sure, being considerably lightened by the transaction ; and we had in this way £500 to start with. This more than warranted me in having not only the foundation stone laid, but the whole foundation finished, and accordingly the work was pushed on with vigour, so that the stone might be ready by Jubilee Day. The foundation was broad and massive, and reposed upon a bed of gravel, which a few feet deeper ended in solid rock, and this first part of the work cost just £200. The design approved was for a stone building under a roof of galvanized iron. Its exterior length was to be eighty feet, and its breadth thirty-eight, with clergy and choir vestries on the north side, and a sacristy and porch on the south, and there was to be a baptistery thrown out at the west end. The interior was simple, but effective, and not without a certain dignity of its own. A low stone screen separated the nave from the choir, and the altar was of good proportions and sufficiently elevated. Such a church would cost at least £2,000, and I resolved not to undertake the commencement of the superstructure until at least half the money was ready and waiting in the bank for the purpose.

It seemed in every way a pity to build with brick when beautiful white, grey, and red sandstone was abundant a short distance off, especially as the bricks made in South Africa are so inferior to those used for church building purposes in Europe. We had waited so long for a church, that we were resolved, if possible, to have one which should be strong and durable in its character, now that apparently the opportunity had come to realize the hopes of so many years. So I set to work harder than ever to beg—not of our own people, for they had been already squeezed quite dry, but of our friends and well-wishers in the far off mother country. And I besought everyone I knew above all things to pray—to pray earnestly to the Great Head of the

Church that the money needed for His House might come in. I could not help believing that the Master Whom we served, and Whose interests we were endeavouring, in however poor a way, to promote, would answer such prayers. And really and truly prayer was our only resource, for I had not the vaguest idea where the money still needed (at least £1,700) was to come from. Prayer, and prayer alone, as far as I could see, must bring it to us.

Meanwhile, Jubilee Day had come. The stone was ready, and the Bishop, who had kindly consented to lay it, and had made a special journey for the purpose, had arrived the evening before. A document written in Latin, English, and Sesuto, setting forth the fact that the building now about to be erected was to be dedicated to the worship of Almighty God under the title and dedication of the Church of the All Holy and All Merciful Saviour, was duly prepared. It recorded also the names of the Bishop of the diocese; the clergy and lay-workers, European and native, of the Mission; the Church officers; the principal Government officials; the Paramount Chiefs, both of the whole country and of the division of Leribe; and the principal chiefs and headmen of Thlotse and the Mission district assigned to S. Saviour's. This document, duly signed and attested, was enclosed in a bottle in the usual way, and sealed up; and the bottle, together with most of the coins of the realm, was wrapped in newspapers, English and South African, and encased at the proper moment in the foundation stone of the building.

Jubilee Day will live in the annals of England as a day of rejoicing throughout the whole world-wide British Empire. Without doubt it was a day of rejoicing to us at Thlotse. Though it was mid-winter, the weather was comparatively warm for the time of year, and the sun shone brightly. The day was ushered in by the usual Morning Service in Sesuto, followed by a celebration of the Holy Eucharist, in which the petitions offered for "Victoria our Queen" came home to us with special force; and I am sure that many prayers went up that morning to the Throne of Grace on her behalf, as well as thanksgivings for her long and prosperous reign. We also invoked a blessing on the important work which was to mark the day at S. Saviour's, praying that the building now about to be erected might remain for many generations as a witness of the presence of the Most High, and a house of prayer and praise for all people around; and that the truth as it is in Jesus, peace, unity, and love, might be taught in it, and ever abide in it.

Eleven o'clock was the time appointed for the ceremony, and long before that hour a large number of natives, with Jonathan and the lesser chiefs at their head, had arrived from all parts of the district, and taken up their position in the space allotted to them. They had, of course, never witnessed such a ceremony before, and it greatly excited their curiosity. Cape carts, waggons, and other vehicles soon began to make their appearance, accompanied by a good show of horsemen, the Europeans along the Free State border, besides those resident in Basutoland, having come over to take part in the proceedings. Two Union Jacks were hoisted near the stone, and in front of them were marshalled the school children, all polished up and brightly clad for the occasion, with faces shining like burnished bronze.

At the appointed hour, the clergy and choir issued forth from the temporary church, going in procession to the stone, and singing, as they moved slowly onwards, the Sesuto version of "Onward, Christian soldiers," to Sir Arthur Sullivan's inspiriting music. The beautiful service in use in the diocese of Bloemfontein on such occasions was then commenced, the choral portions being nicely rendered by the choir and school children, and the hymns taken up with heartiness and vigour by the crowd around. The stone was duly laid by the Bishop, with the accustomed formula in the Name of the Ever Blessed Trinity, and his lordship then delivered an earnest and stirring address, thoroughly appropriate to the occasion. After this address, the "Church's One Foundation" was sung with great spirit, and, during the singing of it, many offerings were laid upon the stone. It was a really pretty sight to see numbers of tiny little black dots advance with beaming faces, and deposit their "tickies" (threepenny pieces) in the midst of the small heap of larger coins contributed by their relatives and friends. The "Old Hundredth" was then sung of course in Sesuto, like the other hymns, and taken up with as much force and fervour as it could be in England, the deep voices of the men swelling out at times into a grand wave of sound which must have been heard at a considerable distance in our clear atmosphere. The ceremony was fitly and appropriately concluded by the singing of "God save the Queen," one of the verses of which had been rendered into Sesuto for the occasion, the others being sung, as usual, in English.

Then there followed a big feast of beef, bread, porridge, plain cake and coffee, the most appetising portions of the bill of fare being, as usual, contributed by our kind-hearted churchwarden. The crowd of attendants at this *mokete* contrived, as only natives can, to dispose of a huge pile of provisions in a remarkably short space of time, and certainly the native does not, as the Englishman has been said to do, "take his pleasures sadly." The guests were fed by relays, and the clatter of tongues in the schoolroom where the feast was laid out was deafening and incessant; quips and cranks went merrily round, and quiet jokes and good-natured "chaff" provoked continuous sallies of wit and bursts of laughter. The hundreds of faces presented one great united good-humoured grin, and I think everyone enjoyed himself right heartily.

Cheers for the Church, the Queen, and the Bishop followed, and games and athletic sports concluded the happy day. The "tent-pegging" of the native mounted police was a great attraction, both from its novelty and from the dexterity and skill

T

displayed by the horsemen, who had only recently begun to take lessons in it.

Thus we kept the Queen's Jubilee in our little corner of her mighty empire.

The pressure of work upon my colleague and myself at this time was unusually great. The school, in every way the right hand of the Mission, was without a master, our native catechist at Thlotse having no knowledge of English, and very little capacity for the difficult task of teaching the young. Nor had he, able as he was in some ways, the gift of keeping a number of boys, some of whom were almost little savages, in anything like order. So we had to put the school work into commission, I taking the morning duty and Mr. Champernowne the afternoon. Added to this, there was the additional correspondence involved in writing numberless begging letters on behalf of the building fund of the new church—a task which had to be performed if the church was to be erected at all. We did what we could of the most pressing work, leaving altogether for the present such things as the translation of the Book of Common Prayer (which had largely occupied our spare time for several years), and reducing our visits to out stations, all important as that work was, to a minimum.

Early in December the Bishop came to us again for Confirmations, bringing with him Mrs. Knight-Bruce, whose genial cheerfulness and kindly sympathy brightened our little home, and helped to lighten our daily toil. They stayed with us for nearly a week, during which time the Bishop visited all the out-stations, and devoted one day specially to Tsikoane, where a schoolroom was being erected in response to the chief's appeal, by means of some money which had been given for the purpose by an unknown friend in England. We had hoped that the room might be finished by the time his lordship arrived, but the season had been a dry one, and water had become so scarce that there was little or none available for building purposes, and the work was now at a standstill from lack of it. But, unfinished as the building was, the Bishop wished to seize the opportunity, now that he was again on the spot, to hold a special Mission service just in front of it, thus showing the people of Tsikoane how anxious he was to further their interests, and set forward the work of evangelization in their town. So we all rode out to Tsikoane together, taking the choir with us, and held a most impressive open-air service close to the unfinished schoolroom.

The Bishop received the usual hearty welcome from Jonathan and his people, who were one and all specially pleased to see the wife of the "Great Teacher" among them. Seven hundred men—Jonathan's chosen warriors—marched up from the Khothla to the school, with the Bishop and the Chief at their head, and as they were all, *without exception*, heathen, it may be seen at once what a splendid field is open to the Church at Tsikoane for missionary effort. It was arranged that a resident native schoolmaster-catechist should be appointed as soon as a competent man could be found for the post; £25 per annum having been promised towards his support by the same unknown benefactor (whom may God bless!) who had provided the school. I felt that, humanly speaking, it was the Bishop's influence alone that had gained us this start at Tsikoane; and there was now a hope that a response might be made, at least in some degree, to the oft-repeated appeal of the chief for a "Moruti." The future looked hopeful and encouraging, as far as this new undertaking was concerned, and I once more thanked God and took courage.

The Bishop had not been gone from us a fortnight when the Mission was called upon, in the Providence of God, to suffer a great and irreparable loss. My dear brother priest and colleague, Mr. Champernowne, was suddenly called away to his eternal rest.

What a blow this was to myself can be imagined when it is remembered that he and I had been close companions, bound together in love in the same work and the same interests, for more than eight years.

The first time that I met him was at Modder Poort at the end of 1878. I was on the point of starting for England, and rode over from Bloemfontein, which had been for some time my sphere of labour, to say good bye to my old friends at the Brotherhood Farm. Mr. Champernowne was spending a few weeks there at the time, having just come out to South Africa on a visit to a cousin who had been for some years a worker at the Brotherhood station. He was in rather delicate health, and intended, he told me, to stay in South Africa six months, he liked the country and its climate so much. He had suffered severely at times from asthma, and the dry, warm, rarified air of the Orange Free State exactly suited his constitution, and made him feel in better health and spirits than he had been for years. Habitually grave in manner and demeanour, he was not without a keen sense of humour, and dearly relished a good joke.

He already felt a strong vocation for Holy Orders, and he and I had a pleasant chat together over Oxford life, and the admirable training for the ministry which Cuddesdon afforded. He had had the full benefit of that training, after having taken his degree at Christ Church, and I remember how his face glowed with pleasure and affection when he spoke of Dr. King, the present loved and revered Bishop of Lincoln (at that time the Principal of the college), and of his power and influence for good over the men under his charge. This pleasant chat, over a couple of pipes under a blue gum tree, was the commencement of a life-long affection between us.

Soon after this I left for England, and, during my stay in the mother country, was privileged to pay a visit to his father, the Rector of Dartington, an honoured and venerable parish priest, who has only recently passed away to his rest. Nurtured in that lovely Devonshire home, it must have required some heroism in my friend to tear himself away from it, and expatriate himself as he did for good and all when, some years afterwards, the call came to him to go out and labour among the heathen in Basutoland. That he ever "looked back" after having "put his hand to the plough," no one who knew him could for a moment believe.

I do not remember seeing him again, except once, for a short time in Bloemfontein, until the Lent of 1878, when he came to stay with us for a few weeks at Thlotse. His contemplated stay of six months in South Africa had lengthened out into nearly five years! He had been ordained to the diaconate some time before by Bishop Webb; but—partly, I am sure, from humility, and partly because he was not certain how long he might be able to stay in the diocese—he had not yet offered himself for the priesthood. He came to us now while on his way to England, I, for my part, thinking that the mother country would be, in all probability, his future field of labour. Later on in the same year, when we had planned the establishment of a training institution for native catechists, I wrote to him, and offered him the chaplaincy of it, but without stipend, our resources being so few and scanty.

He felt drawn to our diocese, and his father had generously given him permission to return to South Africa, should he decide to do so. But he could not make up his mind. There were not wanting circumstances which pointed to his stay at home; and on the other hand, he did not hear the voice of the Divine Master calling him distinctly to the foreign mission field. So he patiently waited, and prayed for guidance before deciding. He knew nothing of our plans at Thlotse, and had no idea that I was contemplating the possibility of a native training college. He spent a "quiet day" with some friends in the ministry, but was still undecided what to do. At last the call came.

He was in Derbyshire, amid the lovely scenery of Dovedale, at the time. Walking out one day alone, communing with God and seeking for guidance, he heard what he took to be the voice of his Lord speaking to his heart, and saying, "Offer yourself for the work at Thlotse." In a moment his irresolution vanished, and he hastened to obey the call. He went home, told his father, obtained his permission to go, and wrote at once to me offering to come out to the Mission at his own expense and work without stipend, in the event of my being able to find a "vacant corner" for him.

It is noteworthy that, *at the very time* the call came to him, I was writing to him to offer him the appointment I have spoken of. My readers may perhaps remember that, when the idea of establishing a native institution first presented itself to my mind, I called the two Sekubu brethren together and consulted them about it. My letter to Mr. Champernowne was the outcome of our conference by the river side, after that early celebration of the Holy Communion, in which we had prayed together for guidance in so important a matter. Our letters therefore crossed on the ocean, and at the time he received my invitation I was reading his letter to me offering to come. We both regarded this as a sign that he was called to labour at S. Saviour's, and that the voice which spoke to him was no vain or delusive one, but the voice of God. It was, we believed, a direct answer to prayer; for we had been praying together at Thlotse that he might be guided, if it were God's will, to come out to us, at the very time that he was alone seeking Divine guidance in that Derbyshire valley.

He returned to the diocese early in 1879, going first to Bloemfontein to be ordained to the priesthood. By this act he, as it were, "burnt the bridge" behind him, since ordination in that city subjected him to the provisions of the Colonial Clergy Act, should he ever think of returning to England and exercising his ministry there. But he had no such thought or intention. He had given himself to the heathen, and desired to live and die among them as a simple Mission Priest. And his wish was granted. The knowledge that he was, as he believed, so plainly called to S. Saviour's, helped to increase and strengthen his affection for the work there as time went on, and I do not think he ever had a thought of leaving it, though at times other spheres of usefulness were open to him. When the training college scheme came to nought, he still stayed on, choosing rather to remain at the Mission with merely the status of an assistant curate, than to leave and take independent charge of a parish or mission elsewhere in the diocese.

How he worked on steadily, and with one single aim, and that, too, often in failing health, through evil report and good report, through cloud and sunshine, through adversity and prosperity, these pages have already shown. His quiet, patient, unostentatious but persistent work for God, was not marked by any public acclamations, nor did it meet with any earthly reward. Such things are not to be looked for in an obscure corner of a remote and little known heathen country, and perhaps they are not without a danger of their own when they do fall to the minister of Christ. But our brother's ministerial career was not the less a splendid record of toil and devotion, undertaken and continued to the end for the glory of God and the salvation of the poor souls among whom he laboured.

He died—as he had lived—in harness. He was, as I have said, called away to his rest very suddenly, but I cannot doubt that he was ready. Nor, I venture to think, will the reader when he reads the record of his last day on earth.

That last day was Wednesday, the 14th December, 1887. The weather was intensely hot at the time, and had been for several weeks past, no rain having fallen for many months. The thermometer was sometimes as high as 105 degrees in the coolest shade, and the heat tried us sorely—tried him especially—short-handed as we were, and with so much work to be done. I did what I could to spare him from undue pressure, and often suggested the need of more rest, but he could not bear to see anything left undone, or apparently neglected, so entirely absorbed was he in the work. So he laboured on, I fear beyond his strength.

On that last day of his life he had devoted the morning to visiting among the slums—there are, alas, such things at Thlotse—and they were worse then than they are now. In the afternoon he took the school, but for a shorter time than usual, the children coming out on Wednesdays before the ordinary hour of closing in order to attend a short Mission service, with catechising in the church. This service I conducted myself, and when it was concluded, as I was coming out of the church, I met him at the door. He told me that he desired (in the words of our Church) "to receive the benefit of absolution" according to "the ministry of God's Holy Word," and I returned with him into the sacred building to execute this holy ministry. Whether he had any presentiment that his death was so near I do not know. Certainly I had not, when I gave him the absolution he sought, and commended him to God with the accustomed words of peace and blessing. Little did I think that he would never again hear on earth the assurance of pardon through the precious Blood of Christ. Little did I imagine that, in a few short hours, he would be standing in the immediate presence of the Great Absolver Himself, to hear from His Own Mouth the ratification of the words of peace and forgiveness so lately uttered by my unworthy lips. But it was so, though I knew it not, nor had the least conception of it. But, looking back, I see that his Lord was thus preparing him for the end that was so near; and surely it was fitting that so pure and guileless a soul should go straight to Jesus with the words of peace and pardon resting fresh upon him.

It was half-past five o'clock when we came out of church. He went to his study to write a Sesuto sermon for the following Sunday, the 4th Sunday in Advent. The study was a rondavel of which he was very fond, contiguous to the Mission House, and many an earnest conversation had he held in it with our

Christian neophytes, and with those among the heathen whose hearts grace had touched and softened, and who manifested a desire to be led to Jesus. Going into the hut next morning after his death, I found upon the table the unfinished Advent sermon which he had been engaged in writing. His habit was to write out his discourse, learn it by heart (a remarkable gift), and then preach it without note or manuscript.

This, the last sermon that he ever penned, was on death. "It is appointed unto men once to die"* was his text. He had sketched out the skeleton of it, and filled in a portion. The last words he had written were these :—" E, Lefu le thla thla go rona botle." " Yes, death will come to us all." " Empa neneng ? " " But when ? " " Ga re tsebe." " We do not know." " Ekaba le haufi." " Perhaps it is near." " Ekaba le thla thla gosasane." " Perhaps it may come to-morrow." There the pen had been laid down, never to be taken up again. One cannot help again wondering whether he had any presentiment that it was so near to him—that it would come to *him* on the morrow. In any case, it is remarkable that these should be the last words he ever wrote. It was close upon midsummer, at which time the sun sets with us at 7 o'clock. Just as the sun was dipping under the western horizon, he came to me (I was doing a little light gardening work at the time) to tell me that he was suffering from a sick headache, and felt "fit for nothing." I gently chided him for remaining so long at sedentary work in the study in such excessive heat, and after so many hours of unremitting labour—for, of course, we are early risers at the Mission—and advised him to lie down in the shade on the stoep, and rest until supper time. I thought he was suffering from one of those bilious attacks to which all are liable in hot climates such as ours, and which, though severe while they last, are not, as a rule, dangerous. He took my advice, and I

---

* Heb. ix. 27.

remember looking up while weeding the flowers not far from where he was reclining, and observing him gazing at the mountains opposite, whose majestic peaks were at that moment all aglow with the resplendent rays of the setting sun. How little did I think that that was the last glimpse he was destined to have of the glories of earth, and that a vision of beauty far exceeding any that this world can offer would be his ere the sun rose on the morrow!

As evening advanced, feeling no better, he retired to his room. He took a cup of tea, but did not care to have any medicine, saying that it would only weaken him. Rest and sleep were what he most needed—so it seemed—and I hoped that they might restore him, as they had often done before.

He was to have taken the Sesuto Celebration early next morning, but I told him not to think of getting up for it; I would take it myself.

I saw him two or three times during the evening, and when I retired to rest at ten o'clock he was lying on his bed in his cassock in a profound slumber. I thought it a pity to wake him, and left him lying as he was, asleep.

Next morning, just after six, I knocked at his door, and receiving no answer, entered his room. I found him as I had left him, still lying in his cassock, asleep. But it was the sleep of death: he was asleep in Jesus. There was a soft smile upon his lips, and the look of weariness and pain of the night before had passed away. His face now wore an expression of radiant joy, as if he were dreaming a delightful dream, or beholding some fair vision.

Hastily I ran up into the town and summoned the two or three friends at hand to the bedside, and they agreed with me that his spirit had not long departed from its earthly tabernacle, for his body was not yet entirely cold. He had probably died just as the sun was rising, an hour before.

We sent at once to Ficksburg for our kind friend Dr. Taylor, but he was absent from home, and could not come that day. He arrived next morning, and after a post mortem examination, pronounced that our dear brother had died of serous apoplexy; a conclusion which was borne out by the fact that the pillow of his bed was saturated with water.

The last sad offices of love towards the thin, fragile form, were carefully and reverently performed by Mrs. Reeves, the wife of our Postmaster—a good soul, always ready to do any act of kindness in her power—and the body was clothed in the sacred vestments in which our brother had so often ministered at the Altar of God. A continuous stream of people came to take a last look at the face they loved so well, and many and heartfelt were the tears shed by our sorrowing converts as they stood by that couch of death. Many heathen came too, and " smote upon their breasts and returned," sobbing aloud as they did so, for our brother was beloved by all. "If ever there was a saint of God, he was one," said an official to me; and I felt that the testimony was true.

He was buried on the afternoon of the next day. There was a Celebration in the early morning, at which every native Christian who was on the spot or anywhere near was present. The Service was inexpressibly touching, and went home to the hearts of all. I think everyone was in tears, and after the Prayer of Consecration the stillness was for some moments absolute and deathlike. Then, presently, one great sob went up from the whole congregation, and I feared that they would be unable to restrain themselves, and break out into wailing and lamentation; for natives have not been trained in the habit of self-control as we Englishmen have, and, at times of sorrow and bereavement, often give themselves up to passionate and frenzied exclamations of woe and despair. But they had been taught that such violent and outward expressions of grief were out of place in the House of God, and accordingly they mastered their feelings, and behaved with the greatest reverence and decorum to the end.

Our Mission station is so remote that it was not possible for any of the other clergy of the diocese, except those at Sekubu and Modder Poort, to be in time for the funeral. But Mr. Reading, who received the sad intelligence just in time to be present, started at once, and by hard riding accomplished the journey. He was accompanied by Brother Bernard, who came to represent the Society of S. Augustine; for Mr. Champernowne had often spent his holidays at Modder Poort, and was always a welcome guest at the Brotherhood house. Our friend Mr. Ball, of Sekubu, being only four hours' distant, had arrived the evening before, and had assisted at the Celebration in the morning. Wreaths of the choicest flowers were sent by everyone who had a garden, and among them came a beautiful one from Madame Weitzecker, the wife of the French Protestant missionary at Manamasoane. M. Weitzecker himself rode over for the funeral, an act of brotherly sympathy which we gratefully appreciated.

That the funeral procession was followed by a great concourse of people, I need not say. We buried our dear brother by the side of his sister, in the row set apart for the Mission workers, of whom four had now been called away to their rest within ten years; so deeply had the mark of the cross been stamped upon S. Saviour's.

Richard Keble Champernowne was a man of one aim and one object. His character was emphatically a simple one. I never knew a man who cared less for the world and the things of the world. He counted all things as mere earthly dross, so that he could "win Christ and be found in Him." *Personal devotion to Jesus* was at the root of his life and work, and that carried him through all. Without that a mission priest is bound to fail, however much he may seem to succeed. It is the only thing that *wears*; the only thing that endures to the end.

Studious in his habits and scholarly in his tastes, my colleague was a diligent student of the Word of God. That he

THE REV. R. K. CHAMPERNOWNE.

was a man of prayer goes without saying. Though not naturally a brilliant man, he made good, solid progress in the native language, having made up his mind to master it. He studied it daily, and though never an apt or ready speaker of it in ordinary conversation, acquired, perhaps, a more critical knowledge of it than any of us, and preached in it acceptably and with power. That he had his failings may be readily granted. Which of us has not? But they were so trivial, and so unimportant, that they were forgiven and forgotten in the general excellence of his character, and his unwearied, self-sacrificing devotion to his Master's cause. I, who knew him so closely and so intimately for so many years, can bear testimony to his holiness of life. He was one of the purest, truest, most single-hearted followers of Christ that I have ever known.

And now he was no longer with us here. His labours were ended, and he was at rest. As the grave closed over his remains, and I walked sorrowfully homeward from the cemetery in the lengthening shadows of the fast-departing sun on that December afternoon, the loss that the Mission had sustained was borne in upon me in its fulness. I began to realize the fact that I was once more alone. Two men had been working together in the field of the Lord; the one was taken, and the other left. But why? And why should the younger and the better man be taken first? I could not tell, except that it was because he *was* better, and I not worthy to go. I could only say, " It is the Lord; let Him do what seemeth Him good."*

Good bye, brother beloved, good bye. But not for ever! There will dawn upon us in God's own time the Day of Reunion, to which we all look forward with the gaze of faith, and with yearning, hopeful hearts. Meanwhile, for a little space, farewell. *Sala hauthle.* The all-loving Lord grant unto thee light, refreshment, and peace in the abode of the Blessed. *Phomola ka Khotso Paradeising.*

---

* 1 Samuel iii. 18.

As for me, though the cloud has fallen upon me and the mist once more enwraps me, so that I cannot see what lies in the onward path, I know that, spite of all, there is a Hand that will not fail to uphold, and a Light that will shine athwart the darkness to guide me on my way. May that Light not shine across my path in vain.

> Lead, kindly Light, amid the encircling gloom,
>   Lead Thou me on;
> The night is dark, and I am far from home,
>   Lead Thou me on.
> Keep Thou my feet; I do not ask to see
> The distant scene; one step enough for me.
>
> * * * *
>
> So long Thy power hath blest me, sure it still
>   Will lead me on
> O'er moor and fen, o'er crag and torrent, till
>   The night is gone.
> And with the morn those angel faces smile,
> Which I have loved long since, and lost awhile.

CHAPTER XVIII.

Tribulation and Joy.

1888—1890.

Church Building Prospects—The Champernowne Memorial Lectern—Andrew Makhobothloane—Opening of the Tsikoane School—Scandals—Mrs. Gummidge—Depression—The Church Recommenced—The Salvation Army—Help at Last—Lapse of Alfred Motolo—Completion of the Church—Service of Dedication—Last Words.

The death of Mr. Champernowne gave us our Church. His father received the tidings with the truest Christian resignation, and at once offered to add £500 to the Church Building Fund as a mark of sympathy with the Mission in its loss. Thlotse was now doubly dear to him, and he did all in his power, both by word and deed, to help forward the work there, and to strengthen and sustain my hands. Another member of the family sent me £100, and other friends in England, personally unknown to me, came also to our aid. Among these were the good people of Weybridge, who sent us two handsome offertories. Thus, by the winter of 1888, I had more than the thousand pounds in the bank necessary for the commencement of the building. The church would be now in a double sense a memorial one. It was to be not only a Jubilee Memorial to her Majesty the Queen, but also a Memorial to the workers of the Mission now at rest.

A special memorial to my dear brother priest was also subscribed for by the clergy and others of his friends in the diocese; and this took the form of a handsome brass eagle lectern, which arrived from England before the building was finished.

At the beginning of the year 1888 I was able to secure the services of an assistant for the school, who has since been licensed to the Mission as a catechist. This young native, Andrew Makhobothloane by name, was one of our first boarders, and owed most of his early training to Mrs. Widdicombe. After her death he remained with me until the outbreak of the rebellion, when, as the reader knows, the Mission was broken up, and our boys scattered. Andrew then went down to the Eastern Province of the Cape Colony, and obtained employment for some time as a telegraph messenger at East London and Queenstown. After that he was sent by an uncle, a Wesleyan Christian, to the Wesleyan Training College at Benson Vale. And now, his father having died not long before, he had returned to Thlotse, though his college course was unfinished, in order to support, as far as he could, his widowed mother and his numerous brothers and sisters, most of whom were still very young. He had, of course, no Government certificate, and was not sufficiently educated or experienced to take charge of a large and important school like ours; but I was, nevertheless, glad to accept his services, and he made an efficient assistant to myself in the daily work of the school.

On the Second Sunday in Lent we inaugurated the mission work at Tsikoane with a most hearty and successful service. Our Thlotse Christians went out with me, and some of the Europeans joined us, and we spent a happy day there. Jonathan, his wives, counsellors, and head men were there, and all the people of the place with them; and I arranged for an evangelistic service to be held in the new school-room every alternate Sunday, either by a native catechist or by myself, and for school for the children three days in the week. That was all that could possibly be done under present circumstances.

Soon after this a heavy trial fell upon the Mission, different in character from any that we had hitherto had. The senior catechist, Alfred Motolo, was accused of grievous misconduct, and others of our native Christians, notably the young people, followed his evil example, and were giving trouble likewise. The air was thick with stories, accusations, and rumours, and the scandal to the Mission was great; and that in the face of such a large heathen population at our doors watching our manner of life and conversation day after day.

I investigated everything that was brought to my knowledge most fully and carefully, taking care to have the Church Council present throughout the proceedings. The Council consisted of three of our oldest and most trustworthy men—communicants, and all three Basutos, elected by the congregation to aid me and strengthen my hands by their counsel and advice in matters of discipline connected with the Mission. All the accusations and charges were gone into, with the result that two of our communicants were placed under discipline for a season. But nothing was *proved* against the catechist. The evidence against him was unsatisfactory, and far from clear, and as he stoutly maintained his innocence, I felt bound to give him the benefit of the doubt, and declare him free from blame. Yet I had my misgivings as to the truthfulness of his statements, and feared that there had been prevarication all round ; and time, alas, proved that these fears were far from groundless.

I was sitting moodily one day upon the stoep, " thinking by myself, as the Germans say, and repeating, not, I fear, in a very patient spirit, Keble's lines :—

> Lord, in Thy field I work all day ;
> I read, I teach, I warn, I pray ;
> And yet these wilful, wandering sheep,
> Within Thy fold I cannot keep.

I was, I say, sitting thus, when suddenly poor old Gummidge, whom I had not before seen that day, mounted the steps of the stoep in a limp, feeble sort of way, far removed from her usual springiness and alacrity, and stood before me.

But who is " poor old Gummidge " ? the reader will ask.

Gummidge—or to be respectful, and give her her full name, Mrs. Gummidge—was my best loved and favourite cat. She was twelve years old—very old for a cat, at any rate an African cat ; and she stood before me now, looking up into my face with an expression which it is difficult, if not impossible, to put into words. There was in that look sorrow, affection, suffering, and resignation, all blended into one. She did not utter a sound, but stood gazing into my very eyes with a look that seemed to say, as plainly as words could say, " Farewell, old Master. We have been companions together for many long years, and now I am going to leave you, and you will see me no more. But you will remember me, and the many pleasant hours we have spent together in days gone by for ever."

At once the thought took possession of me that she was going to die, and had come to take a last look at the master for whom, in her poor dim way, she was not without affection, before her life had ebbed away. She turned to go, and I spoke an endearing word to her ; upon which she half bent round towards me, and gave me a last lingering glance, oh, so mournful—so

U

inexpressibly, pitifully mournful — that the tears started unbidden to my eyes. Then she tottered away, slowly and feebly, and went round to a hut at the back of the house which was half full of straw, where she usually slept. I had not the heart to follow her, knowing that I could do nothing for her. She was old, and had suddenly become feeble and decrepit, and her hour had come.

But some time afterwards I summoned up courage enough to go round and see if she were really dead. It was as I thought. Her body was lying cold, rigid, and lifeless upon the straw. I think she must have died as soon as she reached the hut. Perhaps she had risen from her deathbed to creep feebly round and give me that last look. I think it was so. I took up, as tenderly as I could, the poor worn form of my faithful old friend, and carried it into the garden, where I buried it beneath the spreading branches of our best apple tree.

Dear old Gummidge!

How did I get her? you ask; and how came she to have such a singular name? I will tell you.

She was one of the kittens given to us to "start us in life with" (as perhaps the reader may remember), when we first went to Thlotse, by Emma Bell, Colonel Bell's little daughter, and soon learnt to make herself at home in her new surroundings. She was not what would be called a handsome kitten, though her winsomeness, together with her downrightness of character, soon made her a general favourite. She was fawn and white in colour, and prettily marked, and had a pleasant look, and an intelligent, "knowing" face.

As she grew up to mature cathood, we observed that when things went smoothly and easily with her and ourselves, she often manifested a sort of uneasiness, not to say discontent; wandering about and whining in a disconsolate way, as if she were lamenting the prosperous state of affairs. She seemed to be most happy when there was no meat in the house, and not more than a tablespoonful of milk to be poured out for her. She would eat her mealie meal porridge at such times, all sticky as it was, with apparent relish, and lick her lips after it as if it were a toothsome repast of bird, reptile, or fish. Then she would go a hunting; and woe to the mouse, snake, *lebodu*, lizard, or locust which came across her path! Woe, too, to the small birds! A cat is a necessity in our circumstances, and we had several; but she was the cleverest hunter of them all. Nothing escaped her. I fear she rather spoilt her companions by so constantly bringing to them a large share of the prey she captured. She thought more of them and of their kittens than of herself, and it was an everyday sight to see her with a bird or reptile in her mouth, calling them to the feast which she had provided for them. She would look on with the greatest satisfaction while they appropriated and enjoyed the fruit of her labours.

One day, when she was pacing about in a disconsolate frame of mind, one of us remarked, "She is just like Mrs. Gummidge 'crying for the old 'un!'" And forthwith we dubbed her *Gummidge*, after that celebrated creation of one of our greatest novelists.

I have heard it said that cats are not capable of much affection for their masters, and perhaps there is some truth in the assertion. Certainly they are not generally equal to dogs in this respect, but Gummidge was an exception. She knew us all, and was in her way really attached to us. She used to follow us into the veldt for a considerable distance, like a dog, when we took our walks abroad. But she would draw a line at a certain cross road on the way to Leribe: she would not go beyond that. When we attempted to go further she would resolutely sit down, and mew until we turned back, or struck off across the veldt at a right angle in the direction of Sebotoane, when she would bound towards us with grunts of delight, and scamper on in front of us, or trot along with evident satisfaction at our side. She knew well enough, or at any rate seemed to know, that the angle meant another turn further on in the direction of home. But as to advancing further than the cross road, she would not hear of it. We had gone far enough, and if we went further, perhaps we might never come back any more!

At night, when occasionally I went out to the other end of the town to spend the evening with a friend, she would always be waiting half-way up the road, fearing neither dog nor man; and the moment she heard my footsteps she would hurry forward to meet me with her cheeriest mew, and never fail to see me safe home to my study door.

When she grew still older, she became the general mother and nurse of all the kittens attached to the establishment. We were constantly in a state of kittens, and Gummidge did her best to attend to them all. If she had not her own to care for, she had somebody else's, and it was all the same to her. Two of our cats, like some of their betters, preferred to perform their maternal duties vicariously. In particular, there was a naughty black and white huzzy called Spot that liked to do so. She would calmly walk off and leave her offspring, knowing, I suppose, full well that " old Gummidge " would hear the cry of the helpless little things, and hasten to their rescue.

In England most kittens—in fact, all but one I believe— usually meet with an accident at an early stage of their existence; but out in the wilds in Basutoland, where we are less civilized and more primitive, two at least generally contrive to live. Gummidge often had four or five to care for. We used sometimes to think that it was an example of the willing cat being worked to death, but it was not; for she outlived all her companions. While they perished or came to an untimely end by their follies or vices, she believed that it is better to wear out than to rust out, and no doubt she was right.

How she managed to escape during the war I really do not know. She must often have been in peril from the bullets of our enemies, some of which not only ploughed up the garden, but would at times pierce their way through the doors or windows of our huts, and fall at our feet inside. But none of them ever struck her, nor did any of the men of the native contingent ever lay violent hands upon her and broil her upon a spit, fond as they were of *Katse-Katse*. I often trembled for her, but my fears were always groundless. As soon as the noise and hubbub of the fight were over, she would emerge from I know not where—a hole in the ground, or an empty box in a corner of one of the huts, or some other equally safe hiding-place—and walk along demurely at my side, or get in front of me and insist on trying to saw off my legs with her tail (much to my detriment) as I paced up and down the garden reciting my Evensong.

Once she performed a deed of heroism which ought to be related, if only to show that I have not been too lavish in my praises of her.

In February (I think it was), 1883, a terrific hail storm swept across the heights from Tsikoane to Buta-Bute, taking our station on its way. The stones were not those large ones which sometimes come down with a crash upon the heads of people in the veldt and kill them : mercifully for our garden they were small in size—some of them, indeed, quite tiny little things. But the *quantity* that fell was prodigious, and the swiftness with which it was hurled down upon us not less so. It beat down remorselessly every herb and flower, and stripped every shrub and tree of its foliage, leaving nothing visible but a number of hideous and forlorn looking stumps, where before had been masses of the most luxurious foliage. It covered the whole compound with what in the darkness—for it was dusk when it began to fall—looked like one great sheet of shining pearls of ice. The downpour lasted barely twenty minutes, but during that time the sound was deafening, and enough hail had fallen to cover the whole garden to the depth of nearly two feet outside our huts, and more than three at the bottom wall, where the ground sloped gradually down to the end of the compound. And it brought down the temperature in those few minutes nearly forty degrees—from over 70 degrees to 36 degrees.

I thought of my poor pet and her kittens, fearing that they were all outside exposed to the storm. The air was piercingly cold when I went out to ascertain what had become of them. I hoped that they had found their way into a disused dog kennel between two of the rondavels, but, to my distress, I found that they were not there. I knew that they and all our cats had been playing together just before the hail began to fall, and feared that the kittens had been beaten to the earth, and killed by its violence. As I was peering about in the darkness, I heard a faint mew not far from me near the kennel; and on going to the spot I saw a pitiful sight indeed. There was Gummidge, dear, brave old thing, standing almost embedded in the freezingly cold hail, but making no effort to move. I scraped the hail away from her, and then I saw what had kept her there, and prevented her from escaping. *She had gathered together under her, and was standing over, nine tiny creatures*, thus doing her utmost to shield them from the storm, and save them from destruction. Four of the little things were her own, and the remainder, I think, Spot's; though I am not sure whether two of the latter did not belong to Stumps, another of our household pets, and a daughter of Gummidge's. Spot and Stumps had refused to face the storm when it came down in its fury, and had promptly fled into the kitchen and saved their skin, leaving their offspring to their fate. Then Gummidge, perceiving that there was no time to escape with the kittens to the kennel, rather than allow one of the little things to perish unsheltered, gathered them all up together under her, *and stood over them, receiving the whole weight and fury of the hail upon herself.* In this way she succeeded in saving the lives of three. It was, of course, impossible for her to shelter them all; and the other six, notwithstanding all her efforts, were soon beaten down by the tremendous mass of hail and buried under it.

The brave old thing was in a woeful plight when I came to her rescue. She was, as I have said, almost embedded in hailstones, shivering with cold, and her fur all wet and bedrabbled. Think of the hard blows that must have fallen upon her devoted head! Think of their number as well as their force!

Hastily I extricated her and the three still living little mites —they were far warmer than she was, lucky morsels that they were—and carried them all into my hut, and wrapped them snugly up in a thick woollen blanket. They all recovered, though it took days to restore Gummidge to anything approaching to a respectable appearance, and weeks ere her coat assumed its accustomed neatness and gloss.

And now she was dead and buried, and I should see her no more.

I came away from that apple tree with a great lump in my throat, feeling sore at heart, and very low.

This, thought I, is the last straw. The last, last link that remained between the past and the present is broken and gone. Yes, they are all gone—all severed and gone for ever. The bright young friend of the early days of the Mission; the wife so gentle and so dear—dearer to me than life itself; the sister so devoted to the sacred cause of duty; the close companion of many years in the sacred ministry—they are all gone. One by one they have left me.

> They are all gone into a world of light,
> And I alone sit lingering here;
> Their very memory is fair and bright,
> And my sad thoughts doth clear.
>
> It glows and glitters in my cloudy breast,
> Like stars upon some gloomy grove;
> Or those faint beams in which yon hill is drest
> After the sun's remove.

> Dear beauteous Death, the jewel of the just,
> Shining nowhere but in the dark,
> What mysteries do lie beyond thy dust,
> Could man outlook that mark." *

Yes, thought I, and now the only living thing left, my faithful old friend of so many years—she has gone too. Thanks be to God, my child is still left to me; but even she cannot be here. She is hundreds and hundreds of miles away, and who knows whether I shall ever see her more?

If I had felt depressed before, I felt doubly so now. I wished that I could go too. It was very wrong, I know; but I wished it nevertheless. I felt ill in body and in mind; worn out, old, used up, played out, done for. Of what good was I on earth? These very scandals that the Mission was at that moment suffering from—perhaps they might be my fault. Perhaps I had neglected my duty, and taken my ease, when I ought to have been watching over the souls committed to my care, as a good shepherd should do.

In my misery and loneliness I felt like Job. There was a heap of ashes in the yard at the back of the house, and I felt that I should like to go and sit upon it.

But I did not. It was not an English-like proceeding, and I was not Oriental or African enough to attempt it.

I lit my pipe: a never failing solace in moments of depression. But even that faithful friend failed me, and afforded no comfort.

I must indeed be low; and I was.

But I did not go round the house and sit on the ash heap. I had not the moral courage to do it. I did a much weaker thing: I wandered slowly away to my chamber, shut myself in, sat down in the corner, and fairly cried.

Well; I don't know that I am ashamed of it. Why should I not love old Gummidge? And why should I not—if there was no

---

* Henry Vaughan.

other way out of it, and, apparently, there was not—why should I not drop a tear over her departure? I am not ashamed to own it; I loved the dear, faithful, old thing.

Some people love stocks and stones; some old china; and some, extraordinary as it may seem, their *money!* At least, they used to do so long, long ago; for one who knew tells us so, and warns us not to do the same. But, perhaps, no one does that now; perhaps they have grown wiser.

Why should I not love Gummidge? I repeat. I once knew an amiable old lady in a Colonial village who had a great affection for a lame goose. And the affection was reciprocated; for the creature used to waddle and hop, and hop and waddle after her all the way up the High street of the place when she went out shopping, and would insist in following her into every shop she entered. And surely a cat is higher in the scale of creation than a goose—especially a goose with a game leg!

Dear, brave, patient, magnanimous Gummidge; Queen of thy race; I shall never look upon thy like again!

But depression is not good for any man, much less for a missionary. So I made an effort, and shook it off. And there was much that helped me to do so. With the approach of spring, I hoped that the work of building might be resumed, now that we had sufficient money in hand to warrant a recommencement of the church. So I began to look about for a competent and reliable builder willing to undertake the work, and found him in the person of an old friend, Mr. Morgan Harries, a resident of Ficksburg, and a member of the Church. A contract was duly drawn up between us and signed, the Church officers assisting me in the matter with their advice, and entering into the proposal with the utmost cordiality. The work was to be resumed in August, and the building to be finished, if all went well, by the Feast of Epiphany, 1890. Quarrying commenced at once, my old friend Nathanaele Makotoko giving us permission to "break out" stone wherever we pleased round the heights.

Beautiful stone was abundant at a spot about a mile off, and large blocks of it soon began to make their appearance on the building ground. Six men—three whites and three Mauritius Creoles—were at work by the middle of August, cutting and shaping the stone into the required dimensions, and by the end of the year the walls began to rise. I had myself to be clerk of the works, and watch everything, the contractor not being able to be often on the spot; and anyone who has undertaken such a task in a country like Basutoland will readily realize what it involves. The appliances were few, and both Mr. Harries and myself were at the mercy of the men, who worked when they pleased, and idled when they took it into their heads to do so. But still the work went on little by little, the nicely finished blocks of stone accumulated, and the walls grew gradually higher and higher. So, notwithstanding all difficulties and discouragements, I had abundant reason to be thankful, and to look forward hopefully to the completion of the building.

About this time the South African newspapers contained an announcement to the effect that the "Salvation Army" was about "to bombard Zululand and Basutoland." We had read something about this new denomination from time to time, and had noted its advent in South Africa some years before. Up to the present, it did not seem to have accomplished much anywhere in the country. Except at the seaports, and in large centres like Kimberley, its efforts were very few and very feeble. Its methods, certainly, were open to criticism; they did not seem to us to be Pauline. Though the great Apostle of the Gentiles made himself, in the highest and best sense, "all things to all men," that so he might win them to Christ, we can hardly imagine him marching about Antioch or Athens playing a big drum at the head of a procession of "Hallelujah Lasses," or blowing a trumpet at the corners of the streets to give notice that he was about to engage in prayer or address the multitude. Still, we hoped that this new candidate for the public favour might succeed in doing some good in a country like South Africa, where *any* real work for God, however grotesque in some of its methods or details, ought surely to be welcomed. A friend had sent me the "South African War Cry" from time to time, and I observed that it never had anything to say about the vast heathen territories which surrounded the Colonies of the Cape and Natal. But now at length the Army was about to wipe away the reproach, which had been cast upon it, of not venturing out into the depths of heathenism, but contenting itself with processions and "ham teas," and other interesting proceedings in the more prosperous towns and villages. The newspapers told us that a specially trained body of officers was about to undertake the evangelization of Zululand and Basutoland. They were to "bombard the citadel of Satan" in each of these countries, and the enemy of mankind was to be defeated with great slaughter, and his empire destroyed.

I wondered how and when this was to be done, and waited to see. Some little time afterwards another paragraph went the round of the papers to the effect that the training of the officers was completed, and that they were on the point of setting out for the two heathen countries to which they had been commissioned. Satan was about to fall, and to fall ignominiously; for the new missionaries intended "bombarding" him in the only effectual way—a way which, strange to say, had never even been thought of by the missionaries already working among these heathen tribes. This new method, we were gravely told, was to prove invincible, because,

(1) The missionaries were to eat the same food as the natives, and live only upon native fare;
(2) They were to commend themselves to the heathen still further, by *adopting the national costume of the country.*

That was all. Not a word was said about the languages needing to be learnt. No doubt they were mere trifles, though

Sesuto is a language with seven moods and thirty-seven tenses, and possesses a vocabulary of more than ten thousand words. No; our poor heathen were to be converted at once by two or three English men (or possibly women) beating a big drum, and *adopting the food and costume of the Basutos*. That was all; but the reader will see, what no doubt our friends of the "Army" saw when they reflected upon it, that it was *too much*. Certainly it might be possible (some of our own clergy have had to do it at times) for an Englishman to exist for a few weeks, or even a few months, upon the ordinary native food of the country; though I greatly doubt whether any European—at any rate any Englishman—*engaged in active work*, could do so *permanently*. But the "*native costume*"! Dear, dear people, they had evidently no idea how conspicuous it would be by its absence!

When I read this portentous paragraph, I smiled and said to myself, they will never come here upon such terms. And of course they never did. We have not been yet "bombarded," and the tom-tom is still the only big drum we have yet heard in the country.

Whether Basutoland has gained or lost by the non-fulfilment of the announcement I have quoted, the reader, who knows more about the "Army" and its methods than I can possibly do, must determine for himself.

Being now so long single-handed, and with important building operations to superintend, it was impossible to do more than keep up the mere routine work, so to speak, of the Mission— the services, day and night schools, and catechumen and other classes. Ever since Mr. Reading had left us, the Bishop and his Commissary in England had been endeavouring, but hitherto without success, to find a man to succeed him. Several had offered themselves, but they were hardly the sort of men we needed. At last one man was found in every way eligible. I was told that he was really coming. But he did not come after all. He changed his mind at the last moment. They often do;

and perhaps it is as well, as it is a bad thing for a missionary not to be sure of his vocation. Then another offered himself, and was accepted. He was a really good man, but " somewhat of an invalid." But he had really made up his mind to come. I reflected. An invalid, however good and earnest, was a formidable creature to have in our circumstances. But I hoped the best, and was wondering how the experiment would succeed, when at the last moment his doctor stepped in, and forbad him to set foot upon the shores of Africa.

Time went on, until in October a pleasant young fellow, a deacon from the London diocese, joined me. But he was not able to remain permanently in the country. He stayed until the Lent of 1889, when the Mission secured the services of the Rev. Joseph Deacon, who had done good work elsewhere in the diocese for some years. He came to S. Saviour's on Palm Sunday, and we hope that he may be spared to mission work in the Lesuto for many years to come.

How is that so few really strong men—I mean physically strong—come out to us? We need them, but they do not come. Not that I underrate the weak ones. I can call to mind at this moment four of the most devoted of the missionary clergy of our diocese; and one of them is as poor as Job, another has a game leg, the third suffers from a spinal affection which compels him to sit down while preaching, while the fourth is so near-sighted that he is almost as blind as a bat. These four men, " the poor, the maimed, the halt, and the blind," are all of them good men and true, and have all done solid, lasting work for God.

But if such men as these, men compassed about with bodily infirmities, can do so much, I take it that stronger ones could do even more. When will they come out to us, not in twos and threes, but in tens and twenties? When will the great majestic Church of England fully realize the splendid, the unique position which the Lord has given to her in this nineteenth century? When will she rise to the responsibilities which are hers to-day, and send forth into the mission field not two or three here and there, but goodly numbers of her bravest sons and her best, proportionate to the needs which are daily pressing upon her? Such men, strong in body as in mind, men capable of enduring hardness for Christ's sake, are more than ever needed in numberless places in the mission field. I believe that they will come, and perhaps soon, for there are not wanting signs, which cannot be mistaken, that the Church of our fathers is beginning to realize the urgency and the magnitude of the work that lies before her. Meanwhile, let the "poor, the maimed, the halt, and the blind" toil on, strong in faith, if not in body; for to them it is given to lay the foundations; the superstructure will rise in God's Own time.

In September, 1888, I had to dismiss the senior catechist, and request that his licence might be cancelled. It was a great grief to have to do so, but there was no alternative. Poor fellow, he had given himself up to evil courses, and had added dissimulation to his other heinous sins. "The lust of the flesh, the lust of the eye, and the pride of life" had conspired together to slay him. He had grown proud of his position and his influence, for he was in his way a gifted man, and an eloquent preacher in his own tongue, and this pride was his destruction. Within a month of his dismissal from his office he lapsed into polygamy, taking a concubine, for whom he paid cattle in the usual heathen way. I found out afterwards that he had been bargaining to have her even while still holding his position in the Church. It was a sad case, and, unhappily, a not unknown one in the annals of mission work, though it was the first of the kind that had afflicted us at S. Saviour's. Let us pray that our poor friend may speedily "repent, and do the first works;" that so he may be restored to communion with the Church of God, and not after all be a castaway.

The work of building came at length to an end. In spite of many drawbacks and vexations, and much waste of time, the contractor was true to his contract. By the Feast of the Epiphany, 1890, the church was almost finished. It quite realized our hopes and expectations, and has, I think, since won the admiration of all who have seen it. That it was an enormous gain to the Mission goes without saying. Let us hope that it may stand as a beacon light upon the heights of Thlotse for many generations to come. The structure is massive and solid throughout, and the work put into it thorough and good, from the foundation to the wall plates.

And here I may fitly pay a parting tribute of gratitude to our zealous churchwarden, Mr. Richards, not only for his unwearied interest in the work as it progressed from day to day, but also for the many helps he afforded me, both by purse, and by the patient consideration of the many doubts and difficulties which must always attend a work like this. He spared neither thought nor effort on behalf of the house of God, and saved the Mission many pounds in hard cash by procuring for us, and allowing us to purchase, the timber and iron for roofing purposes at cost price. In short, he sacrificed himself in every way for the good of the Mission.

The fabric when finished had cost £1,997, almost the exact amount of our estimate. The floor is simply of beaten earth in the usual African fashion, but covered with cocoa-nut matting, generously given for the purpose, the sanctuary being partially carpeted in addition. Such things as stained glass and encaustic tiles are, of course, things of the future—probably of the far future. The Altar is a memorial to Mrs. Widdicombe, the credence table to Mr. Lacy; the font to a little son of Mr. Charles Vincent, a worthy layman of the Orange Free State, who has always been a sympathetic friend and helper of the Mission. A pulpit, of very simple design, is to be given by the contractor; and the lectern is, as the reader knows, a special memorial to the Rev. R. K. Champernowne. The seats are at present only ordinary school forms, with the exception of two or three deal benches in the chancel for the choir, and a couple of faldstools for the clergy. Wood is very expensive everywhere up country, and we could not think of having costly oak benches or stalls, either in the nave or the choir.

On the application of the Bishop, the Society for Promoting Christian Knowledge, always ready to help, as far as possible, the many poor and struggling missions of the Church at home and abroad, generously made a grant of £200 to our building fund, but the grant is not available until we are in a position to declare that on its receipt the church will be free from debt. After the offerings at the Dedication Services had been added to our funds, it was found that there remained a debt of £600 upon the fabric and its furniture, which, deducting the grant from the Society for Promoting Christian Knowledge, left us with a net liability amounting to £400. For the payment of that liability we had, and still have, to rely upon the charity of the faithful in England, our local efforts having become, as no doubt my readers will see, entirely exhausted. As I write I find that the above amount is now reduced to £166, and I pray that God may put it into the hearts of some of His servants in the mother country, blessed with this world's goods, to come forward and help us, so that we may soon be enabled to draw the £200 granted by the Society, and thus set our house of God entirely free from debt.*

The dedication of the church took place on the 1st Sunday after Epiphany, the 12th January, 1890, the Bishop having fixed that date for the solemn setting apart of the building to the worship of Almighty God. I will not weary my readers with the details of the ceremony, or of the feast that followed it. Suffice it to say, that the town was full of people the whole day; and that, at the Dedication Service, seven hundred people, white and black,

---

* I am thankful to be able to add that, while these sheets are passing through the press, this debt has been extinguished.

Christian and heathen, were crowded into a space arranged for four hundred. Hundreds of natives stood outside round the door, and hundreds more, seeing no chance of observing or hearing anything that was going on, stood some distance off, patiently waiting (thoughtful souls!) for the bread, beef, and coffee which were to follow in the afternoon.

That the singing was joyous and hearty, and the whole service edifying and beautiful, my readers may be assured. Jonathan and all his under chiefs and head men were present, and all took care to drop their coins into the offertory bag.

As to the feast, one can only say that it was the talk of every black-skinned brother and sister, great and small, for days afterwards, simple as the viands were which constituted it. Our Christian women, and some of their heathen friends, were up the whole night before cooking meat, baking bread, and making porridge, but they did not seem the least fatigued with their prolonged labours. Nothing tires a native when a feast is under way.

Altogether the day was by far the greatest and most important in the history of Thlotse.

Our buildings at the main station of S. Saviour's were now complete, and all that now remained was to erect, in process of time, as our means might allow, the school-chapels still needed at the various out-stations. The Bishop told me on the day of dedication that he hoped to repair the little temporary church which had served us so long, and use it in future as the lecture room of a native training college, which he trusted he might be able to establish at Thlotse. May this wish be speedily carried into effect, and his most excellent proposal become an accomplished fact.

With the opening of the church this narrative must come to an end. My task is finished: I have said my say, and have done. My readers and I have travelled together in a remote region, and over a considerable period of time. I have

x

tried to give them some idea of what mission life is like to-day in one of the heathen countries of Southern Africa ; and some conception of its successes and failures, its hindrances and encouragements, its sorrows and its joys, among one of the most important and most intelligent of the native tribes of the Dark Continent. The picture I have drawn is a true one. If there is much of shade in it, there is also, thanks be to God, some light. Come what will, the cause of Christ will triumph in the end; and even now, paradoxical as it may seem, the Cross often wins through apparent failures.

It only remains for me to commend S. Saviour's, and its work for God, to the sympathies and the prayers of my readers, and to wish them one and all a courteous and friendly farewell.

THE END.

A GLOSSARY

OF

SOUTH AFRICAN WORDS USED IN THIS BOOK.

Africander. A person of European descent born in South Africa.

Assagai. A spear or javelin. From the Portuguese.

Bantu. A generic term describing the Kafir, Basuto, and Bechuana races and their various sub-divisions.

Berg, pl. *Bergen.* A mountain. Dutch.

Biltong. Strips of sun-dried beef or venison. From Dutch sources.

Boer. A farmer. Now generally used to denominate the Dutch speaking Africanders of the country districts of the South African Republic and the Orange Free State. Dutch.

Bogobe. The bread of the Basutos; an insipid, pasty substance made of millet, compressed into the shape and size of a cannon ball. Sesuto.

Burg. Village. Sometimes a stronghold. Dutch and German.

Commando. A military force called out for active duty. From Dutch sources.

Disu (sometimes *Lisu*). The dried and prepared dung of the cattle kraals used in the treeless parts of South Africa as fuel. Sesuto.

Donga. A water course with steep, high banks. A ravine. Zulu.

Drift. The ford of a river or spruit. From the Dutch.

Inspan. To harness horses to a vehicle, or yoke bullocks together to a waggon. From the Dutch.

Joala. The strong beer made by the Basutos. Sesuto.

Kafir-corn. The Colonial name for Mabele.

Kaross. A robe of furs or skins sewn together. Probably Hottentot.

Khothla (or *lekhothla*). The open court or enclosure in which a chief gives public audiences, or administers justice.

Koppie (or *Kopje*). An isolated conical or dome-shaped hill, usually visible from a considerable distance, and sometimes rising to a considerable height. Dutch.

Kraal. A cattle fold. Also in Colonial parlance a native village. Probably from the Portuguese.

Lager. A military encampment, usually formed by arranging bullock waggons in a circle and interlocking their wheels. Sometimes applied to a more permanent military camp, the walls of which are of stone or earth. Dutch.

Lekhoa, pl. *Makhoa*. The native name for a white man. Sesuto.
Lesiba. A musical instrument. Sesuto.
Leting. The light beer of the Basutos. Sesuto.
Mabèlè. Millet, the principal cereal of Basutoland. Sesuto.
Mabelete. The name given by the Basutos to the rebels in the "Gun War" in 1880-81. Sesuto-Dutch.
Mafi. The curds of fermented milk. Sesuto.
Matikete. The name given by the Basutos to the loyal natives in the "Gun War" of 1880-81. Sesuto-English.
Mealies. The Colonial name for maize or Indian corn.
Mest. (*Vide* disu.) Dutch.
Mokete. A feast. Sesuto.
Monere. The title usually given by the Basutos to their missionaries. Sesuto-Dutch.
Outspan. To unharness horses, or unyoke oxen. From the Dutch.
Pitso. A Basuto Council. Sesuto.
Poort. A passage between two mountains. French porte.
Riem, riempe. A prepared thong of bullock hide used as a rope.
Rondavel. The name given by Colonists to the round huts of the Basutos. Perhaps a corruption of the English *round hovel*.
Schans, pl. *schansen*. A small temporary fort or breast-work usually erected on a hill or mountain side. Dutch.
Seruto. A native basket. Sesuto.
Siboko. The crest of the Basutos, the creature held in veneration by the tribe.
Sjambok (pronounced by English settlers *shambuck*). A short buffalo hide whip, used chiefly for cattle.
Sloot. A watercourse. Dutch.
Spoor. A track. Dutch.
Spruit. A tributary stream. A short river which disappears suddenly underground. Dutch.
Stoep. The raised stone terrace in front of Colonial houses. Dutch.
Thomo. A native musical instrument. Sesuto.
Trek. To pull. Used of bullocks when drawing a waggon. Also as a substantive denoting a journey. Dutch.
Veldt (pronounced *felt*). Open grass land. The prairie. Dutch.
Vlei (pronounced *fley*). A shallow lake. Dutch.
Volksraad. The Parliament of the Orange Free State, or the South African Republic. Dutch.

INDEX.

	PAGE
Abandonment of the Orange River Sovereignty	38
Africanders and Missionaries	245
A Friend in need	230
Agriculture of the Basutos	47
Alfred Motolo	199, 288
Amahlubi	20
Amangoane	20, 26
Andrew Makhobothloane	287
Anecdotes of Moshesh	28, 30
Animals of Basutoland	3
Architecture of first Mission Buildings	90
Atrocities	225, 236
Attack on Thlotse, First	154
,, Second	166
,, Third	173
,, Fourth	221
Audacity of Tukunya	232
Award, Governor's	191
Balfour, Rev. Canon	98, 100, 123, 269
Balfour, Mr.	99, 119
Baphuti	17, 28, 129
Barolong	17, 31, 246, 251
,, territory	246, 250
Bantu Races	15
Basutoland, Climate of	2, 12
,, Fauna of	3
,, Flora of	5
,, Mountain fortresses of	10
,, Physical characteristics of	1
,, Population of	41
Basutos, Common law of	45
,, Government of	41
,, Land tenure of	43
,, Occupations of	46
,, Prosperity of	31
,, Social life of	41
Batlokoa	23
Beautiful, The Native conception of	115
Bechuanas, The	17
Beckett, Rev. Canon	70, 75, 109, 253
Beer, Native	55
Bell, Colonel	78, 128, 169, 188
Bell, Mrs.	78, 123, 128, 188
Berea, Battle of	35

	PAGE
Bishop Gray and Moshesh	68
Bishop Knight-Bruce's visits	259, 271, 274, 304
Boast, A	220
Boers, The	33, 39, 248
Brand, President	40, 246
Brotherhood of S. Augustine	71
Burning of Molapo's house	227
Bushmen, The	13
Buta-bute	23
Call to Basutoland, The	73
Calvary Group	95
Cannibal caves	24, 264
Cannibals	24, 27
,, Story of	265
"Cape Smoke"	179, 238
Capetown Cathedral	90
Cathcart, Sir George	33
Cetywayo's Ambassadors	126
Chaka	27, 28
Chamberlain, Molapo's	82
Champernowne, Miss	127, 161, 199
,, Rev. R.	276, 286
,, Rev. R. K., Arrival of	127
,, ,, Visit to England	244
,, ,, Return of	254
,, ,, Early career of	276
,, ,, Call to S. Saviour's	277
,, ,, His life and work	278
,, ,, Last day on earth	279
,, ,, Last sermon	281
,, ,, Illness and death	282
,, ,, Funeral of	283
,, ,, Character of	284
Chapel, Mission	90, 198
Choir, Mission	114, 259
Christmas Day, 1880	171
Church, Permanent	268, 297, 303
Circumcision Rites	50, 264
Clark, Sir George	37
Clarke, Sir M., Arrival of	241
,, His Influence	243
,, and the Liquor Traffic	255
Clothing, Native	55
Coast Tribes	16
Combined Attack on Thlotse	221
Compensation Question, The	200

INDEX.

"Cookies and Born Days"...... 102
Cooking, Native..................... 55
Crocodile, Basuto veneration of 63

Dances, War 57
Daniel and his son................. 107
David Mogotsi 97
Deacon, Rev. J. 301
Death of Mr. Lacy 110
,, Rev. R. K. Champernowne 282
,, Mrs. Widdicombe 122
,, Mrs. Woodman 201
Dedication of Mission Buildings 95
Defence of Thlotse 151
Despondency 296
Destruction of new Compound 193
Disarmament Act, The...... 130, 133
Dishonesty. Prevalence of 197
Diviners, Native... 63
Donovan, Major..................... 33
Drink Traffic, The................. 255
Drum, Native........................ 58
Drunkenness 181, 238
Dust Storm, A 262

Earthquake, Superstition concerning............................ 137
Escape. A Remarkable........... 182
,, of Pitso 158

Famine, Results of.................. 24
"Fat Daniel"........................ 106
Fever 195
Ficksburg............................ 108
Fight, Last 188
,, over the Thlotse 223
Finery, Native love of 56
Fine levied by Governor 33
First Convert, The 97
First Attack on Thlotse 154
Food. Native 55
,, Scarcity of................... 178
Frere, Sir Bartle 134
Fugitives, Crowd of 195

Garden, The Mission 92
Girls, Native 51, 56
Gipsy Life 84, 88
Gordon, General, Visit of 202
,, Conversations with......... 204

Gordon, General, Bible Knowledge of 204
,, and frequent Communion 204
,, "An instrument in God's Hands" 205
,, His sympathy with the Loyals 206
,, His advice to Jonathan ... 207
,, His sympathy with the Mission..................... 208
,, His interview with Masupha 209
,, His departure from Basutoland 210
,, calumniated 210
Government, Action of........... 135
Governor's award, The.......... 191
Gray, Bishop, and Moshesh ... 68
Greatest Peril of Thlotse 227
Green Mealies....................... 55
Griffith, Col. 40, 151, 191, 192
Griquas, The................... 26, 31
Gummidge, Mrs. 289

Hailstorm, Terrific 293
Half Brothers, Hatred of ... 53, 216
Hanson, Capt. 176
Harvesting, Native 48
Hermanus Norkie 230
Heroic conduct of a cat 293
Hogge, Major....................... 33
Houses of the Basutos 53
Hurricane, Terrific 112
Huts, Mission...................... 89

"I am not a Mealie" 104
Inter-Tribal Warfare............. 214

Joel Molapo......... 99, 148, 216, 227
Jonathan Molapo 148, 208, 213, 214, 263, 275
Josefa Molapo 148
Journey to Basutoland.......... 76
,, Modder Poort 74
,, Thlotse Heights 84
Jubilee Day (Queen Victoria's) 271

Khethisa...................... 152, 216
Kimberley Horse, Gallant conduct of 168
Knight-Bruce, Mrs., Visit to Thlotse........................ 274

INDEX.

	PAGE		PAGE
Korannas, The	26, 31	Moshesh, Youth of	22
		,, Career of	23
Lacy, Mr.	73, 110	,, Irony of	28, 30
Lancer's Gap, The	35	,, Letter of	36
Language of the Basutos	17, 19	,, Death of	40
,, Bechuanas	17, 19	Motlomi	20
,, Coast Tribes	17, 19	Motsuene	222, 226
Laurence, Major	168, 176	Mountain of Night, The	25
Lekhalong	263	,, Tribes, The	17
Lepoko	221, 225	Mrs. Gummidge	289
Leribe, District of	72	"Murdered in his Nightshirt"	249
,, First Visits to	78, 79		
Lerothodi	148, 188, 189, 242	Musical capacity of Basutos	115
Letsema	47	Musical instruments, Native	58
Letsie	40, 147, 220		
Letter of Moshesh to the Governor	36	Nathanaele Makotoko 21, 67, 165, 196, 223, 297	
Lightning, Native idea of	64	Native Contingent, the	165
Loathsome Diseases	197	,, ornaments	56, 115
Love-songs, Native	59	,, Training Institution 120, 127, 201, 305	
Loyals, Abandonment of	214		
		Nausea, Attacks of	196
Mabelete, Defeats of	223, 235, 257	New Church, Dedication of	304
Ma-Churche, Advent of	81	New School-room	251
"Making his pile"	245	Night School work	119
Makotoko, Nathanaele 21, 67, 165, 196, 223, 297		Ntoana	84, 85, 94, 177
Malutis, The	2, 93	Ophthalmia	196
Manamasoane Loyals eaten up	165	Orange Free State, See of	70
Ma-Ntati	24	Orange River Sovereignty	38
Marriage, Basuto	52	Ornaments, Native	56, 115
Masite, New Station at	256	Outbreak at Thaba 'Nchu	246
Masupha 40, 150, 153, 219, 240, 257		Owen, Mr.	33
,, and Tukunya	154		
Masupha's Sons	243, 268	Pakalita	26
Matebele	17, 29	Palm Sunday, 1881	188
Meteors, Brilliant	117	Peace, Pleasantness of	258
Missionaries, French Protestant	65	Pete	21
,, Roman	66	Pete and Ramanella	268
,, Anglican	68, 71	Pictures, Love of Natives for	117
Missions, English Church, during the Rebellion	142	Pitso, The	42, 130, 239
		Pitso's Escape	158
Modibetsana and his Money	105	Poet, A	180, 183
Mohale's Hoek, Destruction of	142	Polygamy	53
Molapo	40, 72, 80, 136	Population of Basutoland	41
"Moral Force"	237	President Brand's arbitration	246
Moroka	31, 246		
Morosi	14, 40, 129	Queer Companions	180
Moselekatse	29	"Queen's Church"	69
Moshesh, Birthplace of	21	Queen Victoria's Jubilee	271

INDEX

	PAGE
Rain Makers	63
Rain, Persistent	178
Ramanella	39, 162
Reading, Rev. M. A.	127, 132, 153, 228, 267
Rebellion, The	133
Rebellion, The results of	194
Red clay	56
Relief of Thlotse	168
Religion of the Basutos	59
Remarkable escape	182
Results of the First Attack	160
Reversal of Government policy	192
Richards, Mr.	103, 113, 260, 303
Robinson, Sir Hercules	189
Rules for guidance	75
Salvation Army, The	298
Samuel Lefulere	246
Saunders, Commandant	175
Sebotoane, Battles of	175, 217, 235
Sekubu, Mission of	101, 142, 170, 201, 260
Sesuto	17, 19
Setebele	17, 19
"Shaver," The	21
Siboko	63
Siege of Thlotse	166
Sikonyela	27, 38
Sovereignty, Abandonment of	38
S.P.C.K. Grant of	304
S.P.G. Grant of	71
Spirit Worship	60
S. Saviour's	95
Stanton, Capt.	151, 157
Stanton's Horse	151
Stenson, Rev. E. W.	72
Superstitions, Native	62
Taylor, Dr.	109, 196, 232, 282
Thaba Bosigo	25
,, ,, Storming of	29
Thaba 'Nchu	31
Thlotse Heights	82
,, Attacked first time	154
,, Besieged	166
,, Relieved	168
,, Third time	173
,, Fourth time	221
Thlotse Saved	233
Tlasua	152, 216

	PAGE
Tlaputle	21
Traders, Losses of	146
Training Institution, Native	120, 127, 201, 305
Transvaal Horse	169
Treachery and atrocity combined	163
Trials and scandals	288
Tsikoane, Bishop's first visit to	263
,, Opening of school at	288
Tsipinare and Samuel	246
,, Tragic death of	248
Tukunya	150, 232, 252
Ultimatum of Sir G. Cathcart	34
Unburied corpses	196
Viervoet, Battle of	33
Villages, Native	54
Visit of General Gordon	202
Volunteers, Varieties of	186
Vomiting, Attacks of	196
War dance, A great	236
Warden, Major	34
Webb, Bishop, his care for Basutoland	71
,, First visit of to Thlotse	94
,, Second visit of to Thlotse	130
,, Mrs., visit to Thlotse	109
Wesleyan Missionaries	31
Western Tribes	17
White, Bernard	173
Widdicombe, Mrs.	113, 122
Witchcraft	62
Witch doctors	63
Wives of Molapo	81
Wodehouse, Sir Philip	39
Women, Basuto	48, 50
,, Native, great at haggling	86
Woodman, Mrs., Death of	201
Woodman, Rev. T.	103, 109, 142, 170, 201, 251
Work among lepers	268
Workers, Need of more	301
Worship of Ancestors	60
Zulu Ambassadors	126
Zulus	17
,, Language of	18
Zulu War, The	125

www.ingramcontent.com/pod-product-compliance
Lightning Source LLC
Chambersburg PA
CBHW030732230426
43667CB00007B/679